Steve,

Thank you for the support, guidance, and inspiration.

No one was more supportive of this project when I started it (a few years ago) than you.

Oct. 2020

Roy

LAW AND REPUTATION

The legal system affects behavior not just directly, by imposing sanctions, but also indirectly, by producing information on how people behave. For example, internal company documents exposed during litigation will help third parties assess whether they trust a company and want to keep doing business with it. The law therefore affects behavior by shaping reputations. Drawing on economics, communications, and a nascent multidisciplinary literature on reputation, Roy Shapira highlights how reputation works, and how information from the courtroom affects the court of public opinion, with a particular emphasis on the role of the media. By fleshing out interactions between law and reputation, Shapira corrects common misperceptions about the ability of market forces to discipline corporate behavior and adds to timely, ongoing debates such as the desirability of heightened pleading standards or mandatory arbitration clauses. *Law and Reputation* should interest any scholar who invokes notions of market discipline in their work.

Roy Shapira is at the Harry Radzyner Law School, Interdisciplinary Center (IDC), Herzliya. He has focused on the interactions between law and reputation over the past decade: teaching it at Harvard Economics Department, consulting on it for private firms, and publishing in various law reviews and business publications.

Law and Reputation

HOW THE LEGAL SYSTEM SHAPES BEHAVIOR BY PRODUCING INFORMATION

ROY SHAPIRA
Interdisciplinary Center (Israel)

CAMBRIDGE
UNIVERSITY PRESS

CAMBRIDGE
UNIVERSITY PRESS

University Printing House, Cambridge CB2 8BS, United Kingdom

One Liberty Plaza, 20th Floor, New York, NY 10006, USA

477 Williamstown Road, Port Melbourne, VIC 3207, Australia

314–321, 3rd Floor, Plot 3, Splendor Forum, Jasola District Centre, New Delhi – 110025, India

79 Anson Road, #06–04/06, Singapore 079906

Cambridge University Press is part of the University of Cambridge.

It furthers the University's mission by disseminating knowledge in the pursuit of education, learning, and research at the highest international levels of excellence.

www.cambridge.org
Information on this title: www.cambridge.org/9781107186507
DOI: 10.1017/9781316890653

First published 2020

A catalogue record for this publication is available from the British Library.

Library of Congress Cataloging-in-Publication Data
NAMES: Shapira, Roy, 1976– author.
TITLE: Law and reputation : how the legal system shapes behavior by producing information / Roy Shapira, Interdisciplinary Center (Israel)/University of Chicago.
DESCRIPTION: Cambridge, United Kingdom ; New York, NY, USA : Cambridge University Press, 2020. | Based on author's thesis (doctoral – Harvard Law School, 2014). | Includes bibliographical references and index.
IDENTIFIERS: LCCN 2020007266 | ISBN 9781107186507 (hardback) | ISBN 9781316637258 (paperback) | ISBN 9781316890653 (ebook)
SUBJECTS: LCSH: Corporate governance – Law and legislation. | Corporate image. | Corporations – Public relations. | Corporations – Public opinion. | Corporate governance – Law and legislation – United States.
CLASSIFICATION: LCC K1327 .S53 2020 | DDC 346/.066–dc23
LC record available at https://lccn.loc.gov/2020007266

ISBN 978-1-107-18650-7 Hardback
ISBN 978-1-316-63725-8 Paperback

To Moran, Amit, Noya, and Noam

Contents

Acknowledgments

This book's core insight was developed during my SJD years at Harvard Law School, and I am indebted to the many who facilitated my growth there. First and foremost, my academic supervisors – Mark Roe, Lucian Bebchuk, and Robert Clark – were a fantastic source of feedback and inspiration. The school's graduate program provided financial and academic support. And many other faculty members, particularly Jesse Fried and Steve Shavell, were kind enough to offer a constant, high-quality sounding board. The eclectic nature of my work pushed me to interact also with many outside the law school, and I specifically thank the late Richard Hackman for his feedback on the social psychology angles presented here. Finally, Jeff Miron and the Economics Department gave me the opportunity to hone my ideas by teaching a seminar on them at Harvard College for six years.

Following the completion of my doctoral dissertation, I worked as a consultant on corporate reputation, mostly with Reputation Institute. Working there has greatly benefited my perspective on how law and reputation interact, infusing the abstract nature of my ideas with a much-needed reality check. I have also served as a research director at the Stigler Center at the University of Chicago's Booth School of Business, and learned many valuable lessons there, both substantive and methodological. I am specifically indebted to Guy Rolnik for his on-the-ground insights on political economy and the role of the media, and to Luigi Zingales, who headed the center, for giving me the opportunity and for providing a rare blueprint for academic work that is both rigorous and accessible. In the last couple of years I have been a part of the Interdisciplinary Center's (IDC) Law School in Israel, where I enjoyed the support of Dean Amnon Lehavi and all other faculty members, with Amir Licht providing constant feedback on all matters corporate governance and beyond.

Numerous colleagues have read drafts or offered advice in various stages of the project. I especially benefited from the contributions of: Craig Carroll Mike Hatcliffe, Yuri Mishina, Rowena Olegario, Rupert Younger, and Batia Wiesenfeld (for the insights developed in Chapter 1, regarding how reputation works); John Coates, Jonathan Glater, James Hamilton, Shay Lavie, Ariel Porat, and Dean Starkman (Chapter 2, on how the law affects reputation); Jennifer Arlen, Tamar Frankel, Renee Jones, Kobi Kastiel, Vic Khanna, and Edward Rock (Chapter 3, on corporate law); Howell Jackson, Harvey Pitt, and Andrew Tuch (Chapter 4, on securities regulation); Yochai Benkler, Scott Hirst, and Rick Cohen (Chapter 5, on corporate philanthropy); Adam Shinar, Oren Tamir, Adrian Vermeule, and Wendy Wagner (Chapter 6, on administrative litigation); Laurie Dore and Verity Winship (Chapter 7, on the openness of dispute resolution); and John Armour, Brian Fitzpatrick, Jesse Fried, Joel Friedlander, Jill Gross, and Ann Lipton (Chapter 8, on mandatory arbitration). I am also thankful to many research assistants, especially Bernat Nasca and Dor Marinovsky for their help with content analysis of prizewinning investigative reports.

I also thank the various editorial boards that have published previous iterations of insights I present here, helping me in honing them. Especially relevant articles include: *Corporate Philanthropy as Signaling and Co-optation*, 80 *Fordham L. Rev.* 1889 (2012) (an earlier version of the insights developed in Chapter 5 here); *A Reputational Theory of Corporate Law*, 28 *Stan. L. & Pol'y Rev.* 1 (2015) (pertinent to Chapters 3, 4, and 8 here); *Reputation through Litigation: How the Legal System Shapes Behavior by Producing Information*, 91 *Wash. L. Rev.* 1193 (2016) (Chapters 1, 2); *Law as Source*, 37 *Yale L. & Pol'y Rev.* 153 (2018) (Chapters 2, 7); and *Mandatory Arbitration and the Market for Reputation*, 99 *B.U. L. Rev.* 873 (2019) (an earlier version of the insights developed in Chapter 8).

Above all, thanks go to my family. To my parents, for who I am. To my kids, for who they are. And to my life partner, Moran, for her never-ending patience and support (and for being an amazing person, regardless). This book is dedicated to them.

Introduction

Back in 2009 when I was starting my doctoral studies, I sat through my first ever law and economics seminar. Two of the field's founding fathers – Polinsky and Shavell – were presenting their proposal to abolish product liability.[1] A heated debate over the outcomes ensued in the room: how abolishing liability could affect access to justice or distribution. But I was still stuck on the logic, namely, how Polinsky and Shavell treated reputation as an alternative to the legal system. Manufacturers, their argument went, will invest in the quality and safety of their products even without the threat of legal liability, simply because they care about maintaining their reputation. And in markets where these nonlegal (reputational) forces are strong enough, it is not cost-effective to keep a costly adjudication system merely for the sake of an incremental contribution to deterrence. Reputation serves as justification for reducing legal intervention. A quick search revealed that such reputation-instead-of-litigation logic is actually prevalent in economic analysis across various legal fields. I then realized what was bothering me about the logic, and found my academic calling.

At the heart of the argument lies an implicit assumption that the legal system and the nonlegal system are independent of each other. Law and economics scholars were assuming that we can remove the law – remove the background threat of litigation – and the market forces will continue to function just the same. But in reality the strength of market forces is (among other things) a function of the existing legal system. If we remove the background threat of litigation, reputational sanctions may become more strident.

This book represents the culmination of my efforts in the decade that has passed since that law and economics seminar to better understand the

[1] Mitchell Polinsky & Steven Shavell, *The Uneasy Case for Product Liability*, 123 HARV. L. REV. 1437 (2010).

interactions between legal and reputational systems. The book makes three major contributions, along the following dimensions: how reputation works, how the law interacts with reputation, and how a social planner can harness these interactions.

First, the book shows that *nonlegal systems of control are costly too (just less transparently so)*. Legal scholars are usually aware of the costs of legal systems, and can relatively easily quantify them. But the costs of nonlegal systems are less transparent to us, and we tend to underplay them.[2] This is especially true for reputational systems, where the legal literature suffers from an "indefensible optimism about the actual operation of information markets."[3] The legal and economic literature often treat reputation as a straightforward, binary process: if you misbehave, your future business opportunities diminish; if you behave well, your future business opportunities flourish. This book draws from an emerging interdisciplinary body of research to show that in reality reputation is rather inherently noisy. Market players often lack the incentives and information needed to accurately update their willingness to do business with the company in question. As a result, the market systematically overreacts to certain types of behaviors, and underreacts to others. Stakeholders may stop doing business with perfectly fine companies or ignore warning signals and continue doing business with rotten companies.

Second, *Law and Reputation* fleshes out how *the effectiveness of nonlegal systems is affected by the legal system*, and vice versa. Reputational sanctioning does not operate in a vacuum. The same bad news that ignites an initial market reaction may also get the legal system involved in litigation or regulatory investigations. Then, in the process of determining whether to impose legal sanctions, the legal system produces as a by-product information on the behavior of the parties to the dispute: what top managers knew about the problem, when they knew it, whether they could have stopped it, and so forth. This information is available to outside observers and affects the way that these third parties treat the parties to the dispute. In other words, the legal system provides better information to the public for them to base reputational judgments on. Law and reputation are not independent of each other, but rather complement each other.

Finally, recognizing the informational role that the law plays in facilitating reputational sanctions carries important policy implications. On

2 John C. P. Goldberg & Benjamin C. Zipursky, *The Easy Case for Products Liability Law: A Response to Professors Polinsky and Shavell*, 123 Harv. L. Rev. 1919, 1929 (2010) (criticizing the conventional approach for not running market systems of control through the same wringer as it does legal systems).

3 Cass R. Sunstein, On Rumors 22 (2009).

a general level, the book calls for a more cautious approach to advocating for nonintervention. Scaling back litigation or regulation may have the unintended consequences of raising the costs of nonlegal sanctions. On a more specific level, the book uses the reputational framework to reevaluate key doctrines according to how they contribute to the quality and quantity of information produced. In the process we get to revisit timely questions such as the desirability of the recent wave of mandatory arbitration provisions, the proper scope of the judicial review of the Securities and Exchange Commission's (SEC) actions, and whether to assess director liability individually or collectively.

The broad focus of this book is *diffusion of information*. Business law scholars tend to rely on classical economics and agency theory, and this focus has hindered them from grappling with informational issues: market players are assumed either to have information or not to have it. *Law and Reputation* shifts our focus to questions such as how information is diffused (contrary to popular belief, information does not fall on individuals like manna from heaven), what is the role of information intermediaries such as mass media, and what types of messages are perceived as being more credible than others. For example, the book conducts content analyses of prizewinning investigative reports, showing how and how much these impactful media stories relied on information coming from the legal system.

This chapter proceeds in three parts. The first provides an overview of the main themes and questions that motivate each chapter The second explains the methodology – how I approached the questions. The third clarifies the scope of inquiry and original contributions, by juxtaposing my arguments with the extant related literature.

OVERVIEW

The book lays out the theory of law and reputation (Chapters 1–2), applies the theory to specific legal fields (Chapters 3–6), and offers big-picture policy implications (Chapters 7–8).

Chapter 1 starts with the basic questions of what reputation is and why it is noisy. Why do similar behaviors lead to different reputational outcomes? Everyday experience and systematic empirical evidence tell us that not all bad news is created equal. Some companies and businessmen emerge from failures unscathed while others go bankrupt. To better understand why the market reacts negatively to some bad news but not to others, we need to break the process of reputational sanctioning into its different components, and reveal how noisy it is.

The first component is those who dispense reputational sanctions (the company stakeholders: consumers, workers, investors, and so on). Stakeholders often do not have enough information to judge correctly what happened and how it happened. Even when stakeholders do have information, many times they ignore it or process it imperfectly due to well-documented behavioral biases such as focusing too much on available and salient issues. The second component of reputational sanctioning is intermediaries who disseminate information on corporate behavior, such as mass media or corporate watchdogs. These intermediaries have incentives to cater to their audiences' biases. They tend to exaggerate certain criticisms and downplay others, as a function of what sells newspapers or attracts donors and volunteers. Finally, those who are sanctioned – the companies themselves – invest heavily in distorting the information environment with tactics such as smokescreens and scapegoating.

Evidence is thus mounting that the market, when left alone, has trouble calibrating reputational sanctions/rewards correctly. But in reality the market is rarely left alone. In reality reputation operates in the shadow of the law.

This is where Chapter 2 enters, explaining how the law affects reputation. If you read only one chapter of this book (a pity), read this one, as it contains the core elements of the arguments that appear throughout. The law affects reputation in various ways. First, it reveals new damning information about the misbehavior of powerful players in society. The legal system confers fact-generating powers on litigants, judges, and investigators. As a result, the legal system often gives stakeholders access to facts that they were not privy to when they initially reacted. Think, for example, of internal email communications exposed during the discovery stage, showing how top managers knew but did not stop the misconduct. The law can also affect stakeholders' beliefs without producing any new information, simply by shaping the saliency, credibility, and framing of issues in stakeholders' minds.

In particular, the law shapes the scope and tone of media coverage. Chapter 2 presents evidence gathered by interviewing forty investigative reporters, going over members-only databases of reporters' tip sheets and how-to manuals, comparing course syllabi in leading communication schools, and conducting content analysis of prizewinning investigative projects from the past twenty years. The triangulation of these methods yields a clear conclusion: in today's world, legal sources – court documents, regulatory reports, freedom-of-information requests – are the single most important source of investigative reporting. The law facilitates effective media scrutiny, which in turn facilitates effective reputational deterrence.

Chapter 2 then provides a blueprint to applying the law-and-reputation framework to specific legal fields and situations. The key insight is that information flows from the courtroom to the court of public opinion in counterintuitive ways, which need to be taken into account before applying the theory. Not every legal dispute affects reputation. And when they do, they do not necessarily hurt it – some actually improve the disputants' reputation. For example, judicial scolding sometimes helps a defendant company recover its lost reputation, by creating scapegoating dynamics (singling out an individual manager for opprobrium). Thus, companies often lose the legal battle but win the reputational battle, and vice versa.

Chapter 3 starts the applications part of the book with the most natural candidate: fiduciary duty litigation in corporate law. Directors of publicly traded companies are more likely to get struck by lightning than pay legal fines for mismanaging their company. Acknowledging this curious feature of corporate law – the lack of direct sanctions – has led corporate legal scholars to look at the law's indirect effects on nonlegal sanctions and rewards. But so far most accounts have dealt only with how corporate litigation shapes *morals*. Under the prevalent approach, judges who scold misbehaving managers make directors internalize better norms of behavior (framing effects) or behave better out of fear of social disapproval from their peers (shaming effects). The problem with existing accounts is that they focus solely on what judges say rather than on what relevant audiences – the directors themselves, their peers, and the public at large – actually hear. Analyses of the content of media coverage and law firm memos show that in reality moral rebukes often get lost in translation and do not reach their presumed audiences.

In effect, the main function of corporate law is not to shape moral beliefs (finger-wagging theory) but rather to shape factual beliefs (information–production theory). By shifting the focus to information production, we get a fresh perspective on much-debated features of Delaware corporate law, such as the increased reliance on open-ended standards and the liberal use of shareholders' inspection rights, both being doctrines that boost the amount and quality of information production.

Chapter 4 shifts our attention from private litigation to public enforcement, within the context of the SEC's settlement practices, which became the center of national debate in the wake of the 2008 financial crisis. While the existing debate revolves around the amount of money being paid or admissions being collected, the reputational framework offers an alternative way to measure the effectiveness of SEC enforcement. The real problem with SEC settlements is not that the SEC leaves money on the table, but rather that the SEC leaves information on the table. Both the SEC and big-firm defendants have incentives to settle quickly and for high amounts, in exchange for limiting the public release of damning information. Such information–underproduction dynamics are good for both parties but bad for society at large. The reputational framework helps us identify solutions, like evaluating the proper scope of the judicial review of SEC actions.

Chapter 5 switches focus from reputational sanctions to reputational rewards. Why do business companies donate to charity? One possibility is that charitable donations serve as a signaling device: by sacrificing profits in the public interest the company conveys messages about its fundamentals. Think, for example, of cash donations as a handicap: when we observe a company substantially increasing its cash donations, we infer that the firm's insiders perceive its future to be good enough to spend these ultra-discretionary funds. In other words, corporate philanthropy is not so much about gaining a reputation for being nice, but rather about gaining a reputation for being financially sound. But corporate philanthropy is not just about signaling or goodwill, and is not unequivocally good for the company. Corporate managers have both the will and the means to strategically select the levels and targets of corporate charity in order to entrench themselves at the expense of shareholders and society at large. Donations to directors' pet charities can co-opt board independence requirements. And donations to certain educational charities can bypass money-in-politics restrictions.

The theoretical arguments on how philanthropy can be good (signaling) or bad (co-optation) for the company strengthen the case for introducing some form of mandatory disclosure. In fact, corporate philanthropy practices around the world serve as a great laboratory to test the reputational theory of the law: they provide a counterfactual, namely, an environment beyond the shadow of the law. In the United States, for example, there is no legal intervention in corporate niceness – not even a requirement to disclose how much or to whom you donate. The regulatory vacuum leads to a "cheap talk" reputation environment: companies get credit for being socially responsible regardless of their actions. Enron, for instance, won numerous accolades for corporate social responsibility in the years leading up to its collapse. By contrast, in countries that introduce some form of standardized, subject-to-legal-liability mandatory reporting, reputation rewarding becomes more accurate. Two opposite experiences in the United Kingdom and Israel illustrate. Israel enacted in 2003 mandatory disclosure of corporate philanthropy, while the United Kingdom dropped its mandatory disclosure requirement in 2013. The chapter uses evidence from these semi-natural experiments to show that the shadow of the law affects both actual behaviors (how much and to whom companies donate) and perceptions (stock price reactions).

Chapter 6 takes the theory outside of its comfort zone, applying it to regulatory behavior. Can judicial review effectively check regulators' behaviors? The answer largely depends on how regulators behave – what motivates them. If, as in traditional economic theory, regulators mostly maximize their narrow self-interest, then there is little that judicial review can do to stop regulatory capture. Judges may invalidate specific regulatory decisions after the fact, but they cannot overcome the inherent advantages that special interests enjoy in the way of offering lucrative future business opportunities or campaign financing. If, however, regulators care not just about material incentives, but also about their reputation, then judicial review can shape regulators' behavior indirectly, by providing information on how regulators behave. Regardless of whether courts intervene and strike down specific regulatory decisions or not, the process of litigation can generate reputational pressures that propel the regulators to change their behavior. Judicial review mitigates the risks of regulatory capture not so much through modifying regulators' material incentives, as through shaping the public's perceptions of regulators.

A burgeoning political science literature empirically documents how regulators proactively react to what the media writes about them. If the media agenda dictates regulatory behavior, then a key question becomes what shapes the media agenda. Here as well, a large part of the answer is litigation. In administrative litigation, for example, regulators are required to provide detailed explanations for why they decided the way they did, and judges provide their own, hard-look assessment of the regulator's competence and integrity. Still, public litigation is limited in its ability to effect change through reputational pressure, for reasons that include the legal doctrine and the (low) saliency of issues. This is why in many instances the real impact on regulators' reputation comes from a less intuitive channel: private litigation to which the regulator is not even privy. Think about a scenario of mass tort litigation between a polluting plant and victims who live in proximity to the plant. Such litigation may reveal information on how the defendant company skirted environmental regulation and got away with it. The litigation may thus affect not just the defendant company's reputation, but also the regulator's reputation, raising questions about how the regulator let the pollution happen under her not-so-watchful eye.

Chapters 7 and 8 sketch big-picture policy implications that cut across legal fields. Chapter 7 cautions us from taking the law-as-facilitating-reputational-deterrence function as given. For law to affect reputation meaningfully, government agencies need to grant Freedom of Information requests, judges need to resist the temptation to approve the sealing of court documents too easily, and regulators need to resist the temptation to quickly settle enforcement actions without releasing a detailed investigatory report. If they do not, the law's role as a source of media scrutiny diminishes, and, in turn, the effectiveness of reputational deterrence diminishes as well. A social planner should therefore take into consideration the information–production function of the law when evaluating the desirability of legal institutions.

Specifically, we revisit the long-standing debate in the legal literature over how publicly available law enforcement records should be. The debate spans multiple applications: settlement versus trial, openness of proceedings, and so on. The reputational framework contributes to the debate along three key dimensions. First, it injects a real-life implications perspective into a too often abstracted debate. Second, it allows us to disentangle the normally comingled facets of the openness versus secrecy debate.[4] Law-as-source dynamics play out differently in questions such as whether to keep the amount of a settlement secret or whether to seal documents already submitted to the court. Finally, the reputational perspective provides a roadmap for concrete steps that can facilitate more law-as-source benefits. One way to mitigate the existing failure-to-warn problem without overburdening courts is to install an information safety valve: pre-specify criteria under which the filing of additional disputes would trigger a mechanism that makes information about previous disputes publicly available.

The timeliest and most critical issue that the reputational framework sheds light on is the proliferation of one-sided arbitration clauses that effectively waive class actions. The heated debate over this recent mandatory arbitration wave concentrates on justice and efficiency toward parties to the dispute: proponents argue that it will streamline dispute resolution and reduce lawyer fees, while opponents argue that it will hurt the already disadvantaged workers, consumers and suppliers, depriving them of their day in court. Yet, as Chapter 8 shows, the existing debate too often misses the forest for the trees. Instead of analyzing fairness and efficiency toward parties to a given dispute, we should focus on effects on the market overall.

The chapter specifically cautions from current proposals to adopt mandatory arbitration in corporate and securities law. Even if shifting from litigation to arbitration may be good for a specific company *and* its investors, it may prove detrimental to the market overall. We will lose the positive externality (in the form of quality information on corporate behavior) that comes with

[4] Laurie K. Doré, *Secrecy by Consent: The Use and Limits of Confidentiality in the Pursuit of Settlement*, 74 Notre Dame L. Rev. 283, 317 (1999) (showing that different facets of the debate are unjustifiably intertwined).

litigation. A shift to mandatory arbitration may reduce the administrative costs of litigation, but hurt the ability of the market to discipline itself. In other words, mandatory arbitration provisions may reduce the effectiveness of reputational deterrence, and therefore be bad for investors as a group.

A short Conclusion offers a recap of the overarching themes and sketches directions for potential extensions of the law-and-reputation framework.

METHODOLOGY

A few words on methodology are in order from the outset. The reason legal scholars have understudied reputation is not because they find reputational incentives to be unimportant, but because scholars find them to be messy. The extant corporate governance literature, for example, deals extensively with "hard" market incentives such as executive compensation or the market for corporate control, which are easier to quantify, but it understudies "soft" market incentives such as maintaining a reputation for integrity. Reputational forces follow fuzzy dynamics and are hard to capture in neat models or direct statistical proofs.[5] My strategy in addressing the gap and fleshing out the important yet understudied reputational forces was therefore to triangulate, examining them from multiple theoretical and empirical angles. The idea behind triangulation is that combining multiple theoretical and empirical materials can minimize the biases of any single theory/method. Triangulation is especially fitting when dealing with messy factors with little existing hard data, as in our case. It bolsters the prima facie plausibility of the argument.[6]

I start every inquiry by synthesizing theoretical insights from multiple disciplines (as any theory about reputation should).[7] The process of reputational judgment involves issues of belief revision, diffusion of information, economic incentives, and feedback. I therefore combine insights from information economics with insights from social psychology, communication science, and management. For example, I delve into attribution and

[5] Heski Bar-Isaac & Steven Tadelis, *Seller Reputation*, 4 FOUNDATIONS AND TRENDS IN MACROECONOMICS 273 (2008) (a survey of the reputation literature, noting how challenging it is to empirically test reputation theories).

[6] THE SAGE ENCYCLOPEDIA OF QUALITATIVE RESEARCH 893 (Given, ed., 2008).

[7] Luis Cabral, *Reputation on the Internet*, *in* THE OXFORD HANDBOOK OF THE DIGITAL ECONOMY 351 (Peitz & Waldfogel, eds., 2012) (a survey of the reputation literature, calling for an economics and psychology multidisciplinary approach); Thomas Noe, *A Survey of the Economic Theory of Reputation: Its Logic and Limits*, *in* THE OXFORD HANDBOOK OF CORPORATE REPUTATION 134 (Barnett & Pollock, eds., 2012) (another survey, advocating borrowing insights from the management literature and practitioners).

impression formation theories, to understand how stakeholders make sense of good/bad news and change their attitudes accordingly.[8]

Existing statistical data can serve as a check, highlighting my theoretical insights' strengths and limitations. In Chapter 5, for example, I show why a signaling explanation is better than a goodwill explanation in accounting for the fact that most corporate philanthropy expenditures are in cash, or that the high-tech and pharmaceutical industries are the biggest donors. In Chapter 2, I use large-N studies of stock market reactions to litigation to identify the set of cases in which my reputational theory applies. Most notably, the fact that the size of the legal sanction is not correlated with reputational sanctions, and that legal disputes that culminate in verdicts are better for shareholder value than disputes that culminate in settlements, illustrate the need to rethink common assumptions and adopt a more nuanced reputational theory.

The core arguments in this book rest on my independent empirical work, which follows a mixed-methods approach. I emphasize three methodologies in particular: interviews, case studies, and content analysis.

Each line of inquiry in this book contains insights from conducting in-depth open conversational interviews with practitioners.[9] The iterative process of picking practitioners' brains about holes in existing theories and then going back to the drawing board generated some interesting insights. For example, I revised the book's core thesis when practically all the interviewees (litigators, crisis management consultants, and journalists) kept raising the same theme: the information flow from the courtroom to the court of public opinion is badly distorted. In other words, they made me rethink my initial theory: even if the legal system does manage to produce accurate reputation information internally, such information does not necessarily reach stakeholders and affect their beliefs. This insight redirected my attention and I began searching for patterns of distortions in information flows using other methodologies, such as conducting content analysis of media coverage.

Another qualitative method that this book frequently invokes is case studies. My mode of case-studies research is "constructivist": I use specific cases to illustrate, shed light, and serve as a check on competing theoretical frameworks.[10] To these ends, I employ several "purposive" selection criteria.

8 Yuri Mishina et al., *The Path Dependence of Organizational Reputation: How Social Judgment Influences Assessments of Capability and Character*, 33 Strategic Mgmt. J. 459 (2012).

9 In this type of interview the researcher introduces a topic in broad strokes, the interviewee talks freely about his experience and insights into the topic, and the researcher further probes specific experiences with follow-up questions.

10 Harry Eckstein, *Case Study and Theory in Political Science*, *in* Case Study Method 80 (2009).

The corporate law chapter, for example, rests on a famous court case that involves the Disney company as a "crucial, 'most likely' case":[11] the Disney case is widely considered the paradigmatic example of an existing theory of how corporate law works. By digging deep into the case I showed how even such a supposedly clear-cut case does not follow the theory's predictions. The case study therefore illustrates the problems in the hegemonic theory and opens up space for my alternative framework. Another case that appears throughout the book, for purposes of highlighting problems with existing theories of deterrence, is that of DuPont. In the process of manufacturing Teflon, DuPont emitted into the environment an extremely harmful chemical. The justification for using DuPont as a case study comes from the richness of detail: twenty years of litigation against DuPont's toxic pollution have unearthed a trove of thousands of internal documents, which give us a rare peek into a large company's decision-making processes. This rare peek is especially valuable when you consider questions of deterrence. Deterrence, after all, is a perceptual process: it is not about the magnitude of sanctions or likelihood of detection per se, but rather about how the intended audience *perceives* the sanctions and likelihood of detection. By reading though the intracompany emails or internal meeting notes, we learn some valuable, disturbing lessons about how companies manage to manipulate public opinion and dilute expected legal and reputational sanctions.

Finally and perhaps most importantly, the arguments throughout the book rely heavily on content analysis. Chapter 2 presents findings from a "law as source" project, where I coded prizewinning investigative projects from the 1995–2015 period. Specifically, I coded the extent to which these exemplary cases of accountability journalism relied upon legal sources, and found that in over half of them the legal sources played a "but for" role. The content analysis therefore gives us a sense of the magnitude of the law's reputational effects, as well as insights into the cross-sectional variation: the areas in which law-as-source dynamics are more or less pronounced. The securities regulation chapter compares the content of the SEC enforcement announcements to preexisting media coverage of the same misbehavior-in-question, to show that the SEC produces mostly stale information. The corporate law chapter examines how newspaper coverage of big corporate debacles changes before, during, and after litigation. The analysis suggests that the dynamics of litigation's reputational impact follow counterintuitive patterns: the process of litigation (pleading, discovery, and trial) is more damaging to companies' reputations

[11] Qualitative Research Encyclopedia, *supra* note 6, at 70.

than verdicts, judicial scolding is not necessarily hurting companies' reputations, and so forth.

I also draw occasionally from my *practical* experience with reputation consulting, especially at the Reputation Institute. This practical experience provided me not just with an opportunity to hone my theory, but also with access to proprietary databases and methodologies on how to measure reputation. The usual caveat applies: the views presented here are my own, and do not represent those of the organizations I worked with on these issues.

I view the fact that my methodology is more qualitative and exploratory in nature not as a bug, but rather as a feature of this book. Qualitative, exploratory elements are necessary given the subject matter and the state of the art. When the phenomenon in question – here, interactions between law and reputation – has received little previous empirical and theoretical attention, more qualitative and exploratory work is especially productive, given the need to stir ideas and develop new hypotheses. Furthermore, because this book does not focus on the average effect of law enforcement on reputation, but rather on the variation and the processes that connect legal enforcement to reputation, it makes more sense to adopt qualitative methods that shed light on the mechanisms that tie causes to effects.

SCOPE

To delineate the scope of inquiry, it is useful to situate *Law and Reputation* within three related literatures: law and social norms, corporate governance, and reputation (at the intersection of economics and management).

At the most basic level, *Law and Reputation* fits within a larger literature that deals with interactions between legal and nonlegal systems of control, often grouped together under the "law and social norms" moniker.[12] Adverse actions may trigger three kinds of nonlegal sanctions. When the violator suffers shaming – the opprobrium of others – the sanction is an external moral sanction. When the violator suffers from her own guilty feelings, the sanction is an internal moral sanction. When the violator suffers from diminished business opportunities in the future, the sanction is reputational.[13] Among the scholars who acknowledge that legal and nonlegal systems interact, there is

[12] "Social norms" here usually denotes any informal, nonlegal type of control.

[13] For more on the typology, see Robert C. Clark, Laws, Markets, and Morals (Jan. 2010) (unpublished manuscript).

a tendency to focus more on interactions between law and morals. By contrast, we focus on the oft-ignored interactions between law and reputation.[14]

Law and Reputation therefore emphasizes a *belief-shaping role of the law*, while most of the extant literature emphasizes *a preference-shaping role*.[15] Under the prevalent approach the law affects morals by pronouncing the right way to behave, thus inducing social shaming of or guilty feelings in those who misbehave.[16] I agree with the premise that the law affects behavior not just by what it does (sanctions) but also by what it says. But I argue that the law tells us not just what the norms are or ought to be, but also whether the norms were violated in specific instances. To be sure, my emphasis on the informational role of the law does not exclude the possibility of the finger-wagging role of the law. The relative strength of each role depends on the context. I conjecture that my theory is more relevant in environments with diffused and atomistic participants and super-strong economic incentives (think publicly traded companies), where it makes sense to highlight reputational rather than moral sanctions.[17]

[14] In popular language (and sometimes in academic research) "reputation" can also denote the esteem of peers. A reputational sanction, in this sense, would be not getting invited to social gatherings, or getting invited but being frowned upon. I do not treat reputational sanctions here as a "social" sanction, but rather as a "business" sanction: not buying from you/working for you/investing in you. To be sure, in real life the distinction is murky. I adopt it for exposition purposes.

[15] Here as well, the line between belief- and preference-shaping is murky. Stefano DellaVigna & Matthew Gentzkow, *Persuasion: Empirical Evidence*, ANN. REV. ECON. 643, 656 (2010).

[16] *See, e.g.*, Melvin A. Eisenberg, *Corporate Law and Social Norms*, 99 COLUM. L. REV. 1253, 1269–71 (1999).

[17] *See also* Edward M. Iacobucci, *On the Interaction between Legal and Reputational Sanctions*, 43 J. LEGAL STUD. 189 (2014) (noting same). Iacobucci's and Baker & Choi's papers are examples of the exceptions: works that do stress the informational role of the law and its effects on reputation. *Id.*; Scott Baker and Albert H. Choo, *Reputation and Litigation: Why Costly Legal Sanctions Can Work Better than Reputational Sanctions*, 47 J. LEGAL STUD. 45 (2018). My approach can be distinguished from these accounts by the answers to two key questions: what gap in market knowledge is the legal system filling, and how is it filling it? First, other accounts usually assume that market players are not aware of corporate misconduct, and therefore conclude that the role of the legal system is to draw attention to previously unnoticed corporate shenanigans. *See also* JONATHAN R. MACEY, THE DEATH OF CORPORATE REPUTATION 12 (2013). My account, by contrast, assumes that in failures of publicly traded companies, market players often learn about and react to misconduct before the legal system gets involved (for empirical evidence that supports this assumption, see Chapter 2). The role of the legal system in such cases is to provide second opinions on how things happened – reducing the *enforcement costs* rather than the detection costs of reputation systems. Second, other recent accounts tend to focus on the informational role of legal *outcomes*, that is, the signal that legal sanctions send to outside observers. I, by contrast, focus on information disseminated in the *process* of determining legal outcomes (for empirical evidence showing very little correlation between legal and reputational sanctions, see Chapter 2).

Within the accounts that focus on reputation, most focus on close-knit communities with repeated interactions, such as the cotton industry or diamond merchants.[18] I, by contrast, focus on contexts where reputation information travels via intermediaries, relying on technology to reach larger, loose-knit communities. Accordingly, I do not deal with the traditional problems of reputation information, such as local distribution and impermanence, but rather with understudied problems, such as how to make sense of an abundance of ambiguous information, or which intermediary to trust, and corporate reputation rather than individual reputation.

The book's focus on corporate behavior connects it to the corporate governance literature. Corporate governance scholars refer to market/reputational solutions frequently. Yet the focus on agency theory has steered scholars away from grappling with one important precondition of market solutions: the accuracy of market players' beliefs. Pertinently, the corporate governance literature has dealt extensively with the relationship between the board of directors and shareholders, to the point where it neglects the role of other key intermediaries.[19] *Law and Reputation*, by contrast, focuses on the understudied corporate governance *role of the media*.[20]

Finally, the book relates to, and draws heavily from, a fast-emerging reputation literature, which has largely escaped legal scholars.[21] My scope of inquiry here differs from the reputation literature along several key dimensions. For one, much of the practitioner-oriented reputation literature deals with reputational rewards, that is, how companies can develop a good reputation. I focus rather on reputational sanctions. Relatedly, the extant literature has historically focused on how firms' actions shape their reputation in their stakeholders' minds.[22] I, by contrast, focus on the other side of the equation, namely, on those who dispense reputational sanctions (stakeholders), or facilitate reputational sanctions (information intermediaries and, in particular, mass media).[23] Most importantly, the extant literature ignores the role that

18 *Cf.* Lisa Bernstein, *Opting Out of the Legal System: Extralegal Contractual Relations in the Diamond Industry*, 21 J. LEGAL STUD. 115, 116 (1992).

19 JOHN C. COFFEE, GATEKEEPERS 1 (2006).

20 Donald Hambrick et al., *New Directions in Corporate Governance Research*, 19 ORGAN. SCI. 381, 383 (2008) (lamenting the corporate governance literature's narrow focus on formal market incentives and institutions, at the expense of informal intermediaries).

21 For a recent exception, see Yonathan Arbel, *Reputation Failure and the Limits of Market Discipline*, 54 WAKE FOREST L. REV. 1239 (2019).

22 Steve Brammer & Gregory Jackson, *How Regulatory Institutions Influence Corporate Reputations: A Cross-Country Comparative Approach*, *in* OXFORD HANDBOOK OF CORPORATE REPUTATION, *supra* note 7, at 299.

23 The management literature has understudied the role of "evaluating organizations" – those who screen, certify, process and diffuse information for stakeholders. Bar-Isaac & Tadelis,

the law plays in dictating reputation. Focusing on how the legal system shapes media coverage and stakeholders' perceptions provides answers to the key question of why similar behaviors lead to different reputational outcomes.[24]

***

"Reputation matters" has become a mantra in the legal literature. Legal scholars increasingly refer to reputational concerns as important forces that shape our behavior across a wide range of phenomena: from corporate governance and the recent financial crisis to state compliance with international obligations.[25] Mounting empirical evidence shows just how real reputational sanctions can be: news about corporate misbehavior often brings with it declines in stock prices, in consumer willingness to pay, and in employee motivation.[26] Yet so far the literature has stayed remarkably silent on exactly *how* reputation matters, or how reputation interacts with the law. This book explores these two questions in depth. The upshot is that to understand how reputation matters, you need to understand how the law affects reputation, and vice versa.

supra note 5 (noting the gap in the economics literature); Jennifer Bartlett et al., *Reputation and Legitimacy: Accreditation and Rankings to Assess Organizations*, *in* The Handbook of Communication and Corporate Reputation 540 (Carroll, ed., 2014) (noting same for the management literature).

[24] For example, Chapter 2 relays that reputation scholars were puzzled by the fact that Ford suffered reputational damage for its Pinto debacle (defective fuel system leading to explosions), while other car companies with similar problems did not. To solve the puzzle we need simply look at what information from the legal system came out. During the discovery phase in litigation, an internal Ford memo surfaced, showing that the company knowingly took a business decision not to recall the defected cars. This legal document immediately changed the framing of the event and attracted media scrutiny, leading to great reputational damage.

[25] *See, e.g.*, Andrew T. Guzman, How International Law Works: A Rational Choice Theory (2008) (reputation and international relations); Macey, *supra* note 17 (reputation and the financial sector).

[26] *See, e.g.*, Jonathan M. Karpoff, *Does Reputation Work to Discipline Corporate Misconduct?*, *in* Oxford Handbook of Corporate Reputation, *supra* note 7.

PART I

THEORY

1

How Reputation Works

1.1 INTRODUCTION

Reputation matters. Companies invest vast resources in building and maintaining a good reputation. And the threat of losing reputation once bad news about the company breaks disciplines corporate behavior to begin with. Companies anticipate that the release of damning information about them may raise the costs of financing, because investors and lenders now realize that the company has poorer internal controls than they had previously thought. Or it may raise the operational costs of the company, because consumers, suppliers, and employees now perceive the company's operational culture to be more opportunistic than they had initially assumed.

Mounting empirical evidence shows just how real the reputational consequences of corporate misbehavior can be.[1] Event studies, which examine the stock market reaction upon revelation of bad news, show that when publicly traded companies are caught cooking the books or violating securities regulations, the reputational sanction actually dwarfs the legal sanction (six times higher, at least).[2] Other studies show that institutional ownership declines significantly following a restatement, or that the market loses confidence in the firm's earning announcements going forward.[3] Similar dynamics are also

[1] For overviews, see Jonathan M. Karpoff, *Does Reputation Work to Discipline Corporate Misconduct?*, *in* THE OXFORD HANDBOOK OF CORPORATE REPUTATION 363 (Timothy G. Pollock & Michael L. Barnett eds., 2012); CHRISTOPHER HODGES, LAW AND CORPORATE BEHAVIOUR 49 n. 20 (2015).

[2] *Id.*; John Armour et al., *Regulatory Sanctions and Reputational Damage in Financial Markets*, 52 J. FIN. AND QUANT. ANAL. 1429 (2017).

[3] Natasha Burns et al., *Institutional Ownership and Monitoring: Evidence from Financial Misreporting*, 16 J. CORP. FIN. 443 (2010); Deborah L. Murphy, *Understanding the Penalties Associated with Corporate Misconduct: An Empirical Examination of Earnings and Risk*, 44 J. FIN. AND QUANT. ANAL. 55 (2009).

in play with private companies. For example, venture capital companies that are involved in contractual disputes with entrepreneurs suffer heavy reputational damage: investors are less willing to invest in them and entrepreneurs are less willing to work with them going forward.[4] Reputational sanctions are real not just at the company level, but also at the individual level. Directors whose companies are involved in corporate governance debacles lose directorship offers in other companies (their labor-market reputation takes a hit).[5]

Legal scholars are seemingly well aware of the power of reputation. Commercial legal scholars, in particular, invoke it frequently, in analyses of consumer protection, financial markets, and so on.[6] Yet legal scholars usually invoke reputation within the framework of conventional economic models. They treat the process of reputational sanctioning as a straightforward, binary process: as long as market players learn about misbehavior, they will punish the misbehaving entities by withholding future business opportunities.[7] Under this simplistic approach, legal scholars *assume* that reputational concerns shape behavior in a certain scenario, without fully explaining why this is so or examining the social costs of reputational sanctions.

This chapter shifts our approach from making assumptions on whether reputation matters to explaining how exactly reputation matters. By drawing on recent theoretical and empirical insights from the multidisciplinary reputation literature, I show that in reality reputational sanctioning is an inherently noisy process, with the potential to exact heavy social costs. Even when market players learn about certain misbehavior, they often lack the incentives and/or information to properly update their beliefs about the misbehaving company. As a result, the market systematically underreacts to certain types of misconduct and overreacts to others.

Section 1.2 defines reputation, and explains what determines the magnitude of reputational sanctions: the degree to which stakeholders judge the bad news as indicative of the company's future behavior. Section 1.3 details the many biases that plague the process of stakeholder judgments. Section 1.4 explains

4 Vladimir Atanasov et al., *Does Reputation Limit Opportunistic Behavior in the VC Industry? Evidence from Litigation Against VCs*, 67 J. FIN. 2215 (2012).

5 Ian D. Gow et al., Consequences to Directors of Shareholder Activism (2014) (unpublished manuscript), *available at* https://dash.harvard.edu/bitstream/handle/1/13479133/14-120.pdf?sequence=1.

6 *See, e.g.*, Lucian A. Bebchuk & Richard A. Posner, *One-Sided Contracts in Competitive Consumer Markets*, 104 MICH. L. REV. 827 (2006); JONATHAN R. MACEY, THE DEATH OF CORPORATE REPUTATION (2013).

7 Eric Talley, *Disclosure Norms*, 149 U. PA. L. REV. 1955, 1960 n.15 (2001) (collecting references for the common approach).

why the biases do not cancel out, and therefore lead to systematic market under- or overreactions.

1.2 HOW REPUTATIONAL SANCTIONS WORK

A company's reputation can be defined as the set of beliefs that stakeholders hold regarding the company's quality.[8] Without the ability to directly observe the company's abilities and intentions, stakeholders rely on the company's past observable actions as cues to evaluate how the company is likely to behave in the future.

In that sense, a reputational sanction is the product of stakeholders updating beliefs and lowering expectations. Upon hearing bad news about the company, stakeholders infer that the company's "type" is worse than they have realized. The company is now perceived as more likely to defect in the future, and so stakeholders reduce their willingness to interact with the company going forward. Investors hearing about a corporate governance scandal will start demanding higher returns for their investment, customers hearing about a product recall will purchase fewer products, and so forth.[9] The aggregate of diminished business opportunities constitutes the reputational sanction for violating market norms.

So far, the story seems straightforward: if a company misbehaves, it risks losing future business opportunities. But a much more interesting question remains understudied: how exactly do stakeholders update their beliefs? How many business opportunities will the company lose for a given misconduct? After all, we know from everyday experience that *not all bad news is created equal*. Similar adverse actions cause different reputational outcomes. One financial company weathers fraud allegations relatively unscathed, while another goes bankrupt. One top executive takes the fall when her company

[8] Cynthia E. Devers et al., *A General Theory of Organizational Stigma*, 20 ORG. SCI. 154, 156 (2009). While there exist numerous definitions for reputation, most fall into one of two categories: (1) awareness or prominence (how much of a celebrity is this company or businessperson); (2) perceived quality. We focus throughout the book on the latter category. Another point of confusion comes from comingling the notions of reputation and trust. A company's reputation can be thought of as the cash value of the trust that different stakeholders put in the company. Karpoff, *supra* note 1, at 363. But I mostly refrain from using the notion of trust here, in order to avoid unnecessary confusion between Bayesian belief-updating (or: adverse selection-) models and repeated-interaction (or: moral hazard-) models of reputation.

[9] *See generally* CHARLES J. FOMBRUN, REPUTATION: REALIZING VALUE FROM THE CORPORATE IMAGE (1996).

misbehaves while another is unaffected. So what explains the variation in market reaction?

The legal literature tends to boil the answer down to one factor: do stakeholders have information about the behavior in question or not. But *information does not automatically translate into reputational damages*. The fact that bad news broke – that an allegation of corporate misconduct became public – is a necessary, but not a sufficient, condition for meaningful reputational damage to occur. Several additional conditions have to hold: *diffusion*, *certification*, and *attribution*.

Damning information has to be widely diffused so that it reaches a critical mass of stakeholders in order for the reputational sanction to be meaningful.[10] Information that was widely diffused has to be certified as credible for the company's stakeholders to consider it seriously. After all, stakeholders do not change what they think about the company based on any piece of information spread by a fly-by-night rumor propagator. And even information that was diffused and certified has to first be attributed to deep-seated flaws that are likely to reoccur in the future, in order for the company's stakeholders to update their beliefs and act on it.[11]

Notably, the magnitude of reputational sanctions depends largely on how stakeholders perceive the *indicativeness of future behavior*.[12] Reputation sanctioning rests on the "how is it relevant to me" question. That is, stakeholders finding out about a corporate misconduct try to infer how this specific event is indicative of their own future interactions with the company. Some pieces of bad news are deemed more relevant than others. To generalize: when stakeholders attribute the bad news to a one-off mistake, such as a rogue low-level employee who was subsequently fired, the reputational sanction is likely to be small. By contrast, when stakeholders attribute the bad news to a deep-seated flaw, such as a total breakdown of internal checks and balances throughout the corporate hierarchy, the reputational sanction is likely to be large. After all, no one wants to work for, buy from, or invest in companies with deep-rooted problems that will likely resurface.

To illustrate, consider an empirical study of stock market reactions to airplane crashes.[13] The study finds that not all news of crashes is created

10 Julian F. Kolbel, Timo Busch, & Leonhardt M. Jancso, *How Media Coverage of Corporate Social Responsibility Increases Financial Risk*, 38 STRATEGIC MGMT. J. 2266, 2280 (2017).

11 *Id.*, at 2271 (implying that reputational sanctions will be large when shareholders believe misbehaving firms had capacity to act differently but did not).

12 Thomas Noe, *A Survey of the Economic Theory of Reputation: Its Logic and Limits*, *in* OXFORD HANDBOOK OF CORPORATE REPUTATION, *supra* note 1, at 114, 117.

13 Mark L. Mitchell & Michael T. Maloney, *Crisis in the Cockpit? The Role of Market Forces in Promoting Air Travel Safety*, 32 J.L. & ECON. 329 (1989)

equal. The stock price reacts differently based on how the media covers the crash. When the *Wall Street Journal* attributes the crash to internal causes, such as maintenance problems, the stock prices decline dramatically. By contrast, when the *Journal* reports that the crash was caused by external conditions, such as unanticipated weather conditions or a mistake by the ground crew at the airport, the market does not react negatively.

This intuitive point is worth reiterating, as it has largely escaped the legal literature: bad news does not automatically translate into reputational sanctions. For one, certain types of bad news carry zero reputational repercussions. Empirical studies of stock market reactions show that when companies are caught polluting the environment or bribing officials in developing countries (misbehavior against unspecified third parties), there is little to no reputational harm.[14] More pertinently, even for misbehaviors that do carry reputational repercussions (misbehavior against trade partners, as in breaching contracts), the magnitude of the sanction varies greatly as a function of the public perception of what caused the debacle. When stakeholders read bad news, they try to infer the degree of intentionality and controllability involved in the misconduct.[15] The more stakeholders perceive the reported misbehavior as intentional and controllable, the more they will update downward their evaluation of the company – a bigger reputational sanction.[16]

The upshot is that the process of translating bad news into reputational assessments requires *not just facts about what happened but also interpretations and judgments of how things happened*. And the next crucial step is to acknowledge that the facts are often open to multiple interpretations and market players often get the interpretation wrong. Unlike in the airplane crashes scenario, where it is relatively easy to attribute the right cause to the problem, in other contexts there is no black box. Stakeholders often interpret an isolated mistake as a deep-seated flaw and vice versa. There is often a gap between outsiders' perceptions and the reality of how things happened. To better understand reputational sanctions, we therefore need to delve into the sources that bridge gaps between perception and reality.

14 Karpoff, *supra* note 1, at 372.

15 Rebecca Reuber & Eileen Fischer, *Organizations Behaving Badly: When Are Discreditable Actions Likely to Damage Organizational Reputation?*, 93 J. Bus. Ethics 39, 42–43 (2010); Batia M. Wiesenfeld et al., *The Stigmatization and Devaluation of Elites Associated with Corporate Failures: A Process Model*, 33 Acad. Mgmt. Rev. 231, 235 (2008).

16 Timothy Coombs, *Situational Theory of Crisis: Situational Crisis Communication Theory and Corporate Reputation*, *in* The Handbook of Communication and Corporate Reputation 268 (Carroll, ed., 2014).

1.3 WHY REPUTATIONAL SANCTIONS ARE NOISY

Several conditions have to apply in order for a misbehaving company to suffer meaningful reputational damage. Information about the misbehavior has to become public (revelation); reach a critical mass of stakeholders (diffusion); be considered as credible (certification), and indicative of the company's future behavior (attribution); and stakeholders have to be motivated to act on it – punishing the company by taking their business elsewhere.

Yet none of these conditions is automatic. The process of reputational sanctioning is systematically distorted due to issues with asymmetric information, judgment biases, and divergent incentives. To appreciate just how noisy reputational assessments are, it is useful to break down the process of reputational sanctioning into its different components.

1.3.1 *Players Who Dispense Sanctions (Stakeholders)*

Unlike legal sanctions, reputational sanctions are not dispensed by public officials, but rather by the company stakeholders themselves. The stakeholders who reduce their interactions with misbehaving companies have the right incentives: they stand to gain from accurately judging how things happened and from staying away from bad companies. However, stakeholders often lack the right information. In some cases, stakeholders will not even be aware of the misbehavior. When chemical giant DuPont emitted an opaque toxic chemical dubbed C8 into the air while producing Teflon without notifying the public or regulators, it took the outside world decades to find out about it.[17] The asymmetries in information between the company's insiders and outsiders can be extreme.

Even in instances when outsiders know with some certainty *what* happened – that a company granted a big bonus for a failed CEO, or that a certain amount of people were harmed by an auto tire defect – they find it hard to understand *how* things happened. It is especially hard for outsiders to know the inner workings of the company. In other words, stakeholders are not well informed about questions such as what top managers knew, when they knew it, and could they have stopped it. As Oliver Williamson put it, we often lack the "second-level information": we observe the bad outcomes but are unaware of the circumstances that led to them.[18]

[17] Roy Shapira & Luigi Zingales, *Is Pollution Value-Maximizing? The DuPont Case* (Nat'l Bureau of Econ. Research, Working Paper No. 23866, 2017), http://www.nber.org/papers/w23866.

[18] Oliver E. Williamson, Economic Institutions of Capitalism: Firms, Markets, Relational Contracting 396 (1985).

Furthermore, even when stakeholders have information, they process it imperfectly, for various reasons. Judgment biases sway our reputational assessments.[19] For example, we tend to overly focus on issues that can be easily summoned into our memory (availability bias).[20] In other words, we evaluate the likelihood that a certain behavior will reoccur according to our ability to remember examples of it: vividness is an important determinant of reputational sanctions.

To illustrate, consider the difference in public reaction to two Carnival Cruise Line incidents. In 2012, Carnival's ship ran aground, in a calm sea with good visibility. The captain inexplicably delayed the order to abandon ship, and the evacuation took many hours to complete (in violation of maritime laws), culminating in the death of over thirty people. Then, a year later, another of Carnival's ship suffered an engine fire and subsequently lost power during a cruise. This time around, the staff reaction was swift and proper: they extinguished the fire, restored most critical systems, and immediately contacted the coast guard to receive supplies. The company then offered a public apology, refunds, flights home, and credits for future cruises. The 2012 event is a textbook case for mishandling a crisis, while the 2013 event is the opposite. Yet the reputational damage (sales lost) was seemingly *worse* following the 2013 event. The media highlighted vivid images of raw sewage in hallways and on the walls, and nicknamed the ordeal as "the ship of poop" event. The image made the 2013 event more vivid, causing more consumers to book their cruises elsewhere than after the 2012 event.[21]

Another relevant type of biases is *attribution errors*. When stakeholders hear bad news about a company, they ask themselves why the company did that. By identifying the cause of behavior, we hope to gain knowledge of the company's "stable traits and dispositions," and be able to predict how it will behave in the future.[22] Yet attributions are notoriously messy.[23] For instance, when interpreting events stakeholders suffer from what psychologists call the "naïve

[19] Yuri Mishina et al., *The Path Dependence of Organizational Reputation: How Social Judgment Influences Assessments of Capability and Character*, 33 Strategic Mgmt. J. 459 (2012).

[20] Amos Tversky & Daniel Kahneman, *Availability: A Heuristic for Judging Frequency and Probability*, 5 Cognitive Psychol. 207 (1973).

[21] On the crisis communication lessons here, *see, e.g.*, Dov Gardin, *Carnival Cruise Lines: What They Should Have Done*, Risk Management Monitor Blog, Feb. 22, 2013, https://www.riskmanagementmonitor.com/carnival-cruise-lines-what-they-should-have-done/. I thank reputation consultant Mike Hatcliffe for suggesting this example.

[22] Sabine Einwiller, *Corporate Attributes and Associations*, *in* Handbook of Communication and Corporate Reputation, *supra* note 16, at 301.

[23] Donald Lange & Nathan T. Washburn, *Understanding Attributes of Corporate Social Irresponsibility*, 37 Acad. Mgmt. Rev. 300, 302 (2012).

psychologist phenomenon."[24] That is, we tend to adopt causal rather than contextual explanations: we assume that if something bad happened, then the company and businesspersons involved are bad.[25]

In all, all too frequently stakeholders either lack proper information, or process whatever information they have improperly. As a result, stakeholders often fail to calibrate reputational sanctions accurately: they underreact to some misbehaviors while overreacting to others.

1.3.2 *Players Who Facilitate Sanctions (Information Intermediaries)*

Another basic problem with reputational sanctions stems from the narrow incentives of those who provide information and interpretations on corporate misbehavior. Reputational sanctions in today's world are largely determined by "information intermediaries." Back when most of our interactions happened within close-knit communities, we formed impressions of businesses based mostly on our direct experience with the seller (first party) or gossip we heard from our close peers (second party). Yet, in today's world, we often form impressions of companies based on what we gather from third parties: mass media, stock analysts, institutional investors, and corporate watchdogs.[26] The way that these intermediaries screen, frame, certify, and diffuse information dictates the effectiveness of reputational deterrence. The intermediaries often possess more information and expertise than the average stakeholder. However, intermediaries have their own narrow incentives to push the market toward overreacting to some behaviors and underreacting to others.

For large companies in particular, reputation is largely a function of media coverage.[27] Yet the media has difficulties scrutinizing corporate behavior, due to a plethora of factors. For example, the media suffers from dependence on advertisers.[28] A profit-minded media firm will think twice before producing biting watchdog-type reporting on big advertisers, so as not

[24] *See generally* DANIEL KAHNEMAN, THINKING, FAST AND SLOW 85–88 (2011).

[25] Donald Lange et al., *Organizational Reputation: A Review*, 37 J. MGMT. 153, 173 (2011); Andrea M. Sjovall & Andrew C. Talk, *From Actions to Impressions: Cognitive Attribution Theory and the Formation of Corporate Reputation*, 7 CORP. REPUTATION REV. 269, 274–75 (2004).

[26] Stefano DellaVigna & Matthew Gentzkow, *Persuasion: Empirical Evidence*, ANN. REV. ECON. 643, 644 (2010).

[27] David L. Deephouse, *Media Reputation as a Strategic Resource: An Integration of Mass Communication and Resource-Based Theories*, 26 J. MGMT. 1091, 1096 (2000).

[28] *See, e.g.*, Jonathan Reuter & Eric Zitzevitz, *Do Ads Influence Editors? Advertising and Bias in the Financial Media*, 121 Q.J. ECON. 197, 225 (2006).

to risk losing much-needed advertising revenues.[29] Similarly, the media depends on sources.[30] To bring stories about the inner workings of large businesses, journalists frequently rely on insiders. Yet these insiders have little incentives to provide damning information about breakdowns in their own companies. And for the journalist, producing watchdog-type reporting on those who are your main sources is akin to burning a bridge.[31]

Other factors include journalists' own shortcomings,[32] or their need to cater to their audiences' biases.[33] Indeed, one study found that the financial media criticizes executive stock-option plans based on high value at the exercising date (which is a function of external conditions) rather than at the granting date (which is more related to the strength of corporate governance).[34] Another study found that the media criticizes shady accounting practices based on the visibility of companies rather than the size of the discrepancy: large, well-known companies get more negative coverage for more minor deviations.[35] Such studies corroborate our notion that the media targets companies based not on the social harm done, but rather on spurious factors such as the visibility of and resentment toward these companies, or the entertainment value of the story.[36]

Because of all these compromising factors, too often relevant information on corporate misbehavior is not spotlighted and diffused. Similar dynamics are in play with other information intermediaries. As a corporate-watchdog NGO, it pays to publish exaggerated criticisms against the McDonald's-es of the world. After all, eliciting a strong market reaction against visible companies will help you win the competition for donors' money and volunteers'

29 Michael Schudson, The Sociology of News 125 (2003) (citing a survey of television news directors in which over half of the respondents admitted that advertisers pressured them to kill negative stories or put a positive spin on them).

30 Alexander Dyck & Luigi Zinglaes, *The Bubble and the Media*, *in* Corporate Governance and Capital Flows in a Global Economy 84 (Cornelius & Kogut, eds., 2003).

31 Dean Starkman, *Power Problem*, Colum. Journalism Rev. (2009), http://archives.cjr.org/cover_story/power_problem.php.

32 *See, e.g.*, Damian Tambini, *What Are Financial Journalists for?*, 11 Journalism Stud. 158, 159 (2010) (noting that journalists often have too little experience and expertise to be able to report critically on complex topics).

33 DellaVigna & Gentzkow, *supra* note 26, at 659–60.

34 John E. Core et al., *The Power of the Pen and Executive Compensation*, 88 *J.* Fin. Econ. 1, 17 (2007).

35 Gregory S. Miller, *The Press as a Watchdog for Accounting Fraud*, 44 J. Acct. Res. 1001, 1004 (2006).

36 Violina P. Rindova et al., *Celebrity Firms: The Social Construction of Market Popularity*, 31 Acad. Mgmt. Rev. 50 (2006).

time. And stock market analysts have their own well-documented conflicts when reporting about companies.[37]

1.3.3 *Players Who Suffer Sanctions (Companies)*

To debunk yet another simplifying assumption: reputational sanctions are not a one-sided event. Companies do not go down without a fight. Much like legal control, reputational control is a function of ongoing interactions between regulators and regulated players.[38] Corporate insiders invest billions in an attempt to hijack the information flow and influence how their adverse actions are being interpreted by the market.[39]

Companies can dilute reputational sanctions through two channels: (1) avoiding detection, and (2) avoiding enforcement. To borrow crisis communication experts' lingo, this is the "managing information," and "managing meaning" channels, respectively.[40] "Managing information" denotes hiding your misconduct, or at least delaying the revelation of any damning information about you. Consider for example the documented pattern of camouflaging executive pay.[41] Corporate managers anticipate that if news breaks about their inflated pay, it will cause an outrage among stakeholders. In anticipation of the outrage, corporate insiders often manipulate outsiders' perceptions by changing how the pay package looks. By choosing to give the CEO an extra-undeserved $10 million through complex and opaque stock option plans, insiders may prevent an outrage that would have occurred if the CEO had received a less costly but more visible $5 million in cash. To revisit our DuPont–C8 example, there the company's in-house lawyer was conducting internal workshops on what *not* to document, to reduce the chances that any damning information would leak out.[42]

When their "managing information" efforts fail and bad news nevertheless leaks, companies can still resort to "managing meaning:" changing the way

37 *See, e.g.*, Roni Michaely et al., *Conflict of Interest and the Credibility of Underwriter Analyst Recommendations*, 12 Rev. Fin. Stud. 653 (1999).

38 The "New Governance" scholars emphasized this point for legal systems of control. Yuval Feldman & Orly Lobel, *The Incentives Matrix: The Comparative Effectiveness of Rewards, Liabilities, Duties, and Protections for Reporting Illegality*, 88 Tex. L. Rev. 1151, 1174 (2010). It is time we flesh it out for reputation systems of control as well.

39 *Cf.* Jon Hanson & David Yosifon, *The Situation: An Introduction to the Situational Character, Critical Realism, Power Economics, and Deep Capture*, 152 U. Pa. L. Rev. 129, 264–72 (2003).

40 Coombs, *supra* note 16, at 262.

41 Lucian A. Bebchuk & Jesse Fried, Pay without Performance: The Unfulfilled Promise of Executive Compensation 64–70 (2004).

42 Shapira & Zingales, *supra* note 17.

that market players interpret the information. Consider for example companies' investment in corporate social responsibility (CSR) as an image buffer. Stakeholders are less likely to attribute bad intentions to a perceivably nice company, chalking up the bad news to a one-off mistake rather than a deep-seated flaw.[43] When the nice-guy buffer works effectively, the company mitigates the risk of reputational sanctions. Enron serves as a case in point: Chapter 5 discusses one of the least-covered aspects of the heavily covered debacle, namely, that Enron was considered the poster child for CSR before its collapse. Some scholars believe that the accolades showered upon Enron for its CSR image contributed to the slow detection and punishment of Enron's misbehavior.

Companies can affect not only the *revelation* (hiding misconduct) and *attribution* conditions, but also *certification*. A well-developed psychology literature tells us that not all sources of information are created equal: stakeholders are more likely to update their beliefs and act on information when they perceive the source as credible.[44] Companies are well aware of these source-credibility effects, and invest resources trying to discredit any source of damning information about them. The classic example here is the tobacco industry's fight against the evidence on second-hand smoking. An emerging literature now documents more generally how large companies are adept at "manufacturing doubt" on sound scientific evidence.[45]

And, as Section 1.3.2 alluded to, companies can also limit the *diffusion* of damning information about them by capturing the media, as in threatening to sue in libel or to withhold advertising dollars and information.

Agency problems within companies further dilute the reputational deterrence. Sometimes bad news that affects the company's reputation may not affect the company's decision-makers' reputations. For example, one factor that drives a wedge between organizational-level and individual-level reputation is the time lag. When company decision-makers anticipate a big delay between the time they make a decision and the time in which information about their decision reaches the outside world, they may completely discount the threat of reputational sanctions. The executives' labor-market reputation

43 Paul Godfrey et al., *The Relationship between Corporate Social Responsibility and Shareholder Value: An Empirical Test of the Risk Management Hypothesis*, 30 STRATEGIC MGMT. J. 425 (2009); Daryl Koehn & Joe Ueng, *Is Philanthropy Being Used by Corporate Wrongdoers to Buy Good Will?*, 14 J. MGMT. & GOVERNANCE 1 (2010). But I do not wish to overstate the point here: Chapter 5 will delve into, and qualify the "CSR-as-reputational-buffer" argument.

44 DellaVigna & Gentzkow, *supra* note 26, at 657.

45 *See, e.g.*, NAOMI ORESKES & ERIK M. CONWAY, MERCHANTS OF DOUBT (2010); David Michaels & Celeste Monforton, *Manufacturing Uncertainty: Contested Science and the Protection of the Public's Health and Environment*, 95 AM. J. PUBLIC HEALTH 39 (2005).

has an expiration date: reputational concerns only deter them to the extent that the executives expect to be still in the market by the time bad news breaks. Here as well, the DuPont debacle serves as a case in point. DuPont's executives took the critical decision to continue emitting C8 without investing in abatement in 1984. Yet it was not until 2003 that mainline media started seriously scrutinizing the C8 debacle. By then, out of the twenty-nine directors sitting on DuPont's board back in 1984, nineteen had already died or retired from any other professional activity. Labor-market reputation had therefore stopped being a concern for them.[46] Under such scenarios, market discipline loses its force.

*

As reputation scholar Mike Barnett points out, stakeholders are the agents of reputation control, yet these agents are very limited in their ability to patrol (notice), perceive (assess), and punish corporate misconduct.[47] Stakeholders either have limited access to information, or limited attention to deal with the information overload we face nowadays. Part of the reason that stakeholders are so bad at noticing and assessing corporate misconduct is that they cannot consistently rely on the media to spotlight and diffuse information for them, while the misbehaving companies manage to hide critical pieces of information and instill doubt in existing damning information. Importantly, even when stakeholders do notice and properly assess misconduct – that is, even when all four conditions (revelation, diffusion, certification, attribution) are met – stakeholders may still opt to not act on the information. When stakeholders perceive their ability to affect change as limited, they are less likely to bother taking their business elsewhere.[48] A common scenario is that of market concentration: buyers cannot punish a seller by switching to a competitor, if said seller is the only game in town.[49] When stakeholders have no outside option, reputational deterrence loses its effectiveness.

Taken together, the emerging pieces of evidence suggest that reputational sanctions are much noisier than was previously assumed. The next necessary step is to examine why it matters that reputation is noisy: what are the social costs stemming from noisy reputational assessments?

46 And a media search we conducted revealed that none of the 1984 executives who signed the relevant memos and minutes were mentioned in media coverage of the C8 debacle. Shapira & Zingales, *supra* note 17.

47 Michael L. Barnett, *Why Stakeholders Ignore Firm Misconduct: A Cognitive View*, 40 J. MGMT. 676 (2014).

48 *Id.*, at 693.

49 Johannes Horner, *Reputation and Competition*, 92 AM. ECON. REV. 644 (2002).

1.4 THE IMPLICATIONS OF NOISY REPUTATIONAL SANCTIONS

The evidence demonstrates that the market overreacts to some misbehaviors and underreacts to others. Stakeholders may stop doing business with perfectly fine companies, or they may ignore early warning signs and continue doing business with rotten companies.

Polinsky and Shavell's proposal to abolish product liability for widely sold products provides a good case for illustration.[50] In making the argument that the market already monitors and deters misbehavior (whereby we can eliminate litigation without losing much deterrence), Polinsky and Shavell use three motivating examples: Johnson & Johnson's cyanide-laced Tylenol, Audi's self-accelerating cars, and Odwalla's contaminated juice.[51] In all these famous crises, information indeed disseminated quickly when something bad happened to widely sold products. When people died because they took a Tylenol, drove an Audi, or drank an Odwalla apple juice, the media were all over the story, consumers stopped purchasing products, and the stock prices plummeted. But a closer look at these three examples reveals an important yet overlooked point: we cannot assume that reputational forces punished and deterred optimally. In fact, in all these cases the market badly misjudged what happened and how it happened.

The Tylenol poisonings and Audi's self-accelerating cars are good examples of market *over*reaction. In the Tylenol case, Johnson & Johnson initially suffered huge reputational damages for something that it did not do – it was a case of external product tampering that happened on the retailer level.[52] The madman who tampered with Johnson & Johnson products could have tampered with other companies' products. Audi was also initially punished for something it did not do.[53] As was later proven, the self-acceleration allegations were false. Audi's cars did not accelerate by themselves; they accelerated because the accusers mistook the gas pedals for the brakes.

50 Mitchell Polinsky & Steven Shavell, *The Uneasy Case for Product Liability*, 123 HARV. L. REV. 1437 (2010).

51 The Tylenol crisis broke in 1982, when seven individuals died after taking a cyanide-laced drug. The Audi crisis broke in 1986, when Audi was accused of manufacturing a car that accelerated by itself. The Odwalla crisis broke in 1996, when several toddlers were harmed by drinking bacteria-infected juices.

52 Eric Dezenhall & John Weber, DAMAGE CONTROL 13–22 (2007).

53 The details of the Audi case are based on PETER W. HUBER, GALILEO'S REVENGE: JUNK SCIENCE IN THE COURTROOM 57–74 (1991); Greg Farrell, *Lurching into Reverse*, 1 BRILL'S CONTENT 55 (1998).

Odwalla's case is a perfect example of the flip side: the market *under*-reacted to Odwalla's breakdowns in quality control.[54] Odwalla had a preexisting image of a do-gooder, a socially responsible company, and that image served as a reputational buffer of sorts. And so, when top management stated that they could not have anticipated the juice contamination, stakeholders were willing to buy the company's version and interpret the event favorably.

At their core, then, these three famous examples do not tell the tale of optimal reputational sanctioning. They rather tell the tale of distorted reputational sanctioning. We cannot assume that the market reaction to those crises incentivized companies to invest optimally in product safety. If anything, those market reactions only distorted incentives: companies will now invest too much in the safety of certain visible products (following Tylenol); invest less in safety in general because arbitrary allegations against you may erase your reputational capital (following Audi); or invest too much in erecting reputational buffers – focusing on image instead of real quality (following Odwalla).

Importantly, the evidence suggests that the market *systematically* overreacts to certain misbehaviors and underreacts to others. We cannot discard the noise in reputational sanctions as irrational mistakes that cancel each other out. Companies that care about their reputation face incentives to excessively avoid some worthy behaviors (reputational over-deterrence), and excessively engage in some bad behaviors (reputational under-deterrence). For example, the market tends to overreact to failures of well-known companies and vivid failures, and underreact to less visible companies and opaque, complex issues.[55] Another factor to consider is the type of harm done: the market is likely to underreact when the misbehavior causes multiple small harms or concealed harms, and overreact when the victims are easily identifiable.[56] Yet another determinant is the state of the overall economy. Evidence suggests that reputational sanctions follow a supra-cyclical pattern.[57] When the

54 The details of the Odwalla case are based on Mallen Baker, *Odwalla and the E. Coli Outbreak*, CRISIS MANAGER INTERNET NEWSLETTER ABOUT CRISIS MANAGEMENT (Jan. 8, 2002), www.bernsteincrisismanagement.com/newsletter/crisismgr020801.html#3%60; Jon Entine, *The Odwalla Affair – Reassessing Corporate Social Responsibility*, AT WORK (Jan.–Feb. 1999).

55 DEZENHALL & WEBER, *supra* note 52, at 200–01 (detailed examples of how corporate watchdogs selectively bark at visible companies); Reuber & Fischer, *supra* note 15, at 47. To recast the example of criticizing executive pay arrangements: media and activists focus their criticism on the issue of overall *level* of pay, while in reality the *structure* of pay (how managerial incentives are tied to long-term performance) is more relevant to the company's stakeholders. *See* BEBCHUK & FRIED, *supra* note 41, at 121.

56 Polinsky & Shavell, *supra* note 50, at 1444–45.

57 Wiesenfeld et al., *supra* note 15, at 239–40.

economy is down, the public is actively searching for villains, so news about corporate misconduct may attract more attention. As a result, the market may overreact. By contrast, when the economy is booming, stakeholders might be more likely to ignore early warning signs.

As a result, reputational forces may distort primary behavior and hurt allocative efficiency. Companies may pick projects based on their reputational value and not on their "real" value.

The point about potential market over-deterrence is worth emphasizing, as it, too, has largely escaped the legal literature. Existing analyses usually assume that the noise in reputational sanctions leads strictly to under-punishment: large companies enjoy mismatches of information and power versus market players, and so are likely to exploit the holes in reputation systems in their favor.[58] But while it is indeed intuitive to think that companies can camouflage failures, one cannot ignore the dynamics that are in play once their failures are revealed. As scholars in other disciplines have recognized, once bad news breaks, market arbiters face incentives to pile on criticisms. The media tends to favor negative news,[59] and stakeholders suffer from negativity bias as well: we perceive negative information as more diagnostic than positive information.[60] Further, the naïve psychologist bias seems to be stronger for corporate behavior than for individual behavior: we tend to assume that big businesses can control whatever happens to them. As a result, stakeholders may overreact and unnecessarily sever ties with otherwise healthy companies.[61]

To be sure, more (empirical) work is needed to identify the conditions under which the market is under- or overreacting. Still, the basic point about markets for reputation stands: they are much more flawed than was previously acknowledged.

*

My point is not that the invisible hand of the market for reputation never works, but rather that it cannot be assumed to generate optimal deterrence consistently. To recast the example we opened the book with, Polinsky and Shavell anticipated the "market imperfections" rebuttals to their argument that reputational deterrence makes legal liability redundant. To accommodate this potential rebuttal, they limited their proposal to abolish product

58 *See, e.g.*, Robert Prentice, *Whither Securities Regulation? Some Behavioral Observations Regarding Proposals for Its Future*, 51 Duke L.J. 1397, 1429–34 (2002).

59 Kolbel et al., *supra* note 10, at 2269.

60 Shai Davidai & Thomas Gilovich, *The Headwinds/Tailwinds Asymmetry: An Availability Bias in Assessments of Barriers and Blessings*, 111 J. Personality & Social Psych. 835, 847 (2016).

61 *Cf.* Dezenhall & Weber, *supra* note 52, at 52; Wiesenfeld et al., *supra* note 15, at 240–42.

liability only to widely sold products. Their logic was that with widely sold product, there is bound to be ample information on product defects, and so the market for reputation functions well enough to deter misbehavior. Yet our deep dive into the reputation literature reveals the fallacies in logic. For one, we cannot assume that consumers will have access to quality information just because the product is widely sold: if the product causes opaque, latent and dispersed damages, information may not surface even when harm is inflicted upon many victims. More importantly, even if information does surface, information does not automatically translate into reputation. It has to be properly certified, attributed, and diffused – and as we saw here, these conditions are far from automatic.

The lesson for legal scholars and policy makers is straightforward: recognizing an area of market behavior with strong reputational concerns only begins analysis. A full analysis requires identifying whether the reputational forces deter optimally or not. Accurate reputation information is in a sense a public good. It carries social benefits: warning market players of a specific wrongdoer, deterring future potential wrongdoers, and causing market players to switch to doing business with the worthier competitors of the wrongdoer.[62] And it comes with social costs, such as resources spent on certifying rumors or fighting back false allegations. The private players who engage in reputational sanctioning – rumor propagators, media channels, stakeholders – do not fully internalize the *social* costs and benefits. Private players, when left alone, lack the information and incentives to produce accurate reputational sanctions. How can reputation markets function, then?

Part of the answer lies in the fact that in reality the market is rarely left alone. Adverse actions are interpreted and assessed not just by market arbiters, but also by legal arbiters. In the Tylenol, Audi, Odwalla, and many other famous cases, the legal system produced information that propelled market players to revise their initial reaction to the bad news. In order to get a full picture of reputation we therefore need to explore the different channels through which the law generates information and affects reputations.

62 Robert Cooter & Ariel Porat, *Should Courts Deduct Non-Legal Sanctions from Damages?*, 30 J. Legal Stud. 401, 405–06 (2001).

2

How the Legal System Affects Reputation

2.1 INTRODUCTION

Chapter 1 revolved around the question of why similar behaviors lead to different reputational outcomes. This chapter suggests that a large part of the answer is the legal system. When stakeholders hear about a good or bad deed done by a company, they update their beliefs about the company's quality and consequently update their willingness to interact with the company. But this process of belief revision – the process of reputational rewarding/sanctioning – does not operate in a vacuum. The legal system generates new pieces of information on the behavior in question and adds saliency and credibility to existing information. Stakeholders can then rely on the information that was generated by the legal system to reassess their beliefs about the company. In other words, the law dictates the market reaction.

Section 2.2 breaks down the law's reputational effects into two categories: where information comes from, and how the information shapes reputation. The first category concerns the distinction between legal institutions that are primarily geared to produce information, such as disclosure requirements, and legal institutions that produce information as a by-product. The second category concerns the distinction between breaking new information, and shaping the saliency, credibility, and framing of given pieces of information in stakeholders' minds. Throughout all these different conduits, the legal system produces a positive externality: quality information that facilitates effective reputational deterrence.

Evaluating the magnitude of this informational positive externality is a daunting task, though. Deterrence is hard to measure, and reputation is an even fuzzier concept. To provide some sense of reputational deterrence, I resort to using a proxy: media coverage. A multidisciplinary literature documents the important role that media scrutiny plays in holding powerful players to account. Effective media scrutiny facilitates reputational control. I ask the prior question, namely, what determines the effectiveness of media scrutiny. Section 2.3 presents evidence from interviewing reporters, going over a reporters-only database of tip sheets, scouring course syllabi in journalism schools, and conducting content analysis of prizewinning journalistic projects. The triangulation of these methods suggests that litigation is a key source of impactful media coverage, and therefore a key part in well-functioning reputation markets.

Section 2.4 refines our theory by accommodating potential limitations. The legal system does not always manage to produce relevant information. And even when it does, information from the legal system cannot cure all the biases in reputational sanctioning. It can help consumers understand whether a given product defect is endemic or idiosyncratic, but it cannot improve their bounded attention span, or make the media cover opaque topics. The key is to remember that the legal system does not have to be perfect in order to facilitate a well-functioning market for reputation. All it takes is that the legal system's flaws are imperfectly correlated with the market system's flaws. In other words, the interactions between the two systems operate as a diversified portfolio, mitigating the risk of extreme under or overreactions.

Section 2.5 increases our resolution, by focusing on factors that determine the variation in reputational effects: some types of legal disputes generate a big effect on disputants' reputations, while others do not affect reputations whatsoever; some disputes actually boost the reputation of the defendants, while others hurt them greatly.

2.2 THE BASIC STORY

The legal system affects reputation in various ways. This section breaks the different reputational effects down by asking two straightforward questions. First, *where* the information is coming from – what type of legal institution produces it? Does it come from legal institutions that are primarily geared to produce information ("direct sources" – as in disclosure requirements), or does it come from legal institutions that produce information only as a by-product ("indirect sources" – as in litigation). Second, *how* the information affects reputational assessments. Does the legal system break news – reveals new information that was not previously available ("first-opinion effects") to the market, or does it shape the framing and saliency of preexisting pieces of information ("second-opinion effects").

2.2.1 Where Information Comes From

Various legal institutions are primarily geared to make information about the behavior of powerful players available to the public. An obvious example is the Freedom of Information Act (FOIA).[1] Congress explicitly envisioned FOIA as contributing to the ability of the public to hold government players to account.[2] Another classic example is mandatory disclosure requirements. Disclosure requirements incentivize corporate decision makers to publicly reveal information about their own misconduct. Yet another example is whistleblowing laws. Whistleblowing laws protect the whistleblower from retaliation by her employer, and in some areas even offer substantive monetary rewards for blowing the whistle.[3] As a result, they incentivize employees to flush out information about the behavior of their employers.[4]

When legal scholars write about the information-production effects of the law, they usually focus on these "direct" channels. But if you were to ask investigative reporters, they would tell you that there exist other, "indirect" channels through which the legal system produces information, and that these indirect channels are at least equally important.[5]

On paper, FOIA and public records laws, disclosure requirements, and whistleblowing acts should combine to provide ample information for journalists to hold powerful players to account and for market players to decide with whom they want to keep doing business. Yet in reality, direct sourcing channels are severely lacking. The implementation of FOIA is dysfunctional, fraught with delays and denials.[6] As a result, many journalists give up on using FOIA at the outset.[7] While the government is bombarded with FOIA requests, journalists (not to mention regular citizens) make up only a tiny

1 5 U.S.C. § 552 (2018).

2 NLRB v. Robbins Tire & Rubber Co., 437 U.S. 214, 242 (1978).

3 *See, e.g.*, 31 U.S.C. § 3730(d) (2018).

4 Alexander Dyck et al., *Who Blows the Whistle on Corporate Fraud?*, 65 J. Fin. 2213, 2214 (2010) (providing evidence that whistleblowing is a substantial source of breaking bad news about financial misconduct).

5 *See, e.g.*, Reporters Comm. for Freedom of the Press, Federal Open Government Guide 10 (10th ed. 2009). For concrete examples, see Roy Shapira, *Law as Source: How the Legal System Facilitates Investigative Journalism*, 37 Yale L. & Pol'y Rev. 153, 170–71 (2018).

6 *See, e.g.*, Erin C. Carroll, *Protecting the Watchdog: Using the Freedom of Information Act to Preference the Press*, 2016 Utah L. Rev. 193, 193, 195, 211–15 (2016).

7 David Cuillier, Pressed for Time: U.S. Journalists' Use of Public Records During Economic Crisis 13–16 (May 2011) (unpublished manuscript) (on file with author) (presenting evidence from a survey of 442 journalists).

fraction of FOIA users.[8] Disclosure laws, similarly, look good on paper but suffer from enforcement issues.[9] Pertinently, the useful information – damning information about powerful players – either eludes disclosure altogether or gets buried under an avalanche of useless information.[10]

A fundamental problem with direct sourcing channels is that they work well only when there are preexisting high levels of accountability in the system. A journalist submitting a FOIA request in an attempt to expose government misconduct has to hope that the same powerful players that broke substantive rules will somehow abide by the information-production rules, instead of ignoring, delaying, or watering them down.[11] Similarly, corporate decision makers who engage in shady practices also tend not to be fully transparent when revealing information in their company's official documents. Put differently, transparency requirements cannot bypass asymmetries in power.[12] As long as those in power are the ones in charge of enforcing disclosure requirements, it will be hard to use disclosure requirements to hold them to account.

Fortunately, even when direct sources fail, indirect sources prevail. Law enforcement actions, in particular, produce quality information on the behavior of powerful players in society. When government agencies or business companies misbehave and harm someone, the victim may enlist the help of the legal system. A plaintiff's lawyer may file a lawsuit, or a regulator may initiate an investigation to examine whether the powerful entity broke some rules and needs to pay. In the process of determining whether to impose legal sanctions, the law enforcement action produces information on how the parties to the dispute behaved.

Litigation, especially in the US system, provides strong monetary incentives, such as damages and lawyers' fees, for harmed parties to expose misbehavior in court. These strong incentives increase the chance that information about the alleged misconduct will spread readily and credibly to the court of

8 David Pozen, *Freedom of Information beyond the Freedom of Information Act*, 165 U. PA. L. REV. 1097, 1103 (2017).

9 Omri Ben-Shahar & Carl E. Schneider, *The Failure of Mandated Disclosure*, 159 U. PA. L. REV. 647 (2011) (on the failure of mandatory disclosure to shape business behavior); Pozen, *id.*, at 1108 (on the failure of affirmative disclosure to shape government behavior). For studies criticizing whistleblowing laws, see *id.* at 1109 n.67 (compiling references).

10 Ben-Shahar & Schneider, *id.*, at 737.

11 David S. Law, *A Theory of Judicial Power and Judicial Review*, 97 GEO. L.J. 723, 753 (2009) ("For information about the government, the press must rely to a significant extent upon what the government itself chooses to disclose. The government can be expected to provide the media with a selective and self-serving account of its own activities, to reward sympathetic journalists with preferential access to information, and perhaps even to suppress or censor unfavorable coverage").

12 Amitai Etzioni, *The Capture Theory of Regulations – Revisited*, 46 SOCIETY 319, 321 (2009).

public opinion. And as soon as a dispute enters the legal system, the law vests powers in private litigants to probe and demand relevant information from their rivals.

The last point – about information-extracting powers – is worth emphasizing. While direct sourcing channels often rely on players *volunteering* information, indirect sourcing channels often rely on *forcing* information out of them. This fundamental difference can make information extracted during litigation/regulatory investigation more conducive to market players trying to understand how companies behaved, relative to information selectively released by the companies themselves.

As a result, law enforcement actions are a key source of reputation-relevant information. The immediate upshot is that legal strategies to improve the information environment should focus not just on disclosure requirements, but also on issues such as protective orders, confidential settlements, or mandatory arbitration clauses, which limit the information flows from the courtroom. But before we jump ahead to policy implications (Chapters 7 and 8 are waiting patiently), let us first continue breaking down the "reputation through litigation" dynamics, this time according to the different conduits through which they operate: litigation affects reputations not just by revealing new information, but also by shaping the diffusion, certification, and attribution of existing information.

2.2.2 *How Information Affects Reputations*

We saw in Chapter 1 that one basic problem of reputational control arises from the difficulties of detecting and reacting in real time to corporate misbehavior. Law enforcement helps in revealing new information on corporate misbehavior by offering a bounty: the prospect of getting damages and lawyers' fees in litigation incentivizes victims to expose the misbehavior publicly, in court. Once an issue gets to court, the legal system vests fact-finding powers in private litigants to probe and demand relevant information from their rivals. These facts-generating powers were primarily designed to increase the accuracy of legal adjudication. But they also generate as a by-product information to which market arbiters previously could not have been privy. The classic example here is internal email communications exposed during the discovery stage, showing just how big the organizational cover-up was.

In other words, law enforcement can serve to reduce the *detection costs* of reputation control systems: the costs of revealing misconduct. In such instances, the law sets a reputational sanction in motion, pushing market players to react to corporate misconduct.

In many other situations, however, market players hardly need pushing. Research suggests that market players often learn about misconduct by large public companies – and act upon it – long before a lawsuit is filed. One comprehensive study estimates that the filing of a lawsuit is responsible for breaking bad news in less than 7 percent of financial misconduct cases.[13] In the other 93 percent of the cases market players learn about misbehavior from various other sources, such as whistleblowers, investigative reporters, or financial reports. Still, even when the legal system's reaction is lagged it may nevertheless affect the market, albeit in a different way: shaping the attribution, certification, and diffusion of existing information. In other words, litigation helps not only by revealing new information, but also by processing existing information.

Consider first the *attribution* stage. Judicial opinions are good at fleshing out patterns of misbehavior, organizing large chunks of information, and making it all less complex for outside observers. In particular, judicial opinions often make it easier on market players to assess how intentional the actions in question were – an important determinant of reputational sanctions. Think, for example, about securities litigation, where the judge has to make inferences about *scienter* from the outset. Such reputational impact is not limited to the (rare) disputes that culminate in a judicial verdict. Even in cases that settle early, legal documents that come out during pleading, discovery, or trial help not just by drawing outside observers' attention to a misbehavior they were not aware of, but also by adding detail and analysis on how things happened. To reuse Oliver Williamson's typology, litigation often provides stakeholders with the "second-level information" they too often miss (the context).

To illustrate, consider two of the most famous car company debacles: Ford Pinto's defective fuel system design that led to explosions, and GM's ignition switch recalls. Reputation scholars have wondered why Ford received such a big reputational hit following the Pinto scandal, while other car companies who suffered similar problems did not.[14] The answer comes from litigation. Discovery surfaced an internal company memo, showing that the company *knowingly* opted to not recall or fix Pinto models even though they knew these models had safety issues (specifically, a fuel tank being prone to combust in rear-end collisions). Similarly, the key moment that changed public

[13] Jonathan M. Karpoff et al., *Proxies and Databases in Financial Misconduct Research*, 92 Acc. Rev. 129 (2017). *See also* Dyck et al., *supra* note 4.

[14] Donald Lange & Nathan T. Washburn, *Understanding Attributes of Corporate Social Irresponsibility*, 37 Acad. Mgmt. Rev. 300, 302 (2012).

perception of the GM scandal came when the media spotlighted a deposition given by a company's engineer, suggesting that GM knew about the faulty switches but took a "business decision" not to replace them.[15]

Litigation also affects reputation through *certification*. We saw in Chapter 1 that damning information too often does not result in reputational damages, because stakeholders discount it as not credible. But information coming from the legal system is considered relatively credible, and thereby tends to move the needle. Judicial opinions are normally considered disinterested and fair. In the corporate governance context, for example, the business community considers Delaware judges to be reputable experts, and attaches considerable weight to any opinion they have about companies and businesspersons.[16] Depositions and testimonies are given under oath. Documents are produced under the threat of perjury. Indeed, several journalists I interviewed told me that the mere phrase "according to court documents" is a rhetorical device they use to increase their story's credibility.[17] A journalist may have all the information she needs from another source, but she would still find it valuable to search for corroboration in court documents to increase the chances that her story reverberates.

Finally, litigation affects reputation by shaping the frequency and tenor of media coverage (the *diffusion* stage). Litigation feeds the media with prepackaged information, or, the way that communication scientists call it: "information subsidies."[18] Court documents reduce the costs to journalists of covering the story. They often provide information that is well documented and detailed, and contains good quotes from internal company documents. Importantly, information from court documents is invaluable for investigative reporters because it is practically *libel-proof*; as long as the media reports accurately from court documents, it is shielded from defamation liability.

Indeed, when I analyzed the content of prizewinning investigative reports, I found that over half of them rely heavily on legal sources. In many of them, the most important effects of the law were not in providing the initial tip that led to the story, but rather in providing veracity and depth. The rest of this section expands on this point by introducing the analogy of first-opinion- and second-opinion effects.

15 Doron Levin, *New GM: Same As It Ever Was?*, FORTUNE, Apr. 28, 2014, at 64.

16 Chapter 3 elaborates.

17 *See* Appendix A (Table A1, Ureneck interview).

18 *See generally* Oscar H. Gandy, Jr., BEYOND AGENDA SETTING: INFORMATION SUBSIDIES AND PUBLIC POLICY (1982) (coining term).

2.2.3 *First-Opinion and Second-Opinion Effects*

Bad news about a company often ignites two reactions. First, the market system's reaction: stakeholders reducing their willingness to do business with the company. Then, the legal system's reaction: a plaintiffs' lawyer files a lawsuit or a regulator initiates an investigation to examine whether the company broke some rules and needs to pay for it. Importantly for our purposes, the process of determining whether to impose legal sanctions produces information on questions such as what top managers knew and when they knew it. In that sense, litigation or regulatory investigations often create another "third-party assessment" of the company's behavior. And to the extent that such information is made publicly available, it allows market players to reevaluate their assessment of the company's quality.

In other words, the company's stakeholders can use the legal system's lagged version of what and how things happened as a second opinion on their reputation judgments. In the second-opinion analogy, stakeholders are the decision makers, pondering how to update beliefs about a misbehaving company; market arbiters (media, watchdogs, analysts) are the first-opinion givers; and legal arbiters are the second-opinion givers.

To be sure, the fact that another assessment is available does not mean that it will be used. Not all second opinions are effective. In our context, however, the legal system's version often makes a valuable second opinion, because it complements the market's initial reaction nicely. Based on what Chapter 1 taught us about reputational judgments, we can generalize that the market will have a reasonable sense of *what* happened, but will have problems understanding *how* it happened. When news of corporate misbehavior breaks, stakeholders quickly learn exactly what the product defect was or how hefty a severance package was awarded to the soon-to-be-leaving CEO. But stakeholders have poor information and resort to biased heuristics when trying to interpret whether the event is indicative of future behavior. Perhaps the product defect was an unforeseeable isolated mistake; perhaps the hefty severance package was the only reasonable card that the board could play given the circumstances.

Legal arbiters, by contrast, enjoy more fact-finding powers, expertise, and credibility than market arbiters did when they initially judged the event. The discovery process provides market players with better facts. Judges or regulators provide them with better interpretations, helping them assess the intentionality of the act. Judges are arguably seasoned experts in evaluating intentions: in many scenarios the legal doctrine requires a judge to determine the animus associated with a behavior. The legal system's opinion may thus replace half-truths with verified facts, and bias-laden judgments with expert judgments.

2.2.4 *Motivating Examples*

To illustrate the law's second-opinion effects we can start by recasting the motivating examples we used in Chapter 1. The crisis of Audi's self-accelerating cars illustrates several flaws in reputational sanctioning, such as misinformed stakeholders and allegation-driven media.[19] The major reputational damage to Audi occurred after CBS's 60 *Minutes* picked up the self-acceleration allegations and aired a story with dramatic interviews and a (fabricated) visual illustration of a driverless car accelerating. At that point Audi's reputation among US customers was close to zero. Then, after the immediate market overreaction, the story was picked up by plaintiffs' lawyers who filed lawsuits and government regulators who initiated investigations. During cross-examination a new crucial piece of information came to light: the featured interviewee from the 60 *Minutes* piece admitted to telling the police officer on the scene that she mistook the gas pedal for the brakes. And a thorough investigation by the regulatory agency – the National Highway Traffic Safety Administration – concluded that the cars did not accelerate by themselves. Audi then used the information produced by the legal system to try to correct the noisy information produced by rumor propagators and the media. The company bought full-page ads in major newspapers and simply filled them with quotes from the regulatory report, claiming vindication.

Another earlier example – the Odwalla case – illustrates the flip side: how asymmetric information and judgment biases may lead stakeholders to *under*-react. After Odwalla initially succeeded in convincing the public that the failure was unforeseeable, some of the lawsuits against it reached the discovery stage. The plaintiffs' lawyers then exposed internal company documents showing that Odwalla's managers actually knew about the potential health hazards in advance and chose to ignore the warnings. Consequently, the market rethought the trustworthiness of Odwalla, and the company's reputation took a big dip.

Many other famous corporate debacles display similar second-opinion effects. Chapter 3 delves into the famous corporate law case around the Disney–Ovitz divorce, and shows that the valence of media coverage of the debacle had become more *favorable* toward Disney following the verdict. This is hardly surprising: stakeholders' initial reactions when reading about corporate misbehavior are plagued by attribution errors and hindsight bias. Once bad news breaks, stakeholders often overreact because they tend to downplay

19 The details of the Audi case are based on PETER W. HUBER, GALILEO'S REVENGE: JUNK SCIENCE IN THE COURTROOM 57–74 (1991); Greg Farrell, *Lurching into Reverse*, 1 BRILL'S CONTENT 55 (1998).

the context and attribute negative outcomes to deep-seated flaws. Judges can balance this tendency, because their version usually spotlights the external conditions surrounding the event in question.

In other types of cases, the legal system's second opinion helps stakeholders de-bias the information coming from the misbehaving companies. As the debacles of Salomon Brothers and Arthur Andersen illustrate, the legal system can either lend credibility to or discard a company's version of the events. In 1991, news about Salomon Brothers' trading shenanigans ignited a media firestorm, which in turn resulted in mass sell-offs of the company's shares.[20] The company acted promptly to recover the reputational harm: Warren Buffet took charge and the company offered transparency and full cooperation with the investigation. Salomon's recovery is widely considered a success story. But *why* exactly did the Salomon recovery succeed? After all, many companies follow the same recipe of changing the management and promising to be nice from now on, yet do not recover reputational damages.

In this specific case, the recovery efforts received a boost of credibility from financial regulators. Following the initial outcry, the Justice Department, Securities and Exchange Commission (SEC), and other government agencies started investigating Salomon. Several months later, the SEC announced that Salomon had agreed to pay a $290 million fine to settle the case. More importantly, the SEC chairman included in his announcement an assessment of the company's behavior that pretty much certified what the company was claiming. The SEC lent credibility to the company's attempts to distance itself from the wrongdoing, believing that the "infractions were rooted in individual excess rather than in systemic abuse," and that current management did right in responding to the misconduct and "purging the company of its rogue elements." The stock market reacted very positively to the announcement.

By contrast, when Arthur Andersen followed the same recipe in an attempt to distance itself from the Enron debacle, the market was not convinced.[21] This is partly because the legal system produced information that discredited the company's version. Arthur Andersen claimed that the misbehavior was the work of a single partner, who was subsequently fired. But the prosecutors chose to cut a deal with the singled-out partner, and the trial produced information

[20] The details of the Salomon Brothers case are based on CHARLES J. FOMBRUN, REPUTATION: REALIZING VALUE FROM THE CORPORATE IMAGE 362–85 (1996); Lynn Sharp Paine & Michael A. Santoro, *Forging the New Salomon* (Harv. Bus. Sch., Case Study No. 9-395-046, 2004).

[21] The details of the Arthur Andersen case are based on Rebecca Reuber & Eileen Fischer, *Organizations Behaving Badly: When Are Discreditable Actions Likely to Damage Organizational Reputation?*, 93 J. BUS. ETHICS 39, 42–43 (2010).

about how pervasive the problems were, and how the higher-ups in Andersen were aware of them in real time.[22]

Taken together, all these examples illustrate how the legal system can serve as *a safety valve* for reputation systems. In instances where market players greatly under or overreacted, the legal system later provides a more balanced perspective of how things happened, thereby allowing market players to go back and correct their initial assessment. Perhaps more importantly and beyond the impact of the legal system on specific under or overreactions after the fact, the mere background threat of litigation affects all future reputational assessments to begin with. We turn to these *ex ante* effects now.

2.2.5 Ex ante *Effects*

Studies across various contexts show that when first-opinion givers anticipate the possibility of an accurate second opinion, they invest more in the accuracy of their initial assessments.[23] We have ample reason to believe that the analogy applies to our context of providing information on corporate failures. Both the accusers and the accused are disciplined by a credible threat of second opinions.

The mere background threat of litigation pushes the accused companies to refrain from lying when denying accusations. Indeed, crisis management experts explicitly advise their clients to be disciplined in how they fight accusations, bearing in mind the possibility that their denials will be exposed in discovery as lies.[24]

The background threat of litigation also pushes information intermediaries to make their accusations more accurate. A journalist or a corporate watchdog probably anticipates the possibility that future litigation will surface nuanced information about the behavior it is currently criticizing. Assuming they care about their reputation as a journalist/activist, the possibility of being later exposed as wrong will make them invest more in their initial assessments. It is as if the legal system helps us better assess not only the behavior of business corporations, but also the behavior of corporate watchdogs. Watchdogs that make unfounded accusations can later be exposed as unprofessional. By contrast, high-quality watchdogs can use legal success stories to boast of their

22 Jonathan R. Macey, The Death of Corporate Reputation 141–42 (2013).
23 In the literature on second opinions, such a reaction is termed the *sentinel effect*. Adrian Vermeule, *Second Opinions and Institutional Design*, 97 Va. L. Rev. 1435, 1464 (2011).
24 *See, e.g.*, Michael Regester & Judy Larkin, Risk Issues and Crisis Management 194 (2005).

effectiveness as compared to their competitors, namely, other watchdogs advancing the same cause. In that sense, the legal system facilitates a market for corporate watchdogs' reputation.[25]

Indeed, when I sampled websites of prominent corporate watchdogs, I found that almost every website contains a list of "legal victories" describing how watchdog-initiated fights led to hefty damages awards or changes in regulation.[26] For example, the Natural Resources Defense Council (NRDC), an environmental nongovernmental organization, declares itself "the most effective lobbying and litigating group on environmental issues."[27] What makes them so effective, you may ask? Well, for one thing, they tell you, they have an army of 500 savvy lawyers, scientists, and policy advocates. The website then refers the visitor to a long list of legal battles that the NRDC has won. To be sure, these anecdotal observations are not enough to prove that the legal system facilitates a better market for watchdog reputation, and more systematic evidence is needed.[28] Nevertheless, the observations indicate how watchdogs think that success in the legal arena is a good indicator of their competence.

*

Overall, second-opinion effects reduce the *enforcement costs* of reputational systems: the costs of calibrating and carrying out responses to detected violations of market norms. In doing so, the second-opinion role of the law coexists and complements nicely the first-opinion role, in which the law helps market players detect violations. We cannot determine with certainty which of these two informational effects is more important, as both depend on the company

[25] To illustrate, when Wendy's was accused of selling a woman chili containing a severed human finger, the vivid accusation threatened to kill the Wendy's brand. But Wendy's reputation quickly recovered because journalists found out that the accuser had a record of frivolous lawsuits. The public's attention then shifted from the alleged misbehavior of the company to the bad intentions of the accuser. ERIC DEZENHALL & JOHN WEBER, DAMAGE CONTROL 127–30 (2007).

[26] My sampling criterion was straightforward: all the watchdogs that a notable crisis management book (ERIC DEZENHALL, NAIL 'EM! CONFRONTING HIGH-PROFILE ATTACKS ON CELEBRITIES & BUSINESSES (1999)) mentions as prominent.

[27] *About Us*, NAT. RES. DEF. COUNCIL, http://www.nrdc.org/about [https://perma.cc/3Q47-2P4C] (last visited Aug. 1, 2015). *See also Litigation Project – Current Docket*, CTR. FOR SCI. PUB. INTEREST, http://www.cspinet.org/litigation/current.html [https://perma.cc/S7U9-EG95] (last visited Aug. 1, 2015) (providing an even more straightforward example).

[28] From my anecdotal observation I found little to no reports of legal losses or frivolous suits. Watchdogs report only successes. And it seems like watchdogs take credit even for success stories to which they contributed marginally. The legal success-story signal is thus very noisy. It is better than no signal, though. Fly-by-night watchdogs are not able to boast a long list of legal success stories.

and issue at hand.[29] But we can observe, more generally, a gradual shift in the informational role of the law: in the past, when markets and information technologies were not as developed, the role of the law in reputation markets was mostly to detect violations.[30] Nowadays, the problem is not so much lack of information, but rather sorting out what pieces of information are more relevant and credible. In a "fake news"/"attention deficit" environment, adjudication is needed not so much to add more information, but rather to spotlight, make sense of, and ensure the veracity of given pieces of information.

2.3 EVIDENCE

The abovementioned examples may have convinced you that the law can occasionally produce a positive externality: quality information on the behavior of powerful players, which then turns into reputational deterrence. Yet evaluating the magnitude of this informational positive externality is a daunting task. Deterrence is notoriously hard to measure, and reputation is a fuzzy concept. To provide some sense of reputational deterrence, I therefore resorted to using a proxy: media coverage of powerful players in government and business.[31]

A burgeoning multidisciplinary literature documents the important role that media scrutiny plays in corporate governance and politics. I ask the prior question, namely, what determines the effectiveness of media scrutiny: what types of corporate misconduct will the media cover? How it will cover them? In particular, I look at the extent to which media scrutiny relies on court documents. By triangulating several methods – interviewing reporters, going over a reporters-only database of tip sheets, scouring course syllabi in journalism schools, and conducting content analysis of prizewinning journalistic projects – I make the case that litigation is a key source of impactful media coverage.

Section 2.3.1 presents the evidence gathered by listening to what journalists say about the role of law as source. As a first step, I interviewed forty veteran reporters, asking about their experience using legal sources. To mitigate the

[29] To generalize: first-opinion effects are only relevant when negative events are likely to fly under the radar to begin with. David W. Prince & Paul H. Rubin, *The Effects of Product Liability Litigation on the Value of Firms*, 4 AM. L. & ECON. REV. 44, 64–65 (2002).

[30] Indeed, this is the main theme of historical case studies of *lex mercatoria*, where judges did not sanction but provided information to other merchants on the misconduct of disputants. Law, *supra* note 11, at 745.

[31] The reputation literature has long recognized that the media is not just a recorder of reputation but also an important determinant of reputation.

potential biases in an interview method, I evaluated not only what the journalists said when they spoke with me, but also what they say when they talk among themselves and give advice to their colleagues in memoirs, how-to manuals, and tip sheets. Relatedly, I compared basic Investigative Reporting course syllabi from leading journalism schools. Section 2.3.2 presents evidence about what journalists actually do. I analyzed the content of prizewinning investigative projects over 1995–2015, and coded the extent to which they relied on legal sources. All these different methods led to the same conclusion: legal sources play a significant role in facilitating accountability journalism.

2.3.1 *Findings from Tip Sheets, Course Syllabi, and Interviews*

One way to gauge the importance of law as source is to listen to what investigative reporters say about it. And the best place to pick up pointers on how journalists treat sources is investigative reporters' tip sheets and how-to manuals, whose target audiences are other journalists. The Investigative Reporters' Organization (IRE) has created a members-only database of tip sheets, containing advice from investigative reporters to their colleagues on a wide range of issues.[32] I accessed their database and found no fewer than ninety-two tip sheets under the tag of "court documents." All these tip sheets explicitly refer to the various roles of law as source, underscoring just how important legal sources are to the different phases of the investigative reporter's work.

To illustrate, one tip sheet, titled "Finding the Story," contains advice about the initial phase of investigative work.[33] The tip sheet makes it clear from the outset: whenever you investigate a powerful institution, the first thing you need to do is "pull every related suit," and "scour state agency disciplinary and regulatory reports." This is because "lawsuits connect us to documents, exhibits, depositions and sources of every type," and "[e]nforcement actions are rich repositories." Further, the tip sheet explicitly recognizes the role of lawsuits as a gateway to other sources: "[l]awyers are great sources . . . they are document-based creatures – like us – and they often relish media contact." Then, once lawsuits and regulatory investigations have allowed you to spot a pattern and realize that there is a story, the tip sheet tells you to start researching the story by using another "legal" channel, namely, filing FOIA requests.

[32] The database is available at http://ire.org/resource-center/tipsheets.
[33] Michael Berens, *Finding the Story* 1 (IRE, Tipsheet No. 3764, 2012) (on file with author).

Such explicit references to law as source are not limited to the IRE's tip sheet database. I also found them in multiple how-to manuals, textbooks, and scholarly work on investigative reporting.[34] As one textbook puts it, "Whether in the form of affidavits, motions to sever or judges' opinions, court filings contain clues to solving a case's mysteries."[35]

As another method to gauge the importance of law as source, I interviewed forty investigative reporters. I started every interview with the same big-picture question: "What role does the legal system play in sourcing investigative reports?" Almost every interviewee suggested that the law plays an extremely important role as source. "Huge" and "invaluable" were the most frequently used descriptors.[36] In the reporters' own words: "Most serious investigative stories involve court records."[37] "Journalism rests heavily on legal sources."[38] "[The] relevancy of legal documents is huge . . . it is an essential part of investigative reporting."[39] "The court system is so integrated in investigative reporting – hard to imagine doing it without them."[40] "Going to the courts is ingrained in every investigative journalist. The minute I have an idea [for a story], first thing I do, to research the landscape, I go to the court and look for cases."[41] "[It is] unusual to have a major investigative project without legal documents to buttress some of the findings."[42] "[Legal sources are] more important than just about any other source of information. I don't know an investigative reporter that doesn't rely on documents they get from courts . . . Can't imagine doing an investigative piece without it."[43]

Importantly, several interviewees qualified their answer to the what-role-do-legal-sources-play question along the lines of "it depends."[44] They all shared the same theme, namely, that the legal system allows too much information to remain sealed, thereby limiting the actual role that the law plays.[45] In other

34 *See, e.g.*, William C. Gaines, Investigative Journalism: Proven Strategies for Reporting the Story 139–43 (2008); Toni Locy, Covering America's Courts: A Clash of Rights 71 (2013); David Spark, Investigative Reporting: A Study in Technique 32–40 (1999).

35 Locy, *id.*, at 67.

36 *See* Appendix A (Table A1, Berens interview); Bogdanich interview; McKim interview; Nelson interview.

37 Appendix A (Table A1, McKim interview).

38 Appendix A (Table A1, Mehren interview).

39 Appendix A (Table A1, Lewis interview).

40 Appendix A (Table A1, Nelson interview).

41 Appendix A (Table A1, Berens interview).

42 Appendix A (Table A1, Englund interview).

43 Appendix A (Table A1, Bogdanich interview).

44 Appendix A (Table A1, Daly interview; Eisinger interview; Graves interview; Smith interview).

45 Appendix A (Table A1, Bogdanich interview; Locy interview; Starkman interview).

words, they all agreed that the law can and often does play an important role in sourcing accountability journalism, but lamented that the law's information production does not reach its potential. We will revisit this theme in Chapter 7 when discussing policy implications.

Several of the reporters I interviewed teach investigative reporting in universities. They all mentioned emphasizing the importance of legal sources to their students. In their words: "I currently tell my journalism students that court records are the most valuable tool a reporter can use."[46] "One of the cornerstones of journalism school is [to teach the importance of] going to the courthouse and pulling out relevant records."[47] To corroborate their argument, I looked at the basic investigative reporting course syllabi of leading journalism schools.[48]

In all but one course syllabus that provided detail on the content of the individual sessions, the class had specific sessions dedicated to learning how to use legal sources.[49] In fact, many courses share a similar structure: in week 1 the students learn what investigative journalism is, and already in weeks 2 or 3 they are learning how to cull and use information from the legal system. The Boston University course dedicates week 2 to gathering information from criminal litigation and week 3 to doing the same from civil litigation. The Berkeley course syllabus not only earmarks week 2 for legal sources, but also highlights knowing how to use legal sources in the one-paragraph course objectives description. The University of Texas-Austin course similarly includes finding information in court records in the "course aims" paragraph. The NYU course goes a step further: after students learn about conventional legal sources in week 2, they are introduced to advanced digging techniques in week 3, complete with a tour of the university's law library and a lesson on how to navigate archived dockets. Further examples abound.[50]

46 Appendix A (Table A1, Mehren interview).

47 Appendix A (Table A1, McKim interview).

48 We sampled syllabi that are available online and detail the content of the course, from the top ten journalism schools according to *USA Today* (*available at* http://college.usatoday.com/2016/09/30/best-journalism-schools [http://perma.cc/FJC8-WBMK]) and syllabi compiled by the Investigative Journalism Education Consortium. *Syllabi*, Investigative Journalism Educ. Consortium, http://ijec.org/syllabi [http://perma.cc/3QCS-T3V9].

49 The one syllabus that did not explicitly mention using legal sources in the sessions' descriptions was Deborah Nelson's course at the University of Maryland. Yet, even there, Deborah Nelson is one of the Pulitzer winners that I interviewed for this project, and she mentioned unprompted that using court documents is a topic that she hammers to her students.

50 Northwestern University offers a "lab session" on how to search court records. Princeton offers a specific session on how to triangulate legal sources with other sources. The USC course syllabus details four assignments for the students: besides honing and testing their skills in interviewing, data mining, and ethics, students also have an assignment related to finding and

Taken together, the evidence gathered from tip sheets, course syllabi, and interviews overwhelmingly points to the fact that journalists perceive the role of law as source as a crucial element in effective accountability journalism.[51] Still, a skeptic might argue that journalists do not practice what they preach, namely, that in reality they do not rely on legal sources as much as they think they do. Could it be that, for some reason, journalists systematically overstate the role of law as source? To answer this question, we need to go beyond what journalists say and look at what they do: we need to go over the investigative reports and trace the extent to which they actually rely on legal sources.

As a first, smell-test step, I looked at illustrative case studies of the most famous and impactful investigative reports in history. The single most famous case of holding the government to account – Watergate – is billed in popular culture as a story about anonymous human sources meeting journalists in dark parking garages. Yet a closer look at the story behind the story reveals that Woodward and Bernstein based important parts of their investigative project on documents they received from law enforcement actions. At one point in their memoir, for instance, Woodward and Bernstein describe flying to a Miami courtroom because they wanted to copy the documents produced when the district attorney subpoenaed key bank and phone records.[52] The most famous case of holding big business to account – the investigative project that popularized the term muckraking journalism – is Ida Tarbell's exposé of the Standard Oil Company at the turn of the twentieth century.[53] Here the role of law as source cannot be more pronounced: Tarbell's reporting rested heavily on court documents, regulatory investigation reports, and depositions.[54] The list goes on, and subsequent chapters provide ample examples.[55]

writing a story with legal sources. The NYU course similarly details an assignment in which students need to find a lawsuit involving a company, and write a story based on it.

51 *See also* Kish Parella, *Public Relations Litigation*, 72 Vand. L. Rev. 1285 (2019); Kish Parella, *Reputational Regulation*, 67 Duke L. J. 907, 965 (2018).

52 Bob Woodward & Carl Bernstein, All the President's Men 36–41 (1974).

53 Tarbell's investigations were later collected in Ida M. Tarbell, The History of the Standard Oil Company (1904).

54 *See* Dean Starkman, The Watchdog that Did Not Bark 27, 208 (2014); James T. Hamilton, Democracy's Detectives: The Economics of Investigative Journalism 139 (2016).

55 In Chapter 8, in particular, we discuss examples from a study that documented the lack of watchdog journalism by the financial media leading to the 2008 financial crisis, and singled out four counterexamples of great investigative pieces. As Chapter 8 shows, all four success stories – the rare pieces that did spotlight the shady Wall Street practices that contributed to the crisis – rested heavily on court documents.

Casual observations therefore support what journalists say, namely, that legal sources indeed play a key role in important work in accountability journalism. To further corroborate the law-as-source argument, we now turn to a more systematic examination of the legal system's role in facilitating media scrutiny.

2.3.2 *Findings from Content Analysis of Prizewinning Investigative Reports*

Aside from listening to what journalists say, we can read what journalists produce, and then reverse-engineer to find out how much of the journalistic output is based on legal-sourcing inputs. To this end, I coded prizewinning investigative projects between 1995 and 2015. I went over all the projects that won the Pulitzer Prize for Investigative Reporting or the IRE medal,[56] and supplemented the sample with specific examples of investigative business journalism that won the Loeb award.[57] I asked what legal sources (direct and indirect) allowed the production of such socially beneficial investigative reports. The content analysis shows that legal sources play a strong "but-for" role in over half of the prizewinning investigative projects.

Methodology. Before we get to the findings, a few words on methodology are in order.[58] First, the sampling criterion: why sample only prizewinning investigative reports? After all, prizewinning projects are, by definition, outliers that do not represent the entire population of accountability journalism. Yet, for this book's purposes, there exist at least two good reasons to sample such outliers. Looking at the stories that win journalistic awards can tell us something about industry norms.[59] Award-winning projects may not reflect the average investigative report, but they do reflect the industry's exemplary standards: what journalists think accountability journalism ought to look like. Importantly, prizewinning projects reflect the investigative reports that had the most impact on society. In other words, by sampling Pulitzers we get a good proxy for the kind of journalism that this book focuses on: journalism that holds the powerful to account (in our terms: journalism that generates

56 The IRE medal, granted by the Investigative Reporters and Editors organization, is "the highest honor that can be bestowed" on investigative work. *IRE Awards*, INVESTIGATIVE REPORTERS & EDITORS, http://www.ire.org/awards/ire-awards.

57 The Gerald Loeb Award is billed as the most prestigious business journalism award. *About the Loeb Award*, UCLA ANDERSON, http://www.anderson.ucla.edu/gerald-loeb-awards.

58 For more details, see Appendix B.

59 Hamilton, *supra* note 54, at 44.

reputational deterrence). If we wish to examine the indirect (informational) role of the law in facilitating media-driven reputational accountability, then it makes sense to focus on the kind of media work that produces the most accountability.

In fact, even if we do not treat prizewinning reports as a sample meant to represent a larger "population" (of all investigative reports), but rather treat it as the entire relevant population (of prizewinning investigative reports), we still have a significant finding in our hands. That is, assume for the sake of argument that prizewinning investigative reports are the *only* reports that rely on legal sources. Still, each of these reports – as Hamilton convincingly showed[60] – makes on average an eight-digit-sized impact on society, and thus demonstrates that reliance on legal sources is in itself an important phenomenon worthy of further consideration. Moreover, there is reason to believe that purposively sampling only the top investigative works is likely to *understate* the law-as-source claims. Investigative reporting textbooks, and the Pulitzer winners I interviewed, suggest that the likelihood of winning the Pulitzer category of investigative reporting goes up when the submitted story emanates from the reporter's original digging.[61] Relying on regulatory documents can become a double-edged sword in such contexts: "You win Pulitzers when [new] regulation follows your investigation, not when your investigation follows regulation."[62] The upshot is that if one can find legal sourcing in the investigative reporting awards, one can find it anywhere.

Out of the relevant investigative reporting prizes, I sampled two: Pulitzers and IRE medals. I went over all of the winning projects in the investigative reporting category of the Pulitzers, as well as all of the IRE medals given for print journalism between 1995 and 2015. The sample included twenty-five Pulitzers and thirty IRE medals (as in some years there were co-winners). Once we subtract the redundancies – investigative reports that won both the Pulitzer and the IRE medal in the same year – we have forty-eight unique projects in our sample.

60 *Id.* Hamilton examines the societal changes that the most successful investigative projects – those submitted to journalistic award competitions – bring about. To illustrate, consider one case: a 1998 Pulitzer-winning investigation by the *Washington Post*, which found that DC police officers were shooting and killing civilians at an alarming rate. The *Post*'s investigative series brought immediate changes in how DC police use force. As a result, fatal shootings by police officers dropped dramatically from 1999 onwards. Hamilton puts a number on the benefits from reduced fatalities, using "value of statistical life" measurements. His calculation suggests an estimated $70 million in net social benefits from the *Post* investigation.

61 *See, e.g.*, Gaines, *supra* note 34, at 2; Appendix A (Table A1, Eisinger interview).

62 Appendix A (Table A1, Eisinger interview).

After deciding on the sample, I had to settle on criteria for deciphering the role that legal sources play: first identifying all the sources a story relies on, and then determining what relative weight to assign to legal sources. Prizewinning projects, after all, rest on more than a single source. They usually triangulate various human sources and documents. Deciphering the role of legal sources necessitated distinguishing between documents produced by other state agencies, such as death records, and documents produced by the legal system, such as regulatory investigation reports. Among documents produced by the legal system, I further distinguished between information received through direct sourcing channels, such as FOIA requests, and information received through indirect sourcing channels, such as depositions produced during litigation.

The most challenging and subjective task was assigning relative weight to legal sources. I assigned a "strong" role to legal sources whenever the legal sources seemed to play a "but-for" role, meaning that the story would have been significantly different (or even not published) had it not been for legal sources. I assigned a "medium" role to legal sources whenever the story would have stood on its own even without legal sources, but the legal sources provided an added layer of important detail and credibility. A "weak" role was assigned when the legal sources added detail and background that was of little consequence to the key points in the project. A couple of prizewinning projects did not seem to use legal sources at all, earning them a "nonexistent" role.

While it is true that content analysis done by human coders is always subject to limitations,[63] I took two steps to increase the findings' reliability. First, two coders (a research assistant and myself) went over all the Pulitzer articles, and the intercoder reliability was high.[64] Second, I approached the prizewinners themselves, asking them to evaluate the role they assigned to legal sources in their own story. The majority of reporters assigned similar or stronger legal-sourcing weights to their stories than the ones I had originally assigned. To the extent that my subjective coding misrepresents the true reliance on legal sources, it does so in ways that only understate my claim for heavy reliance.

Findings.[65] In twenty-three of the twenty-five (92 percent) Pulitzer-winning projects, legal sources played some role. In thirteen of them, legal sources

63 *See, e.g.*, Leona Yi-Fan Su et al., *Analyzing Public Sentiments Online: Combining Human- and Computer-Based Content Analysis*, 3 INFORM. COMM. SOC. 406, 408 (2016).

64 Intercoder reliability denotes the level of agreement between different coders. *Id.* at 408.

65 For the full results, see Appendix B.

played a *strong* role, meaning that at least parts of the story could not have been written without them. Similarly, in twenty of the twenty-three IRE medal-winning projects, legal sources were explicitly mentioned in the one-paragraph description of how the story came about.[66] Roughly speaking, it appears that in the majority of paradigmatic cases of accountability journalism, the legal system plays a strong role.

Delving deeper into the stories where legal sources played a strong role, I looked at whether the information came from direct or indirect channels. In four of the thirteen Pulitzers, the strong reliance on legal sources came from the direct channel of FOIA requests, with litigation and regulatory investigations playing smaller roles. A good example is the 2009 project on how the Pentagon used retired generals to influence public opinion. The reporters successfully sued the Defense Department to get 8,000 pages of emails, transcripts, and records. They then presented visuals of the internal emails in small boxes throughout the text, thus adding credibility and packing a punch. The 2015 project about special interest groups influencing state attorneys similarly relied heavily on FOIA requests and, to a much lesser extent, on law enforcement actions. The reporter in this case used open records laws to obtain 6,000 emails exchanged between corporate representatives and attorneys general. This allowed him to make "an airtight case by relying on the players' own words to show how the lobbying worked and how effectively."[67] A similar pattern emerges with IRE medals: in three of the twenty-three stories I sampled, the reporters mention FOIA requests but do not mention litigation when explaining how the story came about.

In seven of the thirteen Pulitzers with heavy reliance on legal sources, indirect sourcing – litigation or regulatory investigations – played a strong role, with direct sourcing channels playing smaller or nonexistent roles. An example of a story relying on regulatory investigations is the 2008 project on toxic ingredients imported from China.[68] There, the reporters drew extensively from investigations of Chinese manufacturers conducted by regulators around the world. An example of a story relying on litigation comes from the 2005 story of an Oregonian governor's sexual misconduct with a teen. There, the story hinges upon information coming from once-sealed documents in

66 With IRE medal projects our work was easier, as the IRE members-only database now includes the entry form of each winning project, and each entry form includes a list of the sources that the story relied on.

67 Eric Lipton of the *New York Times*, Pulitzer Prize (2018), http://www.pulitzer.org/winners/eric-lipton.

68 Walt Bogdanich and Jake Hooker of the *New York Times*, Pulitzer Prize (2008), http://www.pulitzer.org/winners/walt-bogdanich-and-jake-hooker.

a settled lawsuit between the 14-year-old and the governor.[69] The IRE sample offers a similar observation: in nine of the twenty-three winning projects, the reporters explicitly mentioned getting information from law enforcement actions as key to the story.

Some prizewinning projects relied heavily on both direct and indirect legal sources. In two of the thirteen Pulitzers in which legal sources played a strong role, the reporters needed a combination of FOIA legal battles and court documents to make the story impactful. The reporters behind the 2008 co-winner – a project on lax regulation of baby products – started digging by filing a FOIA request to the product safety commission for information regarding unsafe cribs and toddler car seats. The thousands of documents they received led them to specific lawsuits, and the court documents describing lack of care by the manufacturers and lack of diligence by the regulators allowed them to fully flesh out the story. The 2015 project on healthcare providers milking Medicare money was jump-started by direct sourcing channels: the *Wall Street Journal* won a legal battle to get Medicare physician-payment data, and that data formed the basis for the project's earlier reports. In subsequent reports,[70] the journalists concretized and personalized the story by relying on specific regulatory investigation reports. For IRE medals, the results were more pronounced: eight of the twenty-three winning projects mention both FOIA requests and law enforcement actions as key to the development of the story.

Finally, it is interesting to learn from counterexamples: in three of the twenty-five Pulitzers, the legal system played little or no role. These were the 2013 project on Walmart's bribing practices in Mexico, and the 2004 and 2000 projects on atrocities by the US army in the Vietnam War and the Korean War, respectively. In the Walmart bribes story, the reporters relied on interviews with whistleblowers, internal company documents they somehow obtained, and independent work, meticulously matching zoning plans and approvals with corporate payment records. In the war atrocities stories, the reporters relied on declassified military documents and interviews with victims and military personnel. In all three projects, reporters had few legal documents to cull, simply because the victims had no recourse to the legal system.[71]

69 As the Pulitzer-winning reporter told me, "[w]ithout the court documents there would be no story." Appendix A (Table A1, Jaquiss interview).

70 *See, e.g.*, Christopher S. Stewart, *How Agents Hunt for Fraud in Trove of Medicare Data*, WALL ST. J. (Aug. 14, 2014), http://www.wsj.com/articles/how-agents-hunt-for-fraud-in-trove-of-medicare-data-1408069802.

71 As the 2000 Pulitzer winner, Martha Mendoza, explained, "the victims would have been in big trouble if they [had] tried to make a big thing out of it." Appendix A (Table A1, Mendoza interview).

Interestingly, all these stories focus on non-American victims, and so the American legal system was not invoked and did not produce information.

These counterexamples remind us that the legal system's ability to facilitate reputational control is limited, serving as segue to the next section, which refines the theory by accommodating its limitations.

2.4 REFINING THE BASIC STORY: LIMITATIONS AND MULTIPLE LAYERS

So far, we have focused on "success stories," namely, instances where the legal system helped market players judge reputations better. But under certain (not uncommon) conditions, the legal system cannot help the market for reputation. Sometimes the legal system has trouble producing relevant information. Other times, the legal system may produce valuable information, yet stakeholders will not act on it. In other words, the legal system, even when it operates perfectly, cannot cure all the biases of reputational sanctions. Section 2.4.1 identifies the limitations of the legal system's reputational effects. Section 2.4.2 then puts these limitations in perspective: the fact that both the legal and market systems are flawed does not mean that reputational deterrence will not work. As long as each system's flaws are imperfectly correlated with each other's, the interactions between law and reputation will generate valuable deterrence.

2.4.1 *Limitations*

Some of the limitations of the law's reputational effects stem from the legal system's inability to generate relevant information. The legal system's assessments sometimes suffer from distortions similar to the ones that plague reputation systems: asymmetric information, lack of expertise, strategic behavior, and divergent incentives. There exist ample situations where we cannot trust the legal system to produce the positive externality of accurate reputation information. For example, information produced during litigation may be *too lagged*. Often the judge's opinion comes a few years after the initial market reaction, when no one is interested in the matter anymore.[72] Still, while the time lag indeed represents a strong limitation, we should not overstate it. Remember that the relevant event for measuring the lag is not the day on which the legal case is decided,

[72] David S. Ardia, *Reputation in a Networked World: Revisiting the Social Foundations of Defamation Law*, 45 HARV. C.R.-C.L. L. REV. 261, 314 (2010).

but rather any day on which the legal system injects information into the market. Many times valuable facts become available in the earlier stages of the litigation process. Judges also provide interpretations of how things happened long before the final judicial opinion: adjudication often happens in multiple stages, and judges speak their mind during early stages such as motions to dismiss or class/derivative action approvals. Indeed, this will be a recurring theme in Chapters 3 and 8, which deal with (the usually front-loaded) corporate and securities litigation.

Other limitations stem from the fact that even when the law produces quality information, stakeholders may not act on it. There are certain biases in reputational sanctioning that legal information cannot fix. The law can help stakeholders fix some attribution errors, as in discerning whether product defects are endemic or idiosyncratic. But the law cannot solve stakeholders' limited attention problems, or lack of motivation to act. Also, the law will have a more pronounced effect on stakeholders' judgments in areas of corporate behavior that they do not experience directly, such as the company's social responsibility policies (Chapter 5 elaborates), or its management's integrity (Chapters 3 and 4 elaborate), relative to issues that stakeholders experience directly, such as the quality of the product's human–interaction design.

The law also cannot cure some of the key media biases. The law can rid the media from its dependence on inside sources, and reduce the costs of reporting on misbehavior by powerful players. But the law cannot cure the media from the need to cater to their readers' biases, or from inability to report properly on information generated by the legal system. As the next section elaborates, in many cases information from the courtroom gets lost in translation on its way to the court of public opinion. The media will over-report on vivid issues and under-report on opaque issues. Indeed, we should acknowledge that litigation would meaningfully affect reputation only in a small subset of legal disputes (such as with big-firm defendants), which are interesting and important enough for third parties to follow.

Similarly, the background threat of litigation will not be enough to prevent companies from falsely denying accusations, under certain circumstances. Think for example about a CEO nearing retirement, or a company on the brink of insolvency. These actors have a high discount rate: they need to recover their reputation now, and care about the long term less. As a result, they may choose to bend the truth and not worry about the risk that they will be exposed by the legal system further down the road.

In all, the legal system does not always produce valuable information, and even when it does, it cannot cure us of all our emotional and cognitive biases in processing information.

2.4.2 *Multiple Layers of Reputation Information*

We acknowledged that the legal system is not categorically better or more accurate than reputation systems. And so I emphasize that I do not portray here a horserace over who produces better information, with the legal system winning. But I do portray the legal and market systems as providing multiple layers of reputation information.

The value of the legal system to reputation systems stems largely from the fact that the systems' distortions are imperfectly correlated. The market's first opinion enjoys advantages in some areas and disadvantages in other areas compared to the legal system's second opinion. The two systems in effect create one *diversified portfolio* of reputational assessments. Having different types of assessments mitigate the risk of extreme mistakes (that is, the risk that stakeholders will boycott perfectly good companies or interact with rotten companies). The idea of multiple layers of evaluations has been applied to similar contexts such as second opinions in medical treatment and user reviews in online commerce websites,[73] and it lends itself nicely to our context. Consider for example the four traits that were identified as necessary for well-functioning reputation systems: the system has to produce information in a timely, accessible, accurate, and thorough manner.[74] It is easy to envision how the market and legal system complement each other along these dimensions. The market system provides more timely and accessible information, striking fast whenever bad news breaks. The legal system then produces information that is often more accurate and complete than the market's initial version.

Overall, then, the existence of a well-functioning legal system facilitates better reputation systems. Still, in order to move from claims about the average and improve our ability to predict the reputational impact of specific disputes, we need to introduce more context-specific details and focus on one area of market activity and law at a time. The next section shows how to apply the theory to specific contexts and identify the factors that determine the likely direction of reputational impact.

73 Vermeule, *supra* note 23, at 1435 n.1.

74 *See generally* Ling Liu, Systematic Measurement of Centralized Online Reputation Systems 29-31 (Apr. 2011) (published Ph.D. thesis, Durham University), http://etheses.dur.ac.uk/881/ [https://perma.cc/2DTL-XJAT].

2.5 VARIATION: WHAT EXPLAINS THE MAGNITUDE AND DIRECTION OF REPUTATIONAL EFFECTS

To further complicate the basic story, this section fleshes out five factors to consider before we can apply the reputation-through-litigation perspective to specific contexts. The first three factors concern the counterintuitive *direction* of the reputational effects. Litigation does not always hurt the defendant-company's reputation. Section 2.5.1 highlights the wedge between individual-level and organizational-level reputations. Under certain (quite common) conditions, litigation creates a scapegoating dynamic, hurting the individual manager's reputation while boosting the company's reputation. Section 2.5.2 distinguishes between the reputational effects of the process of litigation and those of judicial opinions. Counterintuitively, under certain conditions losing the legal case, or being scolded by the judge, may actually be good for the defendant-company's reputation. Section 2.5.3 emphasizes the forces that drive a wedge between information that is being produced in the legal system and stakeholders' actual reputational decisions. A lot of information gets lost in translation from the courtroom to the court of public opinion, either because the media is not reporting it, or because the company manages to hijack the information flow by producing smokescreens. As a result, even when the legal system produces damning information about the defendant-company, the company's stakeholders may not act on it.

The other two factors concern the *magnitude* of the reputational effects. Not all litigation affects reputation. Section 2.5.4 maps the areas of the law where the magnitude of reputational effects should be higher, on paper. And Section 2.5.5 provides evidence from the law-as-source study, suggesting that litigation plays a bigger role in facilitating reputational control of private business than it does facilitating reputational control of public entities.

2.5.1 *Litigation Affects the Reputation of Individuals Differently than It Affects Companies*

When analyzing reputational impact we have to distinguish between individual-level and organizational-level reputations. Legal scholars tend to assume that any judicial scorning of individuals reflects badly on their companies, and vice versa. And granted, in many cases this intuitive assumption holds. Yet, as reputation and crisis management scholars have long recognized, scolding an individual does not *necessarily* impact the company's reputation negatively.[75] In general, factors such as the scolded individual's place in the hierarchy, whether the individual still holds office, or what other top managers knew about that individual's actions, play an important role in dictating the link between individual scolding and corporate reputation. Specifically in the context of litigation, we can envision common scenarios where dressing down specific managers may actually boost the company's reputation (or at least not hurt it).

First, singling out an individual for scorning may facilitate *scapegoating* dynamics. In typical corporate litigation scenarios – class/derivative actions – the claim is often jumpstarted by a sharp decline in stock prices (which constitutes the harm to the investor and draws the attention of plaintiff lawyers). And because the stock price decline is likely to push the manager out, by the time judges get to write their opinions they probably dress down a manager who is already gone or on the way out of the company. While such judicial scorning probably hurts the ousted manager's chances of being rehired (that is, hurts the manager's labor-market reputation), it could help repair the *company's* reputation.

To understand why, note that the crisis management literature considers "decoupling" as one of the most effective recovery strategies for companies.[76] In decoupling mode, the company is acknowledging the problem while isolating and localizing it, conveying a message along the lines of "this is not who we are as a company going forward." Assigning blame to a single individual who was since purged from the company can be an especially effective form of decoupling, as long as the public believes it.[77] Thus, when judges single out the ousted manager for opprobrium, they lend credibility to the scapegoating attempts, thereby helping the company distance itself from the wrongdoing.

Another common occurrence in judicial scolding involves criticizing a manager for making mistakes out of incompetence. Here again, the individual's chances of being rehired would probably go down as a result of litigation. But the impact on the company's reputation is not necessarily negative, and could even be positive. Crisis management experts maintain that

75 Dezenhall & Weber, *supra* note 25, at 140; E. Deanne Brocato et al., *When Things Go Wrong: Account Strategy Following a Corporate Crisis Event*, 15 Corp. Reputation Rev. 35, 36 (2012).

76 *See, e.g.*, Anna Lamin & Srilata Zaheer, *Wall Street vs. Main Street: Firm Strategies for Defending Legitimacy and Their Impact on Different Stakeholders*, 23 Org. Sci. 47, 61 (2012).

77 *Cf.* Celia Moore et al., Avoiding the Consequences of Misconduct: Becoming Licensed by and Insulated from Stigma 10–11 (2011) (unpublished manuscript) (on file with author) (finding evidence that firing a CEO before announcing failures reduces the reputational harm for the company).

companies in crises stand a better chance of repairing their reputation when individual managers are portrayed as less than perfect.[78] If stakeholders perceive the leader as perfect and in total control, they assume that she could have prevented the adverse outcome. As a result, stakeholders will interpret the company's misconduct as intentional and indicative of future behavior (that is, arising from deep-rooted disregard for shareholder interests and market norms in general). By contrast, if stakeholders perceive the leader as less than perfect, they are more likely to interpret the adverse outcomes as a result of more easily fixable mistakes.[79]

Chapter 3 uses the famous corporate law case of *Disney* to illustrate scapegoating dynamics in play. Without forecasting too much, let us note that while dozens of law review articles referred to the caustic judicial scolding included in the *Disney* opinion, one aspect of the scolding has been grossly overlooked: *whose* reputation was damaged exactly? Who were the targets of the scolding? As Chapter 3 shows, the chancellor's strongest criticisms were reserved for six individuals who were no longer an integral part of Disney when the verdict was issued. Chapter 3 relies on media coverage of the Disney debacle before and after litigation, to show that the company's reputation for management integrity actually gained from the scolding of these already ousted individuals.

The gap between individual- and organizational-level reputations also works in the other direction: litigation may hurt a company's reputation while helping individual managers salvage their own reputations. So far, our discussion has implicitly assumed that corporate insiders try to maximize the firm's reputation. In reality, though, managers may protect their own reputation at the expense of the company's reputation. Agency problems that plague large corporations loom even larger at times of crisis and legal disputes. Decision makers facing an end-game situation think even more than usual about their own interests instead of the company's interests.[80] For instance, corporate managers may push for early settlements even when litigation can recover damage to the company's reputation.[81] This is because litigation may

78 Dezenhall & Weber, *supra* note 25.

79 *Cf.* Kimberly D. Elsbach, Organizational Perception Management 60 (2006). *See generally* John Hendry, *The Principal's Other Problems: Honest Incompetence and the Specification of Objectives*, 27 Acad. Mgmt. Rev. 98 (2002) (identifying contexts where shareholders can more easily replace an incompetent element than root out moral hazard). To be sure, in the business world it is sometimes better to be (perceived as) immoral than incompetent. Still, there are areas where incompetence is considered less deep-seated and easier to root out than lack of integrity.

80 Brocato et al., *supra* note 75.

81 *Cf.* Bruce Haslem, *Managerial Opportunism during Corporate Litigation*, 60 J. Fin. 2013 (2005) (finding that legal disputes that culminate in verdicts are better for shareholder value

harm the managers' individual reputation or because litigation may increase the chances that managers will have to pay out of pocket.[82] Analyses of the relationship between law and reputation should therefore find a way to incorporate agency considerations.

2.5.2 *The Process of Litigation Matters More than the Outcomes*

When we think about the reputational impact of litigation we usually focus on judicial opinions: how the outcomes (legal sanctions) or content (judicial remarks) of opinions shape the reputation of defendants.[83] But in reality judicial opinions are rare. Most legal disputes settle.[84] Yet even cases that settle sometimes affect the market reaction: the process itself prior to settlements (pleading, discovery, and trial) sheds light on reputation-relevant information.

To illustrate, recall that the Odwalla lawsuit settled, but not before the discovery process corrected the initial market reaction by flushing out important information. Another example comes from Selmi's study of stock market reaction to settlements of racial discrimination class actions.[85] The study indicates that similar cases with similar legal outcomes yielded different market reactions, depending on what information was produced prior to settlement. For example, Texaco's reputation took a hit when the media reported about a tape with explicit racial slurs that was exposed in discovery.[86] And we have systematic indications that sophisticated market players indeed constantly monitor disputes and react to events during the early stages of the process.[87]

than disputes that culminate in settlements, and that the effect is more pronounced in companies with weaker corporate governance).

82 Steve Albrecht, Crisis Management for Corporate Self-Defense 180–81 (1996) (insurance considerations sometimes trump corporate reputation considerations).

83 *See, e.g.*, Edward B. Rock, *Saints and Sinners: How Does Delaware Corporate Law Work?*, 44 UCLA L. Rev. 1009, 1116 (1997) (reputational sanctions are affected by the content of opinions); Batia M. Wiesenfeld et al., *The Stigmatization and Devaluation of Elites Associated with Corporate Failures: A Process Model*, 33 Acad. Mgmt. Rev. 231, 244 (2008) (reputational sanctions are affected by legal sanctions).

84 J. J. Prescott & Kathryn E. Spier, *A Comprehensive Theory of Civil Settlement*, 91 N.Y. U. L. Rev. 59, 61 n.2 (2016).

85 Michael Selmi, *The Price of Discrimination: The Nature of Class Action Employment Discrimination Litigation and Its Effects*, 81 Tex. L. Rev. 1249 (2003).

86 *Id.* at 1270–72.

87 Vladimir Atanasov et al., *Does Reputation Limit Opportunistic Behavior in the VC Industry? Evidence from Litigation Against VCs*, 67 J. Fin. 2215 (2012) (noting that events in the early stages of venture capital litigation affect the venture capitalists' reputation). In an interview

Note that the litigation process's impact on reputation differs markedly from the impact of judicial opinions. The process mainly affects what information we have, while judicial opinions mainly affect how we process that information.[88] In disputes with large, publicly traded firms, market players will likely have access to the basic facts about the misbehavior before a lawsuit is even filed. Still, information produced during pleading, discovery, and trial can give market players more raw facts and inside information to work with, such as internal email communications or board minutes that provide details about what top managers did (or did not do) to prevent the failure. In other words, even when the process of litigation does not affect the revelation stage, it can significantly affect the *attribution* stage: providing information not on what happened but rather on how it happened.

By contrast, judicial opinions would affect mainly the *certification* and *diffusion* stages. By the time judicial opinions are released in such disputes, they probably contain mostly stale information; stakeholders with enough stake and expertise to mine verdicts for information could have already accessed prior sources for the same information. To be sure, verdicts still matter in the court of public opinion. But they matter in different and hitherto understudied ways. The main impact of verdicts is not in introducing new information but rather in affecting how existing information is processed.

Judicial opinions shape the scope and content of media coverage by raising the *saliency* of an issue. A certain issue may be long past its days in the sun when a lagged judicial opinion enlivens the media attention to it, providing the media reporters with readymade quotes. Judicial opinions also change reputations by affecting the *credibility* of a given framing of the issue. They certify certain versions of what and how things happened. Recall the source-credibility effects we mentioned in Chapter 1: the same piece of information may be discounted when coming from a non-credible source, yet move the needle when coming from a credible one. When well-respected judges put their name on a certain version of the events, stakeholders are more likely to update

conducted with a representative of Courtroom Connect – a company that streams online webcasts of Delaware trials – I learned that an important clientele of streaming services is institutional investors who monitor legal disputes in real time and alter investment decisions accordingly.

88 *See generally* Timothy D. Lytton, Holding Bishops Accountable (2008) (a detailed case study of the clergy sexual-abuse litigation); Wendy Wagner, *When All Else Fails: Regulating Risky Products through Tort Litigation*, 95 Geo. L.J. 693, 713–27 (2007).

their beliefs based on it.[89] The judge's version therefore affects how market players package an existing set of facts in their minds.

Beyond the content of judicial opinions (the judge's version of what and how things happened), there are also interesting dynamics with the legal outcomes of the case. It is intuitive to think that the legal outcome of a case will determine its reputational outcome: companies that lose in litigation will suffer reputational damage, and those that win will enjoy a reputational rebound.

Yet a deeper look reveals that legal outcomes are imperfectly correlated, and sometimes even negatively correlated, with reputational outcomes. Two enforcement actions with identical legal outcomes may generate completely different reputational outcomes. This is because the legal outcome of a case is based on specific legal doctrines that may not be relevant to the stakeholders' reputation evaluation. For example, a judge may rule in favor of the defendant company, yet the judicial opinion will contain harsh remarks indicating that the company disregarded market norms, though it fell short of violating legal rules. In such cases, the legal consequences will be positive but the reputational consequences negative. Conversely, a judge may assign liability to the company, but the opinion will make clear that the misbehavior was carried out by a rogue employee and is unlikely to reoccur. In that case the legal consequences will be negative, but the reputational consequences are likely to be positive.

Indeed, various empirical studies of stock market reactions to enforcement actions show that there is no systematic correlation between the size of the legal sanction and that of the reputational sanction.[90] To further illustrate we need simply revisit the Salomon Brothers case. As mentioned, the market reacted very positively to Salomon's settlement with the regulators. But the positive reaction cannot be attributed to the legal outcome: Salomon agreed to pay what was then the second-highest fine ever paid in SEC settlements, and had to double its initial charge-out (indicating a higher-than-expected legal sanction).[91] The positive market reaction is therefore more likely attributable

[89] One aspect that makes judges a credible source is that their perceived self-interest in the issue is low. In other words, the audiences know that judges "do not have a dog in the fight," and are therefore willing to trust judges' versions more.

[90] Atanasov et al., *supra* note 87 (on venture capital litigation); Wallace N. Davidson III et al., *The Effectiveness of OSHA Penalties: A Stock-Market-Based Test*, 33 Indus. Rel. 283, 292–93 (1994) (on enforcement by the Occupational Safety and Health Administration); Haslem, *supra* note 81 (on private litigation in the USA); John Armour et al., *Regulatory Sanctions and Reputational Damage in Financial Markets*, 52 J. Fin. & Quantitative Analysis 1429 (2017) (on enforcement by the United Kingdom's FSA).

[91] Paine & Santoro, *supra* note 20, at 19–20.

to the information contained in the settlement announcement, which suggested that Salomon's past mistakes are not indicative of how the company is managed now. Another example – the Bankers Trust litigation – illustrates the flip side.[92] There, a financial giant won a series of legal battles, but the legal victory proved pyrrhic. The process of litigation exposed the pervasiveness of a sucker-punching culture in Bankers Trust, thus greatly damaging the firm's reputation.

2.5.3 *The Information Flow from the Courtroom Gets Distorted*

So far, we have assumed that stakeholders use information from the legal system to revisit their reputational assessments. But in reality information from the courtroom does not simply find its way to stakeholders intact. Individuals rarely read unfiltered court opinions or regulatory reports. They depend on information intermediaries to process and disseminate the main sound bites for them. Yet intermediaries have their own narrow interests to select what parts to highlight and then add their own take. And the misbehaving companies themselves also distort the information flow. As a result, a lot of information gets lost in translation. Consider two especially notable patterns.

First, different types of intermediaries – such as law firms, business media, or regular newspapers – select different pieces of information to convey to their respective audiences. Take for example the lessons learned from my analysis of the coverage of the *Disney* litigation.[93] Big law firms tend to send "a memorandum to our clients" following significant cases, and did so with *Disney* as well. When I sampled these memos, I discovered an "all-rules" approach: the law firms focused on what the verdict means for directors facing similar situations in the future in general terms. They largely refrained from relaying the detailed narrative of what and how things happened in Disney. By contrast, the newspaper coverage of the *Disney* decision focused more on the judge's caustic criticism and vivid descriptions rather than on the legal doctrines. Even there, different types of media outlets produced markedly different types of coverage. The business media's coverage was more favorable to Disney than the regular media's coverage. Business newspapers were forward-looking: they focused on how the bottom line of the verdict is good for Disney and its current directors going forward, while associating the caustic criticism in the verdict with the retiring CEO. Regular newspapers, by contrast, were more backward-looking:

92 Macey, *supra* note 22, at 71–74.
93 Chapter 3.

they focused on the crushing criticism delivered in the verdict, and painted it as bad for everyone involved.[94]

The variation in the coverage of verdicts carries important implications for reputational outcomes. Reputational outcomes vary across the company's different audiences, as each stakeholder group typically taps different intermediaries for information. To illustrate: directors who read just the law firms' memos will have different perceptions of the company than investors who read the *Wall Street Journal*, or customers who read the *HuffPost* online. In the *Disney* case, the reputational outcomes were likely zero for audiences relying on law firms' coverage; negative for audiences relying on regular newspapers; and mixed (or even positive) for audiences relying on business newspapers. The upshot is that future analyses of the reputational impact of litigation should distinguish between different types of audiences and sources of diffusion of reputation-relevant information.[95]

A second important factor to consider is defendant companies' attempts to produce smokescreens that divert the public's attention away from bad information coming out of the courtroom. To go back to the *Disney* example: the verdict was not the only newsworthy event affecting Disney's reputation at the time. At the exact day that the verdict was released, Disney issued a quarterly report announcing strong earnings growth. The media attention quickly turned away from the verdict and to these positive announcements. Disney's stakeholders ended up reading a commingled story of earning announcement and a verdict, framed by the media as a good day overall for Disney.[96]

Encountering the overlooked smokescreen angle of the Disney story illustrates that reputational sanctions are not a one-sided event. As Chapter 1 showed, companies have the incentives and ability (think public relations departments) to hijack unfavorable information flows. When discussing the informational role of the law we should therefore consider what conditions

94 *See also* An Seon-Kyoung & Karla K. Gower, *How Do the News Media Frame Crises? A Content Analysis of Crisis News Coverage*, 35 PUB. REL. REV. 107 (2009) (finding that in general business newspapers tend to adopt an "economic" frame when reporting about crises while regular newspapers adopt a "morality" frame).

95 In other words, any analysis of reputational impact should ask "reputation to whom?" "For what?" FOMBRUN, *supra* note 20, at 395–96. Companies and businessmen may exit litigation with a stellar reputation among one group of stakeholders but a tarnished reputation among another.

96 Kate Kelly, *Disney Earnings Jump on Gains from TV Division*, WALL ST. J., Aug. 10, 2005, at A3 ("Disney's upbeat earnings announcement came on the heels of another victory for the company: a Delaware judge's ruling that Disney's directors didn't breach their fiduciary duty"); Rupert Steiner, *Record Profits Put the Smile Back at Disney*, SUNDAY BUS. (Aug. 18, 2005) ("[H]ours after [the] ruling, all eyes from Wall Street were on the media group's stellar third-quarter results").

make information flows more (or less) likely to get hijacked by companies. I conjecture that companies can control the information flows from verdicts better than they control information flows from continuous discovery or trial processes. Verdicts are one-time, isolated events, so companies can more easily produce a timely smokescreen, issuing an unrelated press release to steer media attention away from the verdict.[97]

At first glance, the observed distortions in information flows cast a doubt on the legal system's ability to impact reputational sanctions. It can be argued that the media will not widely diffuse corrections of market overreactions (because nuanced, contextual explanations do not sell newspapers like vivid, template-like allegations), and that companies' smokescreens will prevent corrections of market underreaction. However, a deeper look reveals the "multiple layers" dynamic we touched on the previous section: the distortions in information flows are imperfectly correlated and somewhat balance each other:

When the media fails to fully diffuse information that is favorable to companies, the companies themselves have incentives and resources to make sure that stakeholders get the message. To illustrate, recall how Audi purchased full-page ads in major newspapers to increase the public exposure to the exonerating regulatory report. The Exxon Valdez Spill serves as another good illustration. Exxon's spokespersons continue to refer to parts of the judicial opinion in the spill-damages litigation that commended Exxon. For example, when an Alaskan politician brought up the Exxon failure in 2004, the company issued a press release quoting the judicial opinion, suggesting that no one can claim that they are the bad guys anymore.[98]

And in instances where companies try to prevent unfavorable information flows, sophisticated intermediaries have incentives to expose the company for the "villain" that it is (recall the Odwalla example).

2.5.4 *The Reputational Impact Depends on the Market Activity and Legal Field in Question*

One final tuning of the reputation-through-litigation argument is in order, before we move to specific legal applications in the next four chapters. The

97 On the different ways in which firms try to control the information flow of bad news to the market, see generally Lauren Cohen et al., *Playing Favorites: How Firms Prevent the Revelation of Bad News* 1 (Harv. Bus. Sch., Working Paper No. 14-021, 2014), http://nrs.harvard.edu/urn-3:HUL.InstRepos:11508220.

98 Press Release, ExxonMobil, ExxonMobil Sets Valdez Record Straight (Oct. 6, 2004), http://ir.exxonmobil.com/phoenix.zhtml?c=115024&p=irol-newsArticle_print&ID=624293&highlight [https://perma.cc/8ZGJ-3NNA].

magnitude of reputational impact varies greatly across different types of legal disputes. One way to identify the conditions that determine whether a given dispute will affect reputations is to adopt a supply-and-demand framework. "Demand" here denotes the extent to which third parties will be interested in reading what the legal system has to say about the litigants' behaviors. Many types of legal disputes interest only the disputants themselves. Classic examples come from family law or torts committed by individuals. Demand for reputation-relevant information in such cases will be low.

"Supply" denotes the extent to which the legal system can actually produce quality information for third parties who are interested. We can envision a scenario such as medical malpractice litigation, where the demand is high, yet supply is low. On one hand, the reputation of caregivers is very important to third parties and hard for them to assess. So the interest in hearing what the legal system has to say will be high. On the other hand, medical malpractice disputes – when they do not settle – are being decided by inexpert jurors who do not produce detailed opinions. The legal system thus supplies little meaningful reputation information.[99]

The legal system meaningfully impacts reputational sanctions only in areas with both high demand and good supply, namely, areas where market players are constantly looking to reevaluate their beliefs, and the legal institutions are perceived as a capable and credible source of information. One example of an area where both supply-and-demand conditions are met is corporate and securities laws. Stakeholders who deal with large publicly traded companies have ample reason to continuously look for new information and interpretation on companies' abilities and intentions, given the high stakes and various asymmetric information problems involved. And the players in the market – private intermediaries such as securities analysts or institutional investors – enjoy enough sophistication and resources to mine legal proceedings for second opinions. Generally speaking, demand for reputation-relevant information on publicly traded companies is high simply because players in the market are more interested in the empirical truth and the de-biasing of information than consumers of news in other contexts.[100]

99 Telephone Interview with Jeff Segal, Founder, MedicalJustice (Nov. 27, 2012); Telephone Interview with Peter Grossi, Drug Liability Litigator (Dec. 12, 2012). In fact, one can claim that medical malpractice litigation only increases the costs of detection for reputation markets *ex ante*: doctors who anticipate the biased judgments of jurors avoid fully reporting on their own errors (even when those errors were unavoidable) for fear of legal liability. Medical malpractice litigation, the argument goes, creates a "deny and defend" culture, which makes it even more difficult to get accurate reputational judgments to begin with. Joanna C. Schwartz, *A Dose of Reality for Medical Malpractice Reform*, 88 N.Y.U. L. Rev. 1224, 1227, 1239–43 (2013).

100 For evidence suggesting that sophisticated investors continuously monitor and react to information disseminated during litigation, see Roy Shapira, *Reputation through Litigation: How*

On the supply side, several factors make the main adjudicators of corporate behavior – Delaware courts – well positioned to provide timely, comprehensible, and thorough reputation information. First, they are respected in legal and business communities.[101] The nonpolitical appointment process (Delaware judges frequently come from the bar) and the specialized docket allow judges to develop expertise and a broad perspective on market norms. Second, they manage to avoid the time lag that usually accompanies litigation: the specialized and small docket also enables Delaware judges to adjudicate disputes relatively quickly, producing information in a timely manner.[102] Third, as Chapter 3 elaborates, Delaware's decisional law has developed in ways that encourage information production. For example, the use of open-ended legal standards, such as the good-faith doctrine,[103] allows plaintiffs to survive motions to dismiss and reach discovery, and gives judges more flexibility to tailor their own narrative of the events. Finally, the legal system is more likely to tell market players something they do not already know when the issue at hand concerns questions like what insiders knew and when they knew it. Corporate law litigation usually provides valuable answers to these questions, as it revolves around questions of management integrity and the quality of checks and balances throughout the hierarchy.

The evidence from my law-as-source study corroborate this supply-and-demand framework: the law indeed plays a bigger role in facilitating media scrutiny of private businesses than it does in other areas. The next section elaborates.

2.5.5 *Evidence: Where Is Legal Sourcing More/Less Likely?*

Section 2.3 introduced evidence that information coming from the legal system plays an important role in sourcing investigative reporting. This section moves from the "on average" claims to the cross-sectional variation: what did the content analysis, interviews, tip sheets, and syllabi tell us about the areas in which law-as-source dynamics are more or less pronounced? Two types of misbehavior stand out: (1) in misbehavior where the victims have little

the Legal System Shapes Behavior by Producing Information, 91 WASH. L. REV. 1193, 1225 n.139 (2016).

101 Edward B. Rock, *Saints and Sinners: How Does Delaware Corporate Law Work?*, 44 UCLA L. REV. 1009, 1102 (1997).

102 Jill E. Fisch, *The Peculiar Role of the Delaware Courts in the Competition for Corporate Charters*, 68 U. CIN. L. REV. 1061, 1086 (2000).

103 Ehud Kamar, *Shareholder Litigation under Indeterminate Corporate Law*, 66 U. CHI. L. REV. 887, 888 (1999).

recourse to the legal system (for various reasons), the law-as-source dynamics apply less forcefully; (2) when the misbehaving entity is not a government agency but rather a private company, the law-as-source dynamics apply more forcefully.

Think first about the category of victims without recourse. The law cannot generate reputational deterrence when the misbehavior in question does not reach the legal system. Certain conditions make victims less likely to file lawsuits and regulators less likely to start investigations, thereby limiting the relevance of legal sourcing. One subset of cases concerns *victims in foreign countries*, who do not enjoy the same right of access to courts (or power to extract information from the other side once in courts) as Americans do.[104] A second subset of cases concerns *victims who are poor* and do not have the resources needed to set the legal system in motion.[105] Substandard housing problems are a case in point.[106] Finally, a big subset of cases concerns scenarios in which the costs of misconduct are *dispersed* among multiple victims, or are so *opaque* that the victims are unaware of the misconduct.[107] In such contexts, even if the victims are not marginalized in society and can theoretically fight back, they lack the information needed to wage a legal battle, thereby making it less likely that the media will scrutinize the misconduct in question. Take for example the case of DuPont's emissions of a toxic chemical used in the process of manufacturing Teflon at its plant in West Virginia.[108] Residents from neighboring communities had the toxic chemical in their drinking water and suffered increased incidences of various diseases, but could not file a lawsuit simply because they did not know that such a chemical existed in the first place.

From a social planner perspective, areas where both watchdogs – the media and the courts – are likely to fail are ones that bear monitoring. Presumably, in contexts where victims lack recourse to the legal system, we would want another system of control – another watchdog – to step in and spotlight the victims' plight. Yet reputational control depends on media coverage – and the

[104] The book's Conclusion offers thoughts on how law-as-source dynamics play differently across countries.

[105] HAMILTON, *supra* note 54, at 60; Appendix A (Table A1, Daly interview).

[106] *See, e.g.*, Kathryn A. Sabbeth, *Public and Private Lawyers for Public Good* (working paper, 2017) (on file with author) (explaining why tenants who suffer from substandard housing are less likely to enlist the help of the courts).

[107] Appendix A (Table A1, Tulsky interview).

[108] Roy Shapira & Luigi Zingales, *Is Pollution Value-Maximizing? The DuPont Case* (Nat'l Bureau of Econ. Research, Working Paper No. 23866, 2017), http://www.nber.org/papers/w23866.

media's reliance on law as source means that exactly in such contexts the media is less likely to facilitate reputational control.

The second dynamic to consider is the difference between public and private entities. Many of my interviewees suggested that law-as-source dynamics play an especially important role in business investigative journalism.[109] The interviews corroborated a notion that reverberates in communication studies: holding big business accountable is actually much tougher than holding big government accountable.[110] The reason for this has a lot to do with sourcing: my interviewees mentioned three types of sources of damning information that are more available on government misconduct than they are on business misconduct: information from *rivals*, information from *insiders*, and publicly available *records*.

First, a journalist looking for information on misbehavior by politicians can usually count on the politician's rivals. Politics is often a zero-sum game, and politicians are quick to point out their rivals' flaws and misconduct to the media.[111] Within the business world, by contrast, tips by rivals are much harder to come by.[112]

Second, my interviewees suggested that government insiders are more likely to blow the whistle than their corporate counterparts are.[113] The reason, they conjecture, lies in the different organizational cultures: people in government have a greater sense of public duty, and so they are more likely to approach the media when observing misconduct by their superiors.[114] Insiders in private business, by contrast, tend to adopt a profit-maximizing mindset and "zealously guard documents."[115]

Finally, direct sourcing tools help with information on government more than with information on private business.[116] A journalist cannot file FOIA

109 Appendix A (Table A1, Blackledge interview; Bogdanich interview; Coll interview; Daly interview).

110 *See, e.g.*, HAMILTON, *supra* note 54, at 60, 151; MICHAEL SCHUDSON, THE SOCIOLOGY OF NEWS 140 (2003).

111 As one reporter put it, "The two-party system is a blessing for journalists. When the government was Democratic, Republicans would leak. When the Democrats held primaries, one side would leak information on the other." Daly interview. *See also* Appendix A (Table A1, Ureneck interview).

112 One potential explanation is that the business world can be less adversarial, less zero-sum than politics: Company X's shenanigans may benefit company X at the expense of, say, consumers/the environment, rather than at the expense of their rivals from company Y.

113 Appendix A (Table A1, Carter interview; Mehren interview; Tulsky interview).

114 Appendix A (Table A1, Tulsky interview).

115 *Id.* There exist other factors making it more difficult to hold businesses accountable that are not necessarily related to sourcing. The one most mentioned by my interviewees is that businesses are more likely to sue the newspaper and the reporter for libel, compared to politicians. Appendix A (Table A1, Bogdanich interview; Lewis interview).

116 Appendix A (Table A1, Blackledge interview; Horvit interview; Jaquiss interview).

requests or rely on open records laws to get information on how companies behave, and the companies tend not to volunteer damning information.[117]

The added difficulty of getting information on big businesses figures to increase the demand for indirect sourcing channels, such as law enforcement actions.[118] And the supply tends to meet the high demand: big businesses are almost always involved in one legal dispute or another. As a 2017 study shows, more than half of all US companies are managing at least one class action against them at any given point in time.[119] It is therefore not surprising that virtually every investigative journalism tip sheet or course syllabus mentions court documents as key for investigating business. In the words of the Dean of Columbia Journalism School: "[when I teach students] the first thing on the slides is: litigation . . . there's hardly a company in this world that is not being sued, and this is where you get a window [into what is going on in the company]."[120]

My content analysis of prizewinning investigative projects lends credence to the journalists' perspective I picked up from interviews, tip sheets, and syllabi. Six of the twenty-five Pulitzer-winning projects in my sample focus on holding private companies to account.[121] Five of them rely strongly on litigation or regulatory investigations. In an attempt to dig further into the specific context of business investigative journalism, I looked beyond Pulitzers to the Loeb awards, considered the premier prize for business journalism. Among the Loeb awards, I looked at investigative projects that targeted a specific firm. Three examples stood out: the 2017 project on Allegiant Air, showing the alarming rate of airplane malfunctions in the low-cost carrier's fleet; the 2010 project on Toyota, investigating complaints of unintended sudden acceleration; and the 2004 project on Boeing, detailing corporate espionage against rival Lockheed Martin. Unsurprisingly, it turned out that all three projects rested heavily on legal sources.

117 Appendix A (Table A1, Boardman interview; Bogdanich interview (big companies "have infinitely more power to hide things"); Coll interview; Daly interview (with private business "you have very few leverage points" to extract information)). We will come back to this point at length in Chapter 6.

118 A tip sheet titled "Investigative Business Journalism" mentions the following as the first tip for dealing with private companies: "Check civil court files. Lawsuits are often a great source of information about a company. They often contain detailed information on a company's finances and practices" (Gary Cohn, *Investigative Business Journalism* (IRE, Tipsheet No. 3390, 2010)). *See also* Appendix A (Table A1, Tulsky interview; Bogdanich interview).

119 *Class Action Survey* (Carlton Fields, 2017), http://classactionsurvey.com/2017-survey [http://perma.cc/4D57-SXPG].

120 Appendix A (Table A1, Coll interview).

121 These are the 2015, 2014, 2013, 2008a, 2008b, and 1998 winners. *See* Appendix B for details.

When Boeing tried to attain proprietary Lockheed Martin documents, Lockheed sued, and the Justice Department and the US Attorney's Office in Los Angeles got involved as well. The reporters could then rely on legal documents to include detail, and showed that the espionage was not merely the doing of rogue low-level employees, as Boeing claimed.[122] The reporters in the Toyota story reviewed thousands of regulatory investigation and incidence reports. These regulatory reports allowed the reporters to benchmark the gravity and frequency of sudden acceleration issues with Toyota against the industry: nineteen fatalities in Toyotas, eleven in all other cars combined.[123] The legal documents were therefore crucial in establishing the storyline and clarifying that the accidents were not just one-off random mistakes, contrary to what the company and the regulators claimed.

We observed a similar pattern of relying on regulatory reports at the Allegiant Air story: the reporters there submitted a FOIA request to get the mechanical malfunction reports that were filed with the aviation regulator. They used the data to benchmark the company's midair malfunctions against the industry, thus establishing the impetus for the project, namely, "[a]ll major airlines break down once in a while. But none of them break down in midair more often than Allegiant."[124]

Armed with a more nuanced version of the law and reputation argument, we can now start applying it to specific legal contexts, starting with where the reputational effects are apparently strongest: corporate law.

122 Andy Pasztor & Anne Marie Squeo, *Boeing Employees Are Disciplined in Espionage Case*, Wall St. J., Sept. 12, 2003.

123 Ralph Vartabedian & Ken Bensinger, *Toyota's Woes May Not End at Floor Mats*, L.A. Times, Oct. 18, 2009.

124 Nathaniel Lash et al., *Breakdown at 30,000 Feet*, Tampa Bay Times, Nov. 2, 2016.

PART II

APPLICATIONS

3

Private Litigation

Corporate Law's Puzzle

3.1 INTRODUCTION

How does corporate law work? This question has puzzled corporate legal scholarship for decades. The puzzle stems from the apparent lack of legal sanctions. Corporate decision makers practically never pay out of pocket for their misbehavior,[1] so presumably the law lacks teeth. An influential strand of the literature suggested that corporate law's teeth consist in facilitating *nonlegal* sanctions. But so far the existing accounts have failed to develop a satisfactory theory of how nonlegal forces work or how exactly the law facilitates them.

This makes corporate law the classic context in which to start applying the reputation-through-litigation theory. Scholars widely agree that in this context reputation matters. They even recognize that the law affects behavior not just through legal sanctions, but also by facilitating nonlegal sanctions. All that is needed is fine-tuning and some empirical work: existing accounts focus on how corporate law affects morals (tells market players how they ought to behave), and do not examine how information from the courtroom travels to the court of public opinion. This chapter, by contrast, focuses on how corporate law affects reputation (tells market players how others actually behaved), and examine media coverage of fiduciary duty litigation. To concretize the argument, the chapter hones in on the famous corporate law case of *Disney*. Applying the reputational perspective to corporate law produces a set of fresh

[1] Bernard Black et al., *Outside Director Liability*, 58 STAN. L. REV. 1055, 1055 (2006) (in a span of twenty-five years only thirteen outside directors paid out of pocket); Margaret M. Blair & Lynn A. Stout, *Trust, Trustworthiness, and the Behavioral Foundations of Corporate Law*, 149 U. PA. L. REV. 1735, 1791 (2001) (directors are more likely to get struck by lightning than pay damages for breaching their fiduciary duties). The main justifications for refraining from sanctioning are discouragement of productive risk-taking in businesses, judicial incompetence, and the ability of shareholders to fend for themselves by diversifying risks.

insights on longstanding debates, such as the role of indeterminacy and open standards, or how to assess director liability (individually or collectively).

The chapter proceeds in four sections. Section 3.2 describes the existing approach to corporate law's impact on nonlegal sanctions. Current accounts focus on how judicial comments induce guilty feelings among misbehaving directors or on social shaming among misbehaving directors' peers. In other words, the current approach deals narrowly with how *verdicts* ramp up the *moral* sanctions for misbehaving. In reality, though, verdicts are rare, and the moral rebukes offered in them seldom reach their presumed audiences. It therefore makes sense to shift our focus to how the litigation process as a whole (not just verdicts) shapes the reputational (not just moral) sanctions for misbehaving. The section then outlines three important factors that determine how information from the courtroom translates into the court of public opinion. A key takeaway point is that, counterintuitively, not every case of judicial scolding hurts the company's reputation. To predict the reputational impact, we need to ask who the judge is scolding (an ousted individual or an unhealthy corporate culture?); what she is scolding for (honest incompetence or calculated disregard for shareholder interests?); and what her scolding adds to the preexisting information environment.

Section 3.3 employs the famous *Disney* litigation as a case study, analyzing how media coverage of the debacle in question changed before, during, and after litigation. Section 3.4 uses the reputational perspective to reevaluate key corporate law doctrines. Section 3.5 applies the reputational perspective to the regulatory competition debate, explaining why Delaware law facilitates better information flows than other state corporate laws, and why getting scorned by Delaware judges may actually be good for corporate America.

3.2 HOW FIDUCIARY DUTY LITIGATION AFFECTS NONLEGAL SANCTIONS: "SAINTS AND SINNERS" REVISITED

3.2.1 *The Existing Approach: Saints and Sinners*

Delaware fiduciary duty litigation features a striking pattern: no sanctioning but lots of talking. Delaware judges usually refrain from imposing legal sanctions on company decision makers, but they do not shy away from criticizing the directors' behavior whenever they see fit.[2] This fact pattern of lengthy, fact-intensive, judgmental verdicts raises a puzzle: what is the

[2] For empirical support for the argument that Delaware courts rely heavily on moralism, see John C. Coates, Managing Disputes through Contract: Evidence from M&A 35 n.54 (Aug. 14,

point in preaching if you are not going to sanction? If Delaware courts are not enforcing fiduciary duties, why do they bother talking about them so much?

Several prominent corporate legal scholars suggest a solution to this puzzle: preaching *is* the point, they claim. Preaching is not an afterthought but rather the main function of Delaware decisional law. It is through richly detailed narratives of good and bad corporate behavior that Delaware judges control corporate behavior.[3] Once the morality tales of corporate saints and sinners become publicly available, they unleash all sorts of nonlegal forces. In one version of this "saints and sinners" approach to corporate law, directors hate being dressed down in verdicts because it reduces the esteem that they get from colleagues and peers ("external moral sanctions").[4] In another version, directors who are subject to judicial scolding suffer not from disesteem of others but rather from their own sense of guilt ("internal moral sanctions").[5] And because judges elicit the opprobrium of third parties and/or guilt feelings of first parties simply by what they say, they get to sanction and deter misbehavior without imposing legal sanctions.

This saints-and-sinners theory of corporate law does a great job of spotlighting one indirect deterrence element of corporate law. It correctly directs our attention to the possibility that corporate litigation shapes behavior not just through the outcomes but also through the content of judicial opinions. But as the following paragraphs explain, the existing approach has too narrow a focus. I propose here a shift in perspective: from focusing just on how judicial comments affect moral judgments[6] to focusing on how the litigation process as a whole affects reputational judgments.

2011) (unpublished manuscript), *available at* http://papers.ssrn.com/sol3/papers.cfm?abstract_id=1975423. *See also* Stephen M. Bainbridge, *Why is the Delaware Judiciary Killing So Many Trees? The Delaware Courts Really Need a Page Limit*, PROFESSORBAINBRIDGE.COM BLOG, Oct. 1, 2018, www.professorbainbridge.com/professorbainbridgecom/2018/10/why-is-the-delaware-judiciary-killing-so-many-trees-the-delaware-courts-really-need-a-page-limit.html (noting and criticizing Delaware's tendency to produce lengthy opinions).

3 The two most representative accounts are Edward B. Rock, *Saints and Sinners: How Does Delaware Corporate Law Work?*, 44 U.C.L.A. L. REV. 1009 (1997), and Blair & Stout, *supra* note 1. While there are various other accounts of corporate law and social norms that vary in nuances, they all share enough similarities to be grouped for our purposes under the "saints and sinners" umbrella term.

4 Rock, *id.*

5 Blair & Stout, *supra* note 1.

6 For acknowledgments that existing accounts focus on moralistic and not reputational consequences, see, for example, Rock, *supra* note 3, at 1013 (focusing on disesteem); David A. Skeel, Jr., *Shaming in Corporate Law*, 149 U. PA. L. REV. 1811, 1814, 1856 (2001) (focusing on moral disapproval).

First, focusing just on judicial opinions is problematic because most legal disputes settle. Judges get very few chances to offer moral rebukes in verdicts.[7] Cases that settle do not produce moralistic impact, but they may nevertheless affect the market reaction: not by shaping moral beliefs but rather by shaping factual beliefs. The process itself prior to settlements (pleading, discovery, and trial) sheds light on reputation-relevant information. Indeed, Chapter 2 showed that market players monitor and react to events during the early stages of the process.

Second, focusing just on moralistic impact is problematic because the typical verdict sends mixed messages: by legally exonerating defendants, the verdict dilutes the power of any moralistic condemnations made in dicta. The magnitude of legal sanctions embodies the blameworthiness of behavior.[8] Directors are less likely to suffer guilt, and third parties are less likely to engage in shaming, when the legal system tells them that the behavior in question is not bad enough to merit legal sanctioning. Reputational sanctions, by contrast, are less strongly correlated with legal sanctions. As Chapter 2 showed, the trial's outcome is based on specific legal doctrines that may not be relevant to reputational evaluations. The legal outcome is usually determined from a backward-looking perspective, while a reputational outcome is usually determined from a forward-looking perspective (how indicative of future behavior the adverse action is). As a result, the correlation between legal and reputational outcomes is very imperfect.

Finally, moral rebukes often get lost in translation. Directors normally do not read judicial opinions. And the lawyers who summarize the verdicts for directors usually screen out the caustic comments in their memos to their clients.[9] The rebukes rarely reach their presumed audiences. The power of moral rebukes to propel individuals to engage in costly punishing depends largely on striking the right tone and tenor – factors that easily get lost in translation. Reputational information, by contrast, is less sensitive to distorted transmission. Reputational sanctioning is an exercise in self-interest, and sophisticated investors do not wait for someone to strike the right tone and propel them to act. They stand to gain from proactively mining litigation for hard information.

These three problems – lack of opinions, sanctions, and communication channels – illustrate why it makes sense to focus on reputational rather than

7 Geoffrey P. Miller, A *Modest Proposal for Fixing Delaware's Broken Duty of Care*, 2010 COLUM. BUS. L. REV. 319, 329 (2010).

8 Lisa M. Fairfax, *Spare the Rod, Spoil the Director? Revitalizing Directors' Fiduciary Duty through Legal Liability*, 42 HOUS. L. REV. 393, 446 (2005).

9 Chapter 2; Lyman Johnson, *Counter-Narratives in Corporate Law: Saints and Sinners, Apostles and Epistles*, 2009 MICH. ST. L. REV. 847, 868–70.

moralistic impact. The next section proceeds to explain *how* we should focus on reputational impact: highlighting the main factors that determine how information from fiduciary duty litigation translates into changes in the reputations of the parties to the dispute.

3.2.2 *The Reputational Effects of Judicial Scolding*

As Chapter 2 showed, we cannot simply assume that litigation would hurt the reputation of the companies and the businesspeople involved. Reputational sanctions work in fuzzy ways that do not lend themselves to generalizations. With fiduciary duty litigation specifically, when trying to predict the reputational outcomes of a given dispute, we should ask three questions: "scolding who?" "Scolding compared to what?" and "scolding for what?"

First, the "*scolding who*" question. To recast our discussion in Chapter 2, sometimes there can be a difference between litigation's effects on individual reputation and organizational reputation. Nowhere is this difference more pronounced than in the context of corporate law litigation, where many disputes are brought as derivative suits. Derivative suits are brought in the name of the company against its managers, and thereby generate information on actions done by managers, supposedly against the company. Such litigation often leads to one of two scenarios with completely different reputational ramifications: either the judge criticizes singled-out individuals (thereby hurting the individuals' reputation), or the judge criticizes the company's systemic failures (thereby hurting the company's reputation).

Second, the "*scolding compared to what?*" question. Corporate law litigation often involves big and visible companies, and comes against the background of an already existing market reaction. When the company is publicly traded, stock analysts, institutional investors, and business media have incentives to quickly find out the facts about what happened and offer interpretations about how it happened.[10] As a result, in many of the cases that make it to court, the defendant-company stakeholders have already learned about the misbehavior and formed opinions. In fact, many lawsuits are filed precisely because the stock market learned about the bad news and dropped the stock price, causing plaintiff lawyers to rush to file a lawsuit. A reputational analysis of litigation therefore should concentrate on relative impact: do not ask whether the judge's version is

[10] A typical example comes from critical editorials that couch the story under some catchable category such as a story about corporate greed or power-tripping CEOs. *See* Eric Dezenhall & John Weber, Damage Control 15, 39 (2007).

unfavorable to the company – ask whether it is more or less favorable than the prevalent version accepted in the market prior to litigation.

Finally, we should ask "*scolding for what?*" as Chapter 1 showed, the type of sin committed affects the reputational outcome. Judicial comments will affect stakeholder attributions; that is, whether stakeholders attribute the bad outcomes to honest incompetence or to calculated disregard for market norms. Here one counterintuitive observation is especially intriguing: the judge's version, even when containing caustic criticism, typically supports a framing that is relatively favorable to the company. The preexisting framing is tilted by market and social arbiters' incentives to pile on criticism once bad news breaks, and the allegation-driven media's incentives to highlight soundbites from the plaintiffs' lawyers post-filing.[11] As a result, the preexisting version usually makes even caustic judicial comments seem nuanced when compared to the baseline.

Therein lies the rub in the saints-and-sinners approach: people are not exclusively saints or sinners, and judges know that. According to the saints-and-sinners argument, the judges' role is to help market players realize that certain defendants are sinners. But in reality the order and roles are reversed: the market reacts first by painting accused businessmen in black. And the judge often repaints a more richly detailed picture in shades of gray. The court of public opinion tends to categorize businessmen/companies as complete heroes or complete villains. And judges' interpretations – even when critical of defendants – tend to be more contextual. Accordingly, the relative effect of judicial comments on reputation is not necessarily negative, and sometimes even positive. For the judge's narrative to affect the company's reputation positively it does not have to be a resounding endorsement of the defendants' behavior. It only has to make the bad situation appear less bad, for example, by showing that the adverse action does not reflect the company's operational philosophy.[12]

To concretize these differences between the saints-and-sinners approach and the reputational approach, let us now delve into the specific case of *Disney*.

3.3 THE *DISNEY* LITIGATION: A CASE STUDY

The *Disney* litigation is one of the most anticipated and discussed corporate law cases in decades.[13] It revolved around the hiring and subsequent firing of

11 Batia M. Wiesenfeld et al., *The Stigmatization and Devaluation of Elites Associated with Corporate Failures: A Process Model*, 33 Acad. Mgmt. Rev. 231, 240–42 (2008).

12 Dezenhall & Weber, *supra* note 10, at 169, 187.

13 Johnson, *supra* note 9, at 860; Renee Jones, *The Role of Good Faith in Delaware: How Open-Ended Standards Help Delaware Preserve Its Edge*, 55 N.Y.L. Sch. L. Rev. 499, 507 (2011);

Hollywood's agent Michael Ovitz as Disney's president. Ovitz failed to perform satisfactorily and was fired after a year, but not before collecting a $140-million termination package from Disney. Disney's shareholders sued the directors for breaching their fiduciary duties in supervising the hiring and firing of Ovitz.[14] After a lengthy battle at the pleading stage, the lawsuit proceeded to a full-fledged trial. Chancellor Chandler then delivered a 170-page fact-intensive decision that was filled with caustic criticism but ultimately exonerated the defendants who walked away winning.

Many corporate legal scholars have since hailed the *Disney* decision as a paradigmatic example of the saints-and-sinners approach: as illustrating how Delaware courts avoid legal sanctions while ramping up nonlegal sanctions, as exonerating while condemning.[15] And this is exactly what makes *Disney* such an interesting case study for our purposes; a deeper look reveals that even this seemingly clear-cut example does not follow the saints-and-sinners theory's predictions.[16] Instead, it corroborates the alternative theory presented here. The *Disney* saga illustrates the reputational dynamics of big-case litigation: the verdict does not add new information because almost every fact cited by the Chancellor had already been covered by the media. *Disney* also illustrates how a seemingly caustic verdict when read in isolation is actually favorable to the company when considering our three key factors: the preexisting information, who the judge is scolding, and what he is scolding them for.

What distinguishes my reading of *Disney* from the numerous previous dissections of the case is the focus on relative nonlegal impact. Many scholars have focused on doctrinal analysis but ignored the decision's nonlegal impact.

Jonathan Macey, *Delaware: Home of the World's Most Expensive Raincoat*, 33 Hofstra L. Rev. 1131, 1131 (2005).

14 *In re* The Walt Disney Company Derivative Litigation, 825 A.2d 275, 281–87 (Del. Ch. 2003) (describing plaintiffs' allegations).

15 *See, e.g.*, Tamar Frankel, *Court of Law and Court of Public Opinion: Symbiotic Regulation of the Corporate Management Duty of Care*, 3 N.Y.U. J.L. & Bus. 353, 363–64 (2007); Johnson, *supra* note 9, at 863 ("[T]he opinion was a paragon of how Rock had earlier described Delaware opinion. It was detailed, normatively saturated, judgmental, and laced with scolding, sometimes acerbic, moral reproof"); Geoffrey P. Miller, *A Modest Proposal for Fixing Delaware's Broken Duty of Care*, 2010 Colum. Bus. L. Rev. 319, 326 (2010); David M. Wilson, *Climate Change: The Real Threat to Delaware Corporate Law, Why Delaware Must Keep a Watchful Eye on the Content of Political Change in the Air*, 5 Entrepreneurial Bus. L.J. 481, 488 (2010).

16 As the Introduction explained, I use *Disney* as a "crucial, 'most likely' case": since it is widely considered the paradigmatic example for an existing approach (saints and sinners), digging deep into it illustrates the problems in the hegemonic theory and opens up space for my alternative framework.

The scholars who have touched on the nonlegal impact simply note the decision's moralistic tone and assume that it ramps up the nonlegal sanctions and deterrence. I adopt a different methodology that shifts our focus to the dynamics of reputational sanctions. Using a content analysis of the media coverage of the Ovitz debacle, I explore how the reputational capital of Disney and its top managers fluctuated before, during, and after litigation. The media coverage analysis, supplemented with insights from my interviews with key players,[17] allows us to decipher the relative reputational impact of litigation. In other words, by examining how the court of public opinion treated the Ovitz affair before the verdict, we can tease out the real difference that the verdict made as a second opinion.

3.3.1 *Information Produced before Litigation Started*

The *Disney* lawsuit was filed in 1997. But by that time the court of public opinion had already been in session for a year. And the company was losing, badly.

The media covered the Disney–Ovitz debacle extensively during 1996. Investigative journalists were the first to uncover the problems with Disney's management. One lead story followed another, and by the second half of 1996, each medium was competing to come up with vivid details about the bad blood between Disney's top managers.[18] The early reports highlighted how Disney's number one (Michael Eisner) ran his own show without checks and balances from the board[19] while Disney's new number two (Ovitz) was in over his head.[20] At the time, the company was denying the stories in an attempt to limit their negative reputational impact. But the denials rang hollow when investigative reporters exposed internal documents (such as Eisner's internal

17 I especially benefited from phone interviews with reporters who covered the Disney–Ovitz debacle throughout the years: Corie Brown, who covered the litigation for Newsweek (Jan. 20, 2014); Kim Christensen, who covered post-verdict developments for the Los Angeles Times (Jan. 17, 2014); Kim Masters, who wrote multiple articles and a book-length account of Disney's debacles (June 14, 2013); and Richard Verrier, who covered the litigation for the Los Angeles Times (Jan. 23, 2014).

18 Ken Auletta, *Marriage, No Honeymoon*, NEW YORKER, July 29, 1996; Kate Bohner, *Michael Versus Michael*, FORBES, July 1, 1996, at 20; Corie Brown, *Clash of the Titans?*, NEWSWEEK, July 10, 1996.

19 T. L. Stanley, *Definite Difference at Disney*, MEDIAWEEK, Apr. 22, 1996.

20 Bernard Weinraub & Geraldine Fabrikant, *A Mouseketeer with an Attitude: Ovitz's Past Haunts Disney's Future*, N.Y. TIMES, June 10, 1996, at D1; Ronald Grover & Elizabeth Lesly, *The Humbling of Mike Ovitz*, BUS. WEEK (May 27, 1996), www.businessweek.com/stories/1996–05–26/the-humbling-of-mike-ovitz.

memos tarnishing Ovitz) and quotes from former insiders going on record about Disney's governance flaws.[21]

Then in late 1996 the company could no longer deny the problems. Ovitz was fired, and the company had to file press releases and submit information to the SEC (in our lingo: direct legal sources). The injection of new information intensified the market reaction. It was then – via the company's own reporting – that the public learned about the hefty severance package awarded to Ovitz after an unsatisfactory year at the helm. Now market and social arbiters were competing over who would offer stronger condemnations of Disney. Large institutional investors claimed to be enraged.[22] The president of the National Association of Corporate Directors said that Disney's board was "living in the dark ages" and was too beholden to Eisner.[23] And practically all the major newspapers ran editorials that attributed the Ovitz debacle to a corporate culture of total disregard for shareholder interests and societal norms.[24]

Overall, the media coverage of the Ovitz debacle was extensive in scope and unfavorable in tone from the get-go. Any stakeholder of Disney had the chance to learn about the problems and downgrade her beliefs about the company's management integrity, before a lawsuit was even filed.

Corporate legal scholars treat the 2005 verdict as setting a reputational sanction in motion.[25] But in reality the reputational system was already in motion in 1996. Those involved in the Ovitz debacle suffered a huge initial reputational hit. Before litigation began, the company was already depicted as the poster child for bad corporate governance, and its top managers were ridiculed.[26] In fact, it was the reputational system that set the legal system in

21 A *Vanity Fair* story, for example, was based on interviews with dozens of former and current Disney insiders. Bryan Burrough & Kim Masters, *The Mouse Trap*, VANITY FAIR, Dec. 1996, www.vanityfair.com/society/features/1996/12/ovitz-199612.

22 Bruce Orwall, *Disney Holders Decry Payouts at Meeting*, WALL ST. J., Feb. 26, 1997, at A3; Bruce Orwall & Joann Lublin, *The Rich Rewards of a Hollywood Exit*, WALL ST. J., Dec. 16, 1996, at B1.

23 KIM MASTERS, THE KEYS TO THE KINGDOM 380 (2000).

24 *Id.* at 376–7; Holman W. Jenkins, *Beavis and Butthead Do the Disney Shareholders*, WALL ST. J., Jan. 7, 1997, at A17 ("[N]obody in the real world ... gets that kind of money for flubbing up after a year on the job," as if the headline was not enough); A. M. Rosenthal, *Hardtack for the Journey*, N.Y. TIMES, Dec. 17, 1996, at A25.

25 Frankel, for example, claims that "[b]y telling the whole world what was happening within Disney the decision allows us to become somewhat of a peeping tom," and that the decision "carves out a process by which the media becomes aware of an issue." Frankel, *supra* note 15, at 365, 367.

26 IESE BUS. SCH. CASE STUDY, MICHAEL EISNER AT DISNEY (2005) (noting in retrospect that Eisner went from being considered a business guru to a regular on Forbes' annual list of World's Worst CEOs, facing a shareholder revolt, and being forced to resign as chairman);

motion: the lawyers based their 1997 complaint on facts and interpretations taken straight from the media coverage.[27]

3.3.2 *Information Produced during the Earlier Stages in Litigation*

Once a complaint was filed, the mere process of litigation (pleading, discovery, and trial) affected Disney's reputation. The media coverage of the *Disney* litigation was not limited to the final verdict: it was in full effect in the discovery and trial stages, voluminous in scope and unfavorable in tone. It impacted the defendants' reputation at least as much as the verdict did.

The first question to consider is *what* information was covered. The answer: almost everything. After the complaint finally passed the motion to dismiss stage in 2003, the media turned their attention back to the Ovitz debacle. Major financial newspapers sent designated reporters to Delaware to report daily from the trial. And almost any meaningful tidbit of information submitted to court – such as plaintiffs' experts' reports or internal documents revealed in discovery – found its way to mass media and was quickly and widely diffused.[28]

The second question to consider is *how* information was covered by the press. The answer: negatively. The media used the information produced during litigation to paint an unfavorable picture of the company's corporate governance and the individual directors' competence and integrity. Media reporters spotlighted three themes in particular. First, reporters painted a picture of disregard for "best practices of corporate governance" at Disney.[29] They highlighted multiple descriptions of how Eisner was an imperialist who did not consult the board enough and how board members failed to do

ROBERT SLATER, OVITZ 301 (1997) (same); Nikky Finke, *Poof! Mike Ovitz, from Sorcerer to Schmo*, N.Y. OBSERVER, Sept. 23, 1996 (describing Ovitz as powerless and Eisner's whipping boy); *The One-Time Lion King*, THE ECONOMIST (Sept. 16, 2004) (noting in retrospect that under Eisner, "Disney became a byword for poor corporate governance").

27 John Gibeaut, *Stock Responses*, 89 ABA J. 38, 38 (2003) (noting that the initial lawsuit relied heavily on "conclusory statements from newspaper editorials about Ovitz's highly publicized exit").

28 *See, e.g.*, Peter Larsen, *Eisner Criticized in Ovitz Report*, FIN. TIMES, Feb. 27, 2004, at 31 (covering experts' reports); Bruce Orwall, *The Mousetrap*, WALL ST. J. Nov. 23, 2004, at A1 (covering internal memos that were exposed during discovery, where Eisner calls Ovitz a psychopath); Christopher Parkes, *Disney Board Backed Ovitz Just Before He Was Sacked*, FIN. TIMES, Nov. 9, 2004, www.ft.com/cms/s/0/9f92bf36–31df-11d9–97c0–00000e2511c8.html #axzz3HHJCAnjm (covering internal memos).

29 David J. Jefferson, *Back in the Hot Seat*, NEWSWEEK, Nov. 1, 2004, at 38; Larsen, *id*; Orwall, *id* (nothing that the trial reveals how Eisner wielded power over the board, operating with "little regard for the conventional rules of corporate play").

their jobs confronting Eisner. A notable example comes from the new revelation (through cross-examinations) that Disney's hiring committee did not even convene before Ovitz's hiring was announced.[30] Second, reporters emphasized how Ovitz was incompetent for the job he was hired to do. The media especially enjoyed covering the juicy details from plaintiffs' experts' testimonies suggesting that Ovitz was a habitual liar and a conspicuous spender.[31] Finally, reporters suggested that the mismatch and eventual breakup with Ovitz could have been anticipated and avoided. Ovitz himself testified that at the time of his hiring, he thought that the "duty of care" applied only to hospitals.[32]

Overall, the onslaught of information substantiated the market's initial (predominantly negative) reaction. The themes highlighted by the media were not new per se. The public knew the main plotlines – the bad blood, Eisner's power-tripping, and Ovitz's powerlessness – before litigation even started. Still, the litigation process added lots of small details and filled in the blank parts of the story.[33] Most importantly, even when litigation did not produce new information, it nevertheless raised the saliency of and removed uncertainty from existing information. Litigation kept the Disney–Ovitz story in the news cycle, recalling the public's attention to it.[34] And it made certain versions of the story more credible and less refutable by giving the public access to direct quotes and internal memos from Disney insiders.

The Disney case study thus illustrates how the informational role of litigation is not limited to the final outcomes (i.e., not limited to verdicts or

30 Christopher Parkes, *The Case of the 140m Dollars Parachute*, FIN. TIMES, Nov. 8, 2004, at 17.

31 Chad Bray & Bruce Orwall, *Ovitz Performance in Disney Role is Faulted at Trial*, WALL ST. J., Oct. 22, 2004, at B2; Parkes, *id.*

32 Bruce Orwall & Chad Bray, *Ovitz's Testimony on Disney Tenure Portrays a Thwarted Deal Maker*, WALL ST. J., Oct. 27, 2004, at A1 (describing that Ovitz himself warned Eisner in advance that he would have a hard time adjusting to the running of a public company); Christopher Parkes, *Disney Executives "Hostile to Ovitz before He Joined,"* FIN. TIMES, Oct. 27, 2004, at 15 (describing that incumbent top executives clarified from the outset that they would not work with Ovitz); Christopher Parkes, *Ovitz "Did Not Grasp Executive Position,"* FIN. TIMES, Oct. 22, 2004, at 24; Christopher Parkes, *Ovitz Was Determined 'Not to Be a Loser,'* FIN. TIMES, Oct. 28, 2004, at 26 (noting that Ovitz asked to change his severance package between signing and starting work); Kim Masters, *Deposed*, SLATE MAG. (Aug. 16, 2004), www.slate.com/articles/news_and_politics/low_concept/2004/08/deposed.html ("The depositions amplify what was obvious from the start: in terms of temperament and experience, Ovitz could not have been more ill-suited for the job").

33 Orwall, *supra* note 28 ("The trial, plus interviews from depositions, provides an unusual behind-the-scenes peek").

34 Richard Morgan, *The Two Mikes*, THE DEAL.COM (Oct. 18, 2004), *available at* PROQUEST, Doc. No. 220383829 ("The story might have ended there were it not for Milberg Weiss' class action. But now, after years of languishing, the suit has a snowball of interest unimaginable when it was first filed").

settlement announcements). To the extent that the legal system had something to add to market players' assessments of Disney, the additions came largely from the process rather than the verdict. As an anecdote: in Michael Ovitz's *Wikipedia* webpage, the description of the Disney debacle relies not on quotes from the 2005 verdict, but rather on a 2004 media story covering the depositions.[35] To me, this anecdote indicates how the process itself often makes a lasting reputational impact, regardless of the verdict.

3.3.3 *The Real Impact of the Verdict*

Recognizing the important informational role of the process pushes us to rethink the role of verdicts. Judges base their interpretations on information gleaned from discovery, testimonies, and experts' reports. In cases with big-firm defendants, such as *Disney*, the same information that the judge relies upon often gets diffused immediately. By the time the judge releases her version, the public is already aware of the information contained in it. Verdicts in big cases thus fulfill a different informational role than previously assumed: they affect reputational sanctions not by providing new information but rather by constructing and disseminating existing information. Here again, the deep dive into the *Disney* affair provides a case in point.

To analyze the impact that the *Disney* verdict had, we have to first appreciate how the court of public opinion treated the Ovitz affair prior to the verdict. Rereading the decision along with the media coverage of it generates one immediate conclusion: the conventional view that sees the verdict as a reputational deathblow to everyone involved is misguided. Granted, Chancellor Chandler's version contains some quotable caustic comments. But it also provides more nuanced and contextual explanations for the Ovitz debacle. Unlike the prevalent preexisting interpretations of what went wrong in Disney, the verdict attributes the bad outcome to rare external conditions rather than to deep-rooted disregard for market norms. And the Chancellor reserves his strongest criticisms for individuals who were already ousted from Disney, thus implicitly creating a separation between bad (ousted) individuals and a good company. As a result, to the extent that the verdict changed stakeholders' beliefs, it probably pushed stakeholders into thinking more positively about the company and its incumbent management, by (1) emphasizing context; (2) scolding for transient, fixable mistakes; (3) and scolding individuals who were not a part of the company going forward.

[35] *Michael Ovitz*, Wikipedia, http://en.wikipedia.org/wiki/Michael_Ovitz (last visited July 27, 2019).

Emphasizing Context. The Chancellor opens his version with an explanation of the hiring: why Disney's board rushed to hire someone with no experience in running a large public company, and then on top of that, signed an outrageous severance package provision. Here the verdict's version differs from preexisting versions by putting more emphasis on the context. The Chancellor highlights from the outset (and then reiterates constantly)[36] the "perfect storm" that pushed Disney into the Ovitz affair: Disney's previous president died in a helicopter crash; Disney's CEO (Eisner) suffered from a heart condition; and the company was in the midst of major expansions. Due to these unusual circumstances, the company desperately needed a new president to take the burden off the ailing Eisner in the immediate term and to provide an insurance and succession plan for the long run. Targeting Ovitz as the quick fix made sense at the time, since he was considered Hollywood's number one power broker.[37] And promising Ovitz a hefty severance package was necessary in order to lure him from his previous lucrative position and away from Disney's competitors who were courting him.[38]

By making the context more salient,[39] the verdict helps stakeholders overcome biases that plague their reputational assessments. Most notably, the Chancellor opens his decision by explicitly warning the readers from hindsight bias: do not ask yourself whether the board's decisions make sense to you now, he tells the reader; ask whether they made sense at the time they were taken.[40] The Chancellor then provides the readers with tools to mitigate their hindsight bias: he extends the timeframe by spotlighting the events that preceded Ovitz's hiring and reminds the reader not to evaluate Disney's

36 *In re* The Walt Disney Co. Derivative Litig., 907 A.2d 693, 699, 702, 762, 770, 771, 778 (Del. Ch. 2005).

37 *Id.* at 701–02, 764–65.

38 *Id.* at 702. The verdict changed the media coverage's tone dramatically. Prior to the verdict editorials explained Ovitz's severance package as a blatant disregard of market norms. Following the verdict editorials explained the package as a reasonable business decision. *See, e.g., The Happiest Board on Earth,* L.A. Times, Aug. 11, 2005, at B12 ("That kind of 'downside protection' was central to getting Ovitz to leave CAA for Disney, and it's endemic to the Hollywood way of doing business").

39 To emphasize: the facts that the Chancellor cites were not new. But by packaging the facts with a seal of approval from a Delaware judge, the Chancellor increased the likelihood that stakeholders would reevaluate their initial assessment. Indeed, the media coverage that never mentioned the "perfect storm" that explains Ovitz's hiring prior to the verdict began emphasizing it after the verdict. *See, e.g.,* Laura Holson, *Ruling Upholds Disney's Payment in Firing of Ovitz,* N.Y. Times, Aug. 10, 2005, at A1.

40 *Disney,* 907 A.2d at 698. The media echoed the call to beware of hindsight: Holson, *id*; Kathy M. Kristoff, *Ovitz Ruling Is a Limited Win for Directors,* L.A. Times, Aug. 10, 2005, at C1; *Regulating Fantasyland,* Aug. 12, 2005, N.Y. Times, at A18.

management integrity according to twenty-first-century best practices (which were not relevant when the Ovitz affair occurred).[41] Most notably, the Chancellor emphasizes that Disney's stock prices jumped through the roof when Ovitz's hiring was announced.[42] Amazingly enough, this important fact was largely missing from the preexisting accounts of the Ovitz affair in the media.

Emphasizing the context also mitigates readers' tendency to adopt causal explanations (recall our earlier discussion of the naïve psychologist bias). The pre-verdict narratives were predominantly causal: if Disney hired an incompetent president only to cushion his way out after a year with $140 million of shareholders' money, then Disney's decision makers must lack any regard for shareholders' interests, right? Wrong, says the Chancellor. No one in Disney set out to hurt shareholders.[43] In fact, Disney decision makers – along with the rest of the world, as the stock price reaction indicates – thought that they were creating shareholder value by hiring Ovitz.[44]

Scolding for Honest and Transient Mistakes. After explaining the hiring, the Chancellor turns to explaining the firing. How come Ovitz performed miserably at Disney? Why was he not fired earlier? Most importantly, why was he not fired "for cause," which could have saved the need to pay his severance package? Here, the Chancellor's answers focus on "mismatch of cultures." Ovitz and the incumbent managers wanted the experiment to work, the Chancellor tells us, but Ovitz simply experienced difficulties assimilating to Disney. Ovitz was flashy, conspicuous, and tried to "agent" his colleagues while the corporate culture was more blue collar and no-nonsense.[45] Corporate legal scholars viewed the Chancellor's vivid descriptions of the mismatch as humiliating the defendants.[46] But such a view misses two important aspects of reputational sanctions: it ignores the baseline (how does the

41 Disney, 907 A.2d at 697.

42 *Id.* at 708 (noting how Disney's market capitalization increased by more than $1 billion upon announcement).

43 *Id.* at 762 ("[C]onsiderations of improper motive are no longer present in this case").

44 This is another point that the media coverage ignored prior to the verdict and embraced after the verdict. *See, e.g.*, Kim Christensen & Richard Verrier, *Judge Rules in Favor of Disney in Ovitz Case but Criticizes Eisner*, L.A. Times, Aug. 10, 2005, at A1 ("Ovitz's 1995 hiring was hailed at the time as a coup for Disney and Eisner . . . Ovitz was a near-mythical figure then, frequently dubbed Hollywood's most powerful executive").

45 *Disney*, 907 A.2d at 713–14; *id* (echoing the mismatch-in-cultures point).

46 *See, e.g.*, Frankel, *supra* note 15, at 358 ("[The Chancellor made Ovitz] look like an incredibly stupid man, who [was] inexperienced in the politics of corporate Hollywood … [T]his description undermines Ovitz's reputation more than any criticizing of his behavior would … He was the punished bad boy").

Chancellor's version compare to preexisting ones?) and the distinction between individual- and organizational-level reputations.

Attributing the failure to unanticipated mismatches and misperceptions is relatively favorable to the company's reputation. Remember that most preexisting versions talked about how Ovitz's failure was well anticipated: Disney's incumbent management hired an obviously incompetent guy and then intentionally tripped that guy. Moreover, according to the preexisting versions, Ovitz was not fired for cause simply because Eisner wanted to protect his personal reputation at the expense of shareholder interests or, worse, because Eisner and Ovitz cynically plotted to transfer millions from shareholders' pockets to Ovitz's.[47]

The Chancellor rejects these versions: Ovitz actually made some positive contributions to the company, he tells us, and neither side was intentionally tripping or foreseeing the failure.[48] At one point the Chancellor describes in detail a seemingly irrelevant tidbit: a company meeting where all the top executives rode the company bus while Ovitz insisted on being chauffeured in his private limo. Legal scholars viewed the inclusion of such a gossipy story as tarnishing Ovitz's reputation.[49] Well, maybe. But how does such a story affect the *company's* reputation? For stakeholders thinking about whether to interact with Disney in the future, framing the debacle as a story about one greedy executive who did not fit in with the rest of the down-to-earth managers (and was subsequently fired) is not alarming; rather, it is assuring.

To answer the "scolding for what" question: the Chancellor is scolding Disney and its directors not for calculated disregard for shareholder interests, but rather for honest, temporary mistakes. Prior to the verdict, market and social arbiters framed the Ovitz debacle as a clear-cut story of corporate villains: managers becoming too entrenched and greedy, losing regard for shareholder interests or societal norms. The verdict, however critical of Disney's directors, tells a markedly different story: a story about making mistakes while pursuing shareholder value.[50]

47 Bruce Orwall & Joann S. Lublin, *Fading Magic*, WALL ST. J., Mar. 1, 2004, at A1; James B. Stewart, *Partners*, NEW YORKER, Jan. 10, 2005, at 46, 53 (suggesting that Eisner foresaw the failure five weeks into Ovitz's hiring).

48 *Disney*, 907 A.2d at 693, 759, 762, 778.

49 *See, e.g.*, Frankel, *supra* note 15.

50 The media picked up the honest mistakes theme. *See, e.g.*, Ben White, *Disney Executive's Severance Ruled Legal*, WASH. POST, Aug. 10, 2005, at A1 ("[W]hile Ovitz's employment turned out to be a disaster, it was reasonable for directors to think, given the agent's reputation as among the most powerful men in Hollywood, that it could have succeeded").

Scolding Individuals Who Were Already Ousted. Up to now I have focused on how the verdict generates a more nuanced and favorable version. But there are specific parts in the verdict that cannot be viewed as favorable to the defendants' reputation. The Chancellor scolded Eisner for disregarding corporate governance and scolded other top executives for not stepping up and raising red flags. His judicial scolding was done in such a catchable manner and came from such a credible source that it captured front pages of major newspapers, increasing public awareness and recalling attention to the defendants' flaws.[51] But while the reputation-damaging effects of these comments were widely recognized, one aspect of them has been grossly overlooked: the identity of the targets.

The Chancellor reserved his strongest criticism for six individuals. He laid most of the blame at Eisner's feet[52] and then named three directors who should have done more to prevent the debacle: Irwin Russell, who did not negotiate hard enough on behalf of the company, and two members of the compensation committee – Ignacio Lozano and Sidney Poitier – for not being involved enough. The Chancellor also scolded two nondirectors: Sandy Litvack, the general counsel, for not informing the board on the possibility to avoid paying Ovitz his severance package; and Graef Crystal, an outside expert hired to help the compensation committee, for providing a faulty and incomplete report.

All of these six scolded businesspeople have one thing in common: *none of them were any longer an integral part of Disney when the verdict was issued.* The Disney 2005 board contained many directors who were part of the company in the Ovitz debacle days. Yet none of the retained individuals were scolded. The scolding was reserved for individuals who were already ousted or on their way out.

The *Disney* verdict thus illustrates how singling out individuals as sinners may actually help the company. Indeed, the media quickly picked up the scapegoating theme promoted by the verdict. The coverage of the verdict highlighted a contrast: a victory to Disney and its board and a blow to Eisner's scorecard on his way out of the company.[53] More generally, the

[51] One sentence made it to the pantheon of judicial scolding and was cited endlessly, describing how Eisner "enthroned himself as the omnipotent and infallible monarch of his personal Magic Kingdom." *Disney*, 907 A.2d at 763.

[52] *Id.* at 760 (writing that Eisner was the "instigator and mastermind" behind the hiring); *id.* at 763 n.488 (noting that Eisner was imperial and Machiavellian, surrounding himself with yes men). Every major newspaper's front-page story about the verdict contained a sentence explicitly mentioning that Chandler saved his strongest criticisms for Eisner.

[53] One L.A. *Times* front-page headline is illustrative: Christensen & Verrier, *Judge Rules in Favor of Disney in Ovitz Case But Criticizes Eisner*, *supra* note 44; *see also* Rupert Steiner, *Record*

verdict's singling out of ousted individuals contributed to the company's ability to convince stakeholders that the company had learned from its past and changed its ways. The media and institutional investors bought into the recovery message, presenting Disney as the perfect example of a corporate governance turnaround: the bad company of the 1990s turned into the role model of the 2000s.[54]

Aside from illustrating how the scolding of individuals does not necessarily translate into reputational damages to the company, *Disney* also generates a much more counterintuitive observation: judicial comments do not automatically translate into reputational damages to the *individual* either. The reputational outcomes to the individual depend, again, on the baseline and the type of sin for which the individual is scolded.

To illustrate, let us consider Chancellor Chandler's treatment of Ovitz. The baseline – the pre-verdict reputational capital of Ovitz – was close to zero. When legal scholars claim that the verdict humiliated Ovitz by presenting him as a powerless whipping boy, they ignore the fact that these depictions were already publicly available and widely accepted in the court of public opinion.[55] The verdict could not have reduced Ovitz's already deflated reputational capital by much (if at all). In fact, the Chancellor's narrative resembles (and thus lends credence to) the narrative that Ovitz himself promoted in an attempt to recover his lost reputation.[56] Unsurprisingly so: it is better for Ovitz to be perceived as powerless or incompetent in a given task than as someone who cynically disregards shareholder interest or is inherently useless. As one

Profits Put the Smile Back at Disney, SUNDAY BUS., Aug. 14, 2005, at C9 (describing the verdict as "good news" for Disney, while "hardly a valediction for [Eisner's] leaving card"). The fact that the sinner – Eisner – was on his way out was highlighted in media coverage. *See, e.g.*, Holson, *supra* note 39 (referring to Eisner as the "departing" CEO, stepping down soon).

54 *Iger Wins over Wall Street and Main Street*, DOW JONES, Dec. 6, 2006 ("Disney has gone from a poster child for bad governance to a model for reform, according to corporate watchdogs"). Disney itself fueled the turnaround theme by feeding the media shortly after the verdict with announcements of strengthening of corporate governance. *See* Kim Christensen, *Disney Board Gives Shareholders More Clout*, L.A. TIMES, Aug. 19, 2005, at C2; Kim Christensen, *Disney Chief Brings Calm to Firm Famed for Discord*, L.A. TIMES, Sept. 28, 2005, at A1; Laura M. Holson, *Disney Renovation: A Master Plan to Restore the Kingdom's Magic*, N.Y. TIMES, Aug. 15, 2005, at C1.

55 Eric Dezenhall, NAIL 'EM! 128–38 (1999); Dominick Dunne, *Sorcerer's Apprentice*, VANITY FAIR, Feb. 2005 ("Ovitz is probably the most humiliated Hollywood figure of the last decade"); Orwall & Bray, *supra* note 32 ("[Ovitz] seemed intent on using the witness stand as a platform to repair a reputation that has taken a beating since he left Disney").

56 *Compare* SLATER, *supra* note 26, at 328, and Orwall & Bray, *id.*, *with Disney*, 907 A.2d 693, 716 (Del. Ch. 2005).

Wall Street Journal columnist quipped: "if Mr. Ovitz does not come out smelling like a rose, he at least gets some of his reputation back."[57]

*

Overall, the *Disney* litigation illustrates how judicial comments do not automatically translate into an increase in reputational sanctions. To the extent that the verdict impacted stakeholders' beliefs, it probably convinced them that Disney's problems are less deep-rooted and more easily fixable than they previously thought. This is not to suggest that the litigation was all fun and games for the defendants. In fact, it probably was a nightmare for them. After all, they were dragged through discovery and cross-examinations, and some of them were publicly scorned by the judge. But remember that from a reputational perspective, Disney and its managers took a lot of criticism for the Ovitz debacle prior to the verdict. Once the verdict got out, it actually silenced some critics by giving a more nuanced and contextual version, allowing the company to turn over a new leaf. And the parts of the verdict that fueled new criticism were directed at individuals who no longer were part of the incumbent management.

3.3.4 *How Generalizable Are the Lessons from* Disney?

Some may claim that we cannot extract general lessons from *Disney* because the case is so singular: no other corporate dispute would similarly capture the public's attention. My response to this argument is twofold. First, remember that I use *Disney* to make a point about the state of current literature. Corporate legal scholars use *Disney* as a paradigmatic example of the saints-and-sinners approach, so it makes sense for me to engage them on their own terms. By showing that even this supposedly clear-cut case does not behave according to the existing theory's predictions, I illustrate the need to adopt an alternative framework. For example, the saints-and-sinners proponents claim that in big-firm defendant cases, litigation ramps up nonlegal sanctions, and use *Disney* as a case in point.[58] But our deeper look into *Disney* suggests that it is exactly in these big and visible cases that the reputational dynamics may flip sides. A verdict may not play a role of informing market players about the bad corporate sinners, if only because the market has already learned about the

[57] Holman W. Jenkins, Jr., *Beavis and Butt-head, Revisited*, WALL ST. J., Aug. 17, 2005, at A11; *see also* Christensen & Verrier, *supra* note 44 ("Chandler's decision provides some comfort for Ovitz, who had sought to use the case to finally tell his side of the story publicly").

[58] Frankel, *supra* note 15, at 376.

misconduct and painted the company and businesspeople as sinners. Any theory of how litigation affects nonlegal sanction should therefore consider the pre-suit benchmark.

Second, and more fundamentally, *Disney*'s uniqueness is a matter of degree, not substance. Even though other large legal disputes are not as extensively debated in mass media as *Disney* was, many of them are nevertheless are tried in the court of public opinion, with the legal system relegated to a second-opinion role. To illustrate how the *Disney* dynamics exist in other cases, consider another iconic corporate law case: *Caremark*.[59]

The bad news that ignited the *Caremark* litigation was the company's failure to comply with healthcare regulations, specifically by paying "kickbacks" to physicians. Shareholders sued Caremark's directors for breaching their fiduciary duty in not monitoring and stopping the illegalities. Like the *Disney* decision, Chancellor Allen's decision in *Caremark* was seen by corporate legal scholars as a "saints and sinners" maneuver: avoiding legal sanctions while generating nonlegal sanctions.[60] But much like in *Disney*, a deeper analysis of the *Caremark* saga reveals the same dynamics that resist the saints-and-sinners assumptions. First, the judicial opinion does not contain new information. By the time Chancellor Allen released his version, Caremark's stakeholders had already formed opinions about the kickbacks debacle and what it meant. The existing information environment was molded by social arbiters ("a spate of negative press");[61] market arbiters (rating agencies lowering Caremark's ratings);[62] and regulators (after the company pled guilty to several criminal counts, the government released a "statement of facts" detailing Caremark's violations).[63] Similarly to *Disney*, parts of the legal complaint were actually based on information gathered from preexisting media coverage.[64] Chancellor Allen's decision thus did not affect what information was available but rather mostly how available information was diffused. Again, the lesson is that analyses of big corporate legal disputes should adopt a second-opinion perspective, considering the baseline.

59 *In re* Caremark Int'l Inc. Derivative Litig., 698 A.2d 959 (Del. Ch. 1996).

60 *See, e.g.*, Mae Kuykendall, *Producing Corporate Text: Courtrooms, Conference Rooms, and Classroom*, 55 N.Y.L. Sch. L. Rev. 593, 609 (2010) (suggesting that Caremark's decision makers paid "psychic costs" for serving as the poster children for law breaking).

61 John Kimelman, *Caremark: Worst Case Looks Fine*, Fin. World, Mar. 28, 1995, at 20.

62 *Moody's Cuts Rating on Caremark's Notes*, Wall St. J., Mar. 25, 1996, at C24.

63 Thomas M. Burton, *Caremark Paid Physicians to Obtain Patients, Governments Documents Say*, Wall St. J., June 19, 1995, at B4.

64 *Caremark*, 698 A.2d at 964.

Second, in *Caremark* too the Chancellor's version is actually favorable to the company when compared with how market and social arbiters previously interpreted the events. Chancellor Allen spends most of his opinion emphasizing how Caremark's problems resulted from rogue, mid-level employees (who were subsequently fired) rather than from systematic breakdowns. He describes in detail how Caremark's directors were proactive in their efforts to stop the problem once they recognized it.[65] Here, too, the Chancellor's narrative comes close to something a company's spokesperson would dictate: acknowledging a problem but isolating and localizing it, thereby assuring stakeholders that the likelihood of future debacles is low.

3.4 IMPLICATIONS

If we agree that reputation matters in the corporate world and that the legal system affects reputation, the next step is reevaluating legal institutions by factoring (inter alia) how they contribute to the production of high-quality information. The need to reevaluate key features of corporate law along these lines is emphasized by the corporate legal scholarship conundrum: most scholars assume that the primary function of corporate litigation is deterrence,[66] yet we have not yet fully developed answers on how to evaluate deterrence.[67] Existing accounts often assume that deterrence can simply be measured through the outcomes of verdicts – through looking at the imposition of legal sanctions.[68] The saints-and-sinners approach adds the angle of measuring deterrence also through the content of verdicts – through looking at indirect deterrence through moralistic comments. My analysis, by contrast, does not limit itself to the outcomes or content of verdicts. I propose to consider also indirect deterrence through information production (reputational sanctions), which occurs throughout the process.

This shift in perspective – adopting the informational/reputational lens – offers unique insights into key procedural and substantial doctrines in Delaware corporate law. This chapter focuses on three issues: the use of good faith

65 *Id.* at 962–63, 971.

66 Darian M. Ibrahim, *Individual or Collective Liability for Corporate Directors?* 93 IOWA L. REV. 929, 952 (2008) (compiling references).

67 James D. Cox & Randall S. Thomas, *Mapping the American Shareholder Litigation Experience: A Survey of Empirical Studies of the Enforcement of the U.S. Securities Law*, 6 EUROPEAN COMPANY & FIN. L. REV. 164, 182 (2009).

68 *See, e.g.*, Urska Velikonja, *The Cost of Securities Fraud*, 54 WM. & MARY L. REV. 1887, 1956 (2013) (arguing that shareholder class actions "fail to deter the wrongdoer managers, as they virtually never pay out of pocket").

doctrine as a pleading mechanism; judicial approval of class and derivative actions; and whether to assess board conduct individually or collectively.

3.4.1 *The Good Faith Doctrine Leads to More Information and Richer Interpretations*

Countless real-time analyses of the *Disney* litigation touted Chancellor Chandler's treatment of the duty of good faith as holding the promise to revolutionize corporate law. From now on, scholars told us, the enforcement of fiduciary duties will be ratcheted up: Delaware courts will not confine themselves to sanctioning just extreme cases of conflicted interests (duty of loyalty) or recklessness (duty of care); they instead will use the flexible duty of good faith to scrutinize a much wider array of misgovernance, including over-deference to the CEO.[69] In retrospect, we know that the duty of good faith did not deliver on its presumed promise: courts still refrain from imposing sanctions on directors.[70] But it would be a mistake to suggest that the good faith notion did not make a difference for enforcement. Sure, good faith may not have altered the legal outcomes of Delaware litigation, but it did shape enforcement indirectly, through allowing for more relevant information production in the process of litigation.

Good faith is best seen not as a substantive doctrine but rather as a pleading mechanism.[71] Following the enactment of section 102(b)(7) of the Delaware General Corporation Law, most Delaware companies put in their charter an exculpatory provision shielding directors from claims of mismanagement. As a result, most lawsuits used to have trouble surviving motions to dismiss. Good faith then emerged as an antidote to the pleading gambit of defendants: when plaintiffs manage to frame their complaint in ways suggesting bad faith, they stand a chance of advancing to discovery.[72] And once a case proceeds to discovery, the horses are out of the barn: a lot of reputation-relevant

69 Jeffrey N. Gordon, *The Rise of Independent Directors in the United States, 1950–2005*, 59 STAN. L. REV. 1465, 1489 n.88 (2007).

70 Claire Hill & Brett McDonnell, *Executive Compensation and the Optimal Penumbra of Delaware Corporate Law*, 4 VA. L. & BUS. REV. 333, 371–72 (2009) (recounting the rise and fall of the good faith doctrine as the great white hope of increased legal enforcement).

71 Hillary A. Sale, *Good Faith's Procedure and Substance: In re Caremark International Inc., Derivative Litigation*, *in* THE ICONIC CASES OF CORPORATE LAW 279 (Jonathan R. Macey ed., 2008).

72 In that respect, the famous *Stone v. Ritter* ruling, which clarified *Disney*, has been a problem in disguise for defendants: Stone clarified that good faith rests under the duty of loyalty, thereby allowing plaintiffs who claim bad faith to sidestep the 102(b)(7) gambit in motions to dismiss. Stone v. Ritter, 911 A.2d 362 (Del. 2006).

information is produced. Through discovery, the legal system manages to tell market players things they do not already know about the company and businesspeople. So even though the threat of legal sanctions stays the same – most Delaware cases still settle, and in the few that do not, defendants win – the threat of reputational sanctions gets a boost from the liberal use of good faith to advance cases beyond the pleading stage.

Beyond facilitating more information production through discovery, the good faith doctrine also facilitates better information production in judicial opinions. Scholars and practitioners have long decried Delaware's reliance on this open-ended standard, arguing that it creates indeterminacy in corporate law.[73] But reliance on open-ended standards also comes with the potential benefit of increasing the richness and relevancy of judges' opinions. When judges rely on flexible doctrines such as good faith, they are relatively free to select the facts and create a version of the events that they deem most relevant.[74] Moreover, an analysis that focuses on good faith notions emphasizes reputation-relevant distinctions, such as whether directors' misconduct was intentional or whether the problems that directors should have monitored are deep-rooted.[75]

3.4.2 *Judicial Monitoring of Settlements in Class/Derivative Actions Is Key*

Another example of procedural mechanisms that affect corporate behavior (without being fully appreciated for doing so) comes from the body of practices and doctrines on how to treat settlements. The overwhelming majority of corporate legal disputes that are not dismissed settle, so the reputational outcomes of litigation depend on what information emerges from settled cases. Three aspects of settlement dictate the quantity and quality of informed production: timing, openness, and judicial reasoning.

The first two aspects are straightforward. Timing matters: *when* the case settles determines the extent of reputational impact. In instances where the complaint was settled after it reached discovery, chances are that quality reputation-relevant information has already emerged (even if the case is settled

73 Marcel Kahan & Ehud Kamar, *Price Discrimination in the Market for Corporate Law*, 86 Cornell L. Rev. 1205, 1233–34 n.120 (2001) (compiling references for the intermediacy debate).

74 Here again Disney serves as a case in point: Chancellor Chandler's reliance on good faith allowed him to convey a fact-intensive, coherent narrative in a way that could not have happened had he couched the legal questions as concerning strictly loyalty or care. Sean J. Griffith, *Good Faith Business Judgment: A Theory of Rhetoric in Corporate Law Jurisprudence*, 55 Duke L.J. 1, 22–23 (2005).

75 *Cf.* Sale, *supra* note 71, at 292.

before trial). Openness matters too: when the parties stipulate confidentiality in their settlement agreements, the prospect of information production takes a hit. Chapter 7 elaborates, but for now suffice to note that litigation produces an informational public good, and so secret settlements are a public bad.[76]

The third factor – judicial involvement – requires some explanation here, as it is especially relevant in corporate law disputes. Because most corporate disputes are filed as class and derivative actions, most settlements are subject to judicial approval. As a result, Delaware judges get an opportunity to voice their opinion – to give their own version of how things happened – even when the parties themselves have settled. *Caremark* is a case in point: Chancellor Allen developed legal doctrines and generated reputation-relevant information (evaluating the quality of internal checks and balances and directors' conduct) even though he was merely approving a settlement in a derivative action. In general, when judges assess whether to approve settlements, they supposedly already incur the costs of gathering information about the dispute. This puts them in a position to provide valuable information to the market.

One policy implication, then, is that we should encourage more detailed reasoning in judicial approvals of settlements.

3.4.3 *Should Director Liability Be Assessed Individually or Collectively?*

Corporate legal scholars deal endlessly with what the standard of review for directors' behavior should be but ignore the question of how to apply the analysis: whether to assess directors' conduct one director at a time, or to look at the whole board collectively.[77] Here again, *Disney* serves as a great case study. Perhaps the most important yet overlooked doctrinal development in *Disney* is the application of a director-by-director analysis, detailing and grading each individual's behavior.[78] The switch from a collective to an individual mode of analysis carries potential legal implications that have been analyzed elsewhere.[79] I want to focus here instead on the reputational implications: how does the mode of analysis affect information production?

At first glance, an individual mode of analysis is good for reputational deterrence since it generates more credible reputation information. A judge who analyzes each director's conduct individually helps market players avoid a "clarity of responsibility" problem. Under a collective mode of analysis,

[76] Steven Shavell, *The Fundamental Divergence between the Private and the Social Motive to Use the Legal System*, 26 J. LEGAL STUD. 575, 605 (1997).

[77] For a notable exception, see Ibrahim, *supra* note 66.

[78] *Id.* at 939–40, 959–69.

[79] *Id.*

individual directors can hide behind the others in an attempt to limit the reputational harm. By contrast, under an individual mode of analysis, market players who read the verdict (or the media's coverage) get credible information on the specific quality and share of the blame for each director.

However, a deeper look reveals contrasting dynamics. An individual mode of analysis actually may be bad for reputational deterrence under certain circumstances. One example that we already touched on (as is evident in *Disney*) is the potential for "scapegoating" dynamics.[80] The individual mode of analysis may deflect attention away from more systematic problems at the company level, giving the media ready-made villains to feed the public. Moreover, directors will anticipate the possibility of being specifically named and compared to other colleagues, and this anticipation may perversely affect the board's day-to-day dynamics *ex ante* – such as in hurting the collegial atmosphere or promoting paper trails and incentives not to know.

The issue of how to assess directors' conduct therefore is much more important than for which we give it credit. I will not develop this complicated issue here, for considerations of brevity and scope, but will take the risk of making some initial conjectures. I conjecture that switching to an individual-based mode of analysis (as in *Disney*) will be good for moral deterrence but bad for reputational deterrence. Director-by-director analysis allows for better social shaming or guilt-inducing since it gives those who dispense sanctions a clearer picture of the blameworthiness of each individual. At the same time, an individual mode of analysis creates a sharp separation between individual-level and organizational-level reputations, thereby diluting the power of reputational forces to control corporate behavior.[81]

3.5 REGULATORY COMPETITION: DELAWARE'S INFORMATION-PRODUCTION AND RINGMASTER ABILITIES

The reputational perspective can also help us shed new light on the endless regulatory competition debate (on whether state corporate law is a race to the top, to the bottom, or not a race at all). This section highlights what makes

80 To be precise, Chancellor Chandler actually applied a hybrid approach in *Disney*: he analyzed the conduct of several directors individually and the rest of the board collectively. Not coincidentally, the directors who were targeted individually were the ones who were already out of the company.

81 *See generally* JONATHAN R. MACEY, THE DEATH OF CORPORATE REPUTATION (2013) (arguing that reputational forces lose their power when individual reputations are separated from corporate reputations).

Delaware different than other states with established business courts. Section 3.5.1 details how Delaware's decisional law provides private litigants with much more fact-finding powers than rival states. Section 3.5.2 explains why the fact that Delaware judges frequently offer scathing commentary can actually be good for corporate America, as it coopts popular backlash and federal intervention.

3.5.1 *Delaware's Information-Production Advantages*

A few paragraphs above we noted that Delaware courts use the good faith doctrine to flush out disputes in courts and provide more granular information. There is a broader point here, which goes beyond a specific doctrine. Delaware courts have traditionally employed a tapestry of doctrines that lead to production of valuable information for the market. Its decisional law is geared toward information production, much more so than the laws of rival states with established business courts. Consider the following three examples: deference to special litigation committees (SLCs), availability of written opinions, and inspection rights.

It starts with pleading standards: Delaware uses a lax standard of review when determining whether to impose legal sanctions but a more stringent standard of review in the pleading stage. While Delaware courts usually defer to the business judgment of directors, they gladly interfere when directors use their judgment to stifle litigation.[82] In other words, Delaware courts let big cases proceed to discovery and trial even when the odds that these complaints will ultimately win are slim. To illustrate, consider Delaware's treatment of SLCs, with doctrines such as *Zapata*[83] (enhanced standard of review to SLC conduct) and *Kaplan*[84] (allowing plaintiffs to seek discovery when challenging an SLC decision). Other states, such as New York, are much more deferential to SLCs.[85]

Nowhere is the differences in information production more evident than when comparing Delaware to its most recent challenger – Nevada.[86] Delaware's corporate law is much more permissive regarding the right to

82 Kuykendall, *supra* note 60.

83 Zapata Corp. v. Maldanado, 430 A.2d 799 (Del. 1981).

84 Kaplan v. Wyatt, 499 A.2d 1184 (Del. 1988).

85 William T. Allen et l., Commentaries and Cases on the Law of Business Organization 392 (4th ed. 2012).

86 Marcel Kahan & Ehud Kamar, *The Myth of State Competition in Corporate Law*, 55 Stan. L. Rev. 679, 716 (2002) ("Nevada is the poster child for those believing that states compete for incorporations. It is the only state other than Delaware that openly endeavors to attract incorporations, and one of few that attract a substantial number of companies headquartered in").

inspect the company's books relative to Nevada.[87] And while Delaware's judicial opinions serve important roles in providing the media with fact-based narratives and quotable censure, Nevada's business court *does not publish opinions.*[88] Delaware's judicial opinions, by contrast, are published in both the state and regional reporters, and are readily available on commercial databases.[89]

The right to inspect the company's books is perhaps the timeliest example of Delaware's liberal approach to information production. A key development in Delaware's law came in the string of rulings of *Corwin*,[90] *Trulia*,[91] and *C&J Energy Services*,[92] which threatened to severely curtail plaintiffs' ability and incentives to reach discovery and produce valuable information on corporate behavior.[93] *Corwin*, in particular, maintains that the deferential business judgment standard of review applies where a "transaction not subject to the entire fairness standard of review is approved by a fully informed, uncoerced majority of the disinterested stockholders."[94] Yet Delaware courts have quickly reversed the trend and restored balance, by granting liberal inspection rights.

Plaintiffs' lawyers reacted to *Corwin* by concentrating efforts on making section 220 demands (i.e., requests to inspect the defendant company's books and records).[95] Delaware's 2017 *Lavin* ruling facilitated this alternative channel of information production, by stating that a *Corwin* defense (i.e., an informed shareholder vote) does not absolve the company from having to produce documents in section 220 demands.[96] Then, the 2019 *KT4*

87 *Compare* Nevada's NRS 78.257 *with* Delaware's section 220.

88 Joshua Halen, *Transforming Nevadainto the Judicial Delaware of the West: How to Fix Nevada's Business Courts*, 16(1) J. Bus. & Sec. L. 139, 165 (2016).

89 *Id.*, at 150 (noting that availability of published opinions is "the feature that most sets the Delaware Court of Chancery apart from other courts").

90 Corwin v. KKR Fin. Holdings LLC, 125 A.3d 304, 306 (Del. 2015).

91 In re Trulia Inc., 129 A.3d at 891–97.

92 107 A.3d 1049 (Del. 2014).

93 Following *Corwin*, plaintiffs (1) have less chances of surviving the motion to dismiss and reaching discovery; and (2) *do not want* to ask for expedited discovery, because even if they find a smoking gun, the defendant companies can simply publish supplemental disclosure, leaving plaintiffs' lawyers with nothing. *See* Joel Friedlander, Friedlander & Gorris, P.A., *Confronting the Problem of Fraud on the Board*, Harv. L. Sch. F. on Corporate Governance & Fin. Reg. (Jan. 3, 2019), https://corpgov.law.harvard.edu/2019/01/03/confronting-the-problem-of-fraud-on-the-board. While *Corwin* limits plaintiffs' chances of reaching discovery post-closing, *Trulia* and *C&J Energy* limit plaintiffs' chances of reaching discovery pre-closing. Roy Shapira, *Corporate Law, Retooled: How Books and Records Revamped Judicial Oversight*, 42 Cardozo L. Rev. (forthcoming, 2020).

94 *Supra* note 90, at 306.

95 Chapter 8 elaborates on the important role that section 220 requests play – as a pre-discovery tool to extract quality information – in facilitating reputational deterrence.

96 Lavin v. West Corp., No. 2017–0547, 2017 WL 6728702, at *7 (Del. Ch. Dec. 9, 2017).

Partners LLC v. Palantir Technologies, Inc.[97] ruling further boosted the chances of information production, by broadening the scope of inside information that should be provided under section 220 demands. The court clarified that companies may have to produce internal emails and other forms of electronic communication, which plaintiffs can then use not only to defeat a *Corwin* defense (showing that the vote was coerced or uninformed) but also to establish breach of fiduciary duty claims. Shortly thereafter we have witnessed several vivid examples for plaintiffs successfully obtaining relevant, damning information through the section 220 channel.[98]

From this Book's vantage point, Delaware's doctrinal developments seem to have struck the right balance between deference to business judgements and ability to extract information on problematic behavior.[99]

3.5.2 *Make It Look Like a Struggle: the Difference between Perceived and Real Enforcement*

Shifting our focus from legal outcomes (direct deterrence) to nonlegal outcomes (indirect deterrence) necessitates a reevaluation of the endless debate on how the content of corporate law is determined – on whether state corporate law is a race to the top, to the bottom, or not a race at all.

Those who subscribe to a saints-and-sinners approach usually advocate against a race-to-the-bottom view. The main argument of the saints-and-sinners approach, after all, has a normative flavor: it calls for a shift of focus from how seldom legal sanctions are imposed to how many nonlegal sanctions are inflicted (through judicial sermons).[100] Such a description of Delaware law is hard to reconcile with a race to the bottom: why should a race-to-the-bottom judge dress down and inflict nonlegal pain on incumbent managers?[101]

97 No. 281, 2019 WL 347934 (Del. Jan. 29, 2019).

98 *See, e.g.*, *KT4 Partners LLC*, 2019 WL 347934, at *1; Morrison v. Berry, 191 A.3d 268, 273 (Del. 2018); *In re* Tesla Motors Stockholder Litig., No. 12711-VCS, 2018 WL 1560293, at *1–10 (Del. Ch. Mar. 28, 2018).

99 To be sure, not all the developments in Delaware law lead to more information production. In 2013, for instance, Delaware attempted to establish a closed-door arbitration program. Yet the Third Circuit brought the program to a halt, and as of this writing, Delaware has not replaced it with another, leaving its information-production edge intact. Del. Coal. for Open Gov't, Inc. v. Strine, 733 F.3d 510, 512 (3d Cir. 2013), *cert. denied*, 134 S. Ct. 1551 (2014).

100 Fairfax, *supra* note 8, at 445 ("[Saints and sinners] scholars argue that legal opinions obviate the need for legal sanctions because communities rely on the norms articulated by such opinions to regulate director conduct").

101 To use *Disney* as illustration: a state that is racing to the bottom and is captured by corporate America could have thrown away the complaint at the motion to dismiss stage; or at least

The infliction of nonlegal pain is seen in this version as proof that judges do not cater to managers.

I want to offer here an alternative perspective. While I agree that Delaware decisional law generates nonlegal sanctions, I think that the saints-and-sinners proponents miss a crucial distinction between *perceived* sanctions and real sanctions. When legal enforcement is done indirectly (through scolding), it becomes far less transparent than when it is done directly (through legal sanctions). The public can easily assess how much a $100 million fine hurts a company. But the public has a hard time assessing how much verbal scolding actually hurts a company or individual.

The reliance on judicial scolding therefore creates *a wedge between perceived and real enforcement*. This wedge, in turn, allows Delaware to be perceived (by the public and Washington) as tougher on corporate America than it actually is.

My argument starts from a general assertion: under certain plausible conditions, it makes sense for a captured regulator to scold his capturers (regulated entities) in public. If Delaware judges do indeed cater to corporate America, then it is in the interests of both sides to be perceived as fighting each other. The emphasis here is on perceived as. If Delaware really fights and hurts corporate America, it risks losing incorporation fees. If, on the other hand, Delaware is perceived by the public as not fighting corporate America at all, it risks a political backlash and eventually getting overruled by Washington.[102]

To be perceived as enforcing without really enforcing, the enforcer has to adopt *low-visibility favoritism*: to treat managers favorably but not openly favorably. In other words, both the regulator and the regulated industry want to "make it look like a struggle."

We all know what "make it look like a struggle" means, even if we are unfamiliar with the exact term. We have seen it played out in countless films or novels.[103] The story is simple: our hero is captured by some bad guys. The guy who guards our hero, however, wants to let him escape. The problem is that the guard does not want the other bad guys to think of him as a traitor (in our terminology, as catering to the hero). As a result, the hero and the guard

refrain from humiliating directors with caustic judicial commentary. Macey, *supra* note 13, at 1134.

102 Mark J. Roe, *Delaware's Competition*, 117 HARV. L. REV. 588 (2003) (arguing that any state that wins the regulatory competition is subject to the risk of being overruled by Washington).

103 See multiple examples of the make-it-look-like-a-struggle trope in the online wiki page for tropes: TV Tropes Found., LLC, Make It Look Like a Struggle, TV TROPES, http://tvtropes.org/pmwiki/pmwiki.php/Main/MakeItLookLikeAStruggle (last visited Jul. 27, 2019).

come to an agreement: "give me a black eye to make it look like a struggle"/"knock me out with a blow to the head"/"trash the room to make it look like a burglary." You get the idea. And you probably also get the analogy: Delaware – or any other state trying to remain on top of a regulatory race – needs to find a method for being perceived by the public and Washington as delivering vicious blows to corporate America while not really hurting companies. And judicial scolding makes for an effective low-visibility favoritism method, for several reasons.

First and foremost, scolding is salient to the public. As the *Disney* case study illustrates, mass media highlights caustic comments much more than it highlights the nuances of judicial decisions and legal doctrines. Scolding grabs headlines. The result is a public perception of Delaware judges being fed up with corporate America and going after the bad corporate villains. Such a public perception reduces the chances of political backlash, keeping Washington at bay and maintaining Delaware's powers. However, what bystanders view as an all-out attack on corporate America actually is not that hurtful to those who are being attacked. Recall our discussion of typical scenarios where scolding is directed at already ousted individuals, or targets less reprehensible sins.

Second, scathing commentary makes a good make-it-look-like-a-struggle tool because its damage is easily reversible. Scolding is a more flexible enforcement tool than are legal sanctions because it has no precedential value. When judges respond to a wave of corporate scandals by imposing more liability, they somewhat constrain their future behavior by creating precedents. By contrast, when judges ratchet up (perceived) enforcement via caustic comments, they can easily reverse the enforcement intensity once the economy is better and public attention drifts away from corporate governance.[104]

The point about reversibility also illustrates, more generally, why enforcement through scolding may be good for Delaware companies *as a group*. A given company or director that suffers uninsurable reputational damage probably hates judicial scolding (ex post). But *ex ante*, Delaware companies and businesspeople as a group are better off with scolding than with legal liability because scolding allows the enforcer not to commit to harsh responses down the road. It makes favoritism more sustainable. In that sense, Delaware operates like a ringmaster for corporate America.

As with any other theory about Delaware's motivations, it is hard to offer conclusive proof that Delaware judges intentionally pursue a make-it-look-like-a-struggle strategy. What I can offer in support of my hypothesis (aside from logic) is circumstantial evidence, such as the explanations that

[104] *Cf.* Griffith, *supra* note 74; Jones, *supra* note 13, at 500.

Delaware judges themselves give. For example, when Chancellor Chandler was asked whether his Disney decision proves that Delaware courts are too favorable to corporate defendants, he responded: "how come, then, I get attacked on all sides? ... maybe that's the best measure that I'm doing right."[105] To me, such an answer indicates that even if Chandler does not intentionally try to make it look like a struggle, he is aware of the dynamics. Delaware judges understand that the best way to protect their unique reputation with the public and Washington is to give corporate America something to attack them for, and vice versa.[106]

To clarify, I do not claim that make-it-look-like-a-struggle dynamics are necessarily bad for overall welfare. When the risk of market or regulatory overreaction looms large, a make-it-look-like-a-struggle strategy actually can increase overall welfare by mitigating the perverse consequences of populism.[107] My goal is rather to present a tool that the Delaware judiciary (or other regulators) can use to fend off threats to their reputations. I cannot predict with certainty whether judges employ this tool cynically or public-spiritedly.[108] But we nevertheless can glean important insights from shifting our focus to the perception and visibility of enforcement methods. Most basically, we learn that recognizing a pattern of judicial scolding is not the same as proving a race-to-the-top theory. Judicial scolding may sometimes go hand in hand with a race-to-the-bottom theory (or a Delaware-Washington competition theory): by reducing the visibility of favoritism, scolding may help incumbent managers extract more rents.

105 Roy Harris, *Delaware Rules*, CFO MAGAZINE, Aug. 1, 2006.

106 Consciousness is not needed for make-it-look-like-a-struggle dynamics to be in play. Judges or regulators do not have to be fully aware of or able to verbalize the dynamics. They only have to act as if they recognize the dynamics. The strategy of appearing to be tougher than you truly are can survive as a crude decision rule, based on past experiences of the judges.

107 Another positive effect of the make-it-look-like-a-struggle strategy is in limiting "reputational spillover effects." The revelation of bad news about one company may cause stakeholders to lose trust in the whole industry or market. These cascading dynamics, caused by biases such as availability heuristics, are bad for the economy as a whole. And to the extent that Delaware manages to convey a message of keeping corporate America in check, it can restore some of the trust and avoid unnecessary punishing of good companies. We come back to this point in the Conclusion.

108 To emphasize: I do not claim that Delaware judges act with Machiavellian intentions to slow down Washington (or reputational markets) by making it look like a struggle. It is certainly possible that Delaware judges employ scolding because they believe that the alternative – intervening and imposing legal sanctions – is too costly.

4

Public Enforcement

The SEC's Settlement Practices

4.1 INTRODUCTION

Public enforcement affects reputations too. The Securities and Exchange Commission (SEC) enforcement actions, in particular, play a key role in shaping the behavior of publicly traded companies. Much like with private litigation, SEC enforcement shapes behavior not just through imposing fines but also through producing information. This chapter examines how effective SEC enforcement practices are in generating valuable information and facilitating reputational sanctioning. Switching our focus from Delaware litigation to SEC investigations enriches our understanding of the law-and-reputation theory and illustrates its broad applicability. Most notably, we learn how regulatory enforcement actions generate different reputational dynamics than private litigation.

Our starting point is the heated national debate that ensued at the wake of the 2008 financial crisis, over the SEC settlement practices. That debate focused on whether the SEC settles for large enough awards (it does). This chapter shifts focus and examines whether SEC settlements produce enough valuable information to facilitate market deterrence (they do not).

Section 4.2 lays the background by describing the common practice of neither-admit-nor-deny settlements. Section 4.3 details the ways in which such SEC settlements underproduce information. Section 4.4 explains *why* the SEC has traditionally opted to underproduce information. Section 4.5 examines whether recent changes to SEC enforcement practices can solve the information-underproduction problem, and finds them wanting. Section 4.6 sketches alternative solutions to information underproduction, such as reevaluating the proper scope of judicial review of SEC actions. Section 4.7 concludes with big-picture observations on the information-production qualities of SEC enforcement actions relative to those of private securities litigation.

4.2 NEITHER-ADMIT-NOR-DENY SETTLEMENTS: THE EXISTING DEBATE

SEC enforcement actions historically followed a distinct pattern: the SEC learns about an alleged misconduct, investigates the matter, and then brings actions (files a complaint) only to simultaneously announce a pre-negotiated settlement with the defendants.[1] The typical settlement contains a three-pronged obligation by the defendant company: paying a fine,[2] agreeing to an injunction barring similar misconduct in the future, and agreeing not to deny the allegations. In return, the SEC terminates the action and allows the company not to admit the allegations. The agreement is then brought before a federal judge who signs it and turns it into a consent judgment (also known as a "consent decree").[3]

This long-standing practice of neither-admit-nor-deny settlements went unchecked for many years, until Judge Rakoff of the Southern District of New York started raising questions vocally. In a sequence of three notable opinions – *Bank of America*,[4] *Vitesse*,[5] and *Citigroup*[6] – Judge Rakoff decried the practice in general and refused to sign specific consent pacts. Other judges quickly followed suit, sparking a trend of increased scrutiny of SEC settlements.[7] In no time, SEC settlement practices had become the center of national attention.[8] A heated debate ensued over the effectiveness of SEC enforcement and the proper scope of judicial review.

Those who argued against current SEC settlement practices (and consequently were in favor of enhanced judicial scrutiny) claimed that the SEC plays favorites with big-firm defendants, allowing them to get off with small fines and not admitting wrongdoing. The SEC and opponents of enhanced judicial scrutiny countered with two types of

1 Stavros Gadinis, *The SEC and the Financial Industry: Evidence from Enforcement against Broker-Dealers*, 67 BUS. LAWYER 679, 698 (2012); Ross MacDonald, *Setting Examples, Not Settling*, 91 TEX. L. REV. 419, 421 n.16 (2012).

2 "Fines" denote here any monetary remedy, including disgorgement orders.

3 Consent decrees/judgments are basically judicially enforced settlements. *See generally* Judith Resnik, *Judging Consent*, 1987 U. CHI. LEGAL. F. 43, 45.

4 SEC v. Bank of Am. Corp., 653 F. Supp. 2d 507 (S.D.N.Y. 2009).

5 SEC v. Vitesse Semiconductor Corp., 771 F. Supp. 2d 304 (S.D.N.Y. 2011).

6 SEC v. Citigroup Global Markets Inc., 827 F. Supp. 2d 328 (S.D.N.Y. 2011), *vacated and remanded*, 752 F.3d 285 (2d Cir. 2014).

7 *See, e.g.*, *Rakoff's Revenge*, THE ECONOMIST, Apr. 13, 2013.

8 Samantha Dreilinger, *Is There a Crowd? The Role of the Courts in SEC Settlements* 5 (Oct. 2010) (unpublished manuscript), *available at* http://works.bepress.com/samantha_dreilinger/1, at 2–3 (providing examples of intensive media coverage); *Examining the Settlement Practices of U.S. Financial Regulators: Hearing before the Comm. on Fin. Services*, 112th Cong. 2 (2012).

arguments.[9] First, they claimed, there is nothing wrong with the amount of awards collected in settlements. When evaluating whether the collected amount makes sense, one needs to consider the alternative to settling: wasting limited resources on a costly litigation while risking not proving violations and collecting nothing. Second, the SEC claimed, SEC settlements contribute to sanctioning and deterrence not just through imposing fines but also through producing information. The SEC announces settlements with a press release that details the allegations, thus putting market players on notice about how the defendants behaved. And since defendants are barred from denying the allegations,[10] the SEC's version goes uncontested and is considered reliable.

Given the theme of this book, we will focus on the second type of arguments – evaluating whether SEC settlements do indeed inform market participants about wrongdoing. I leave aside the first type of arguments not only because of scope but also because I think that there is no real reason to question the SEC's official line.[11] The SEC has incentives to maximize the amounts it collects even without judicial scrutiny, because this is how the SEC's monitors – in the press, Congress, or academia – measure its success.[12] Take the *Citigroup* case as an example. The absolute maximum that the SEC could have collected had it fought and won a trial is $320 million;[13] the amount that the SEC got in settlement was $285 million. The SEC did not leave money on the table with *Citigroup*. It rarely does.[14] Moreover, federal judges are not well positioned to decide questions such as whether to settle and for how much: such decisions require not only factoring the particulars of the case at hand but also prioritizing the budgetary constraints and caseload pressures of the agency.[15] On the other hand, we have plenty of reasons to

9 Brief for Appellant at 14–15, 19, 24, SEC v. Citigroup Global Mkts., Inc., 673 F.3d 158 (2d Cir. 2012) (No. 11–5227) [hereinafter SEC's Brief]; Robert Khuzami, *Remarks before the Consumer Federation of America's Financial Services Conference*, U.S. Securities and Exchange Commission (Dec. 1, 2011), *available at* www.sec.gov/news/speech/2011/spch120111rk.htm.

10 17 C.F.R. § 205.5 (2014).

11 Another good reason to focus on the indirect outcomes of SEC settlements is that most commentators have focused solely on direct outcomes – the severity of fines obtained. David M. Becker, *What More Can Be Done to Deter Violations of the Federal Securities Laws?*, 90 Tex. L. Rev. 1849, 1867 (2012).

12 Jonathan R. Macey, The Death of Corporate Reputation 13 (2013).

13 SEC's Brief, *supra* note 9, at 50–51.

14 MacDonald, *supra* note 1, at 427; Danné L. Johnson, *SEC Settlement: Agency Self-Interest of Public Interest*, 12 Fordham J. Corp. & Fin. L. 627, 661, 672 (2007).

15 SEC's Brief, *supra* note 9, at 43; Sanford Weisburst, *Judicial Review of Settlements and Consent Decrees: An Economic Analysis*, 28 J. Legal Stud. 55, 67, 98 (1999).

question the SEC's claim that its settlements provide useful information. They do not. The rest of this chapter explains why.

4.3 IDENTIFYING THE PROBLEM: HOW SEC SETTLEMENTS UNDERPRODUCE INFORMATION

The SEC's argument about the informative value of settlements misses an important distinction between the quantity and quality of information. More information does not necessarily translate into a better information environment. The SEC is right to suggest that its settlements produce more information than private settlements – as is manifested in summarizing the allegations in press releases and making detailed complaints available. But *the information that the SEC typically releases is not reputation-relevant*. It does not help market players distinguish between good and bad actors. In order for SEC settlements to impact market players' beliefs and facilitate better reputational sanctioning, they have to provide new facts or credible interpretations. The typical SEC settlement fails to do that,[16] for several reasons.

First, putting the public on notice is helpful only if the public has not already noticed the wrongdoing. One influential study that examined how news on corporate fraud breaks, found that SEC actions break the news in only 7 percent of the cases.[17] In general, when the wrongdoing is done on a large scale and by visible companies, the media usually covers it long before the SEC releases information.[18] In the *Bank of America* settlement announcement, for example, every piece of information was stale.[19] The informative value of putting the public on notice thus depends on the baseline. To generalize: the notice has an informative value in actions against small broker-dealers, where but for the SEC announcement the violation would not have been noticed. Conversely, notice by itself has little informative value in settlements of the *Bank of America* and *Citigroup* kind, where the public had already noticed that something wrong had happened, and the role of the SEC was to focus on explaining *how* exactly things went wrong: what

16 Samuel Buell, *Potentially Perverse Effects of Corporate Civil Liability*, *in* Prosecutors in the Boardroom: Using Criminal Law to Regulate Corporate Conduct 87, 99 (Barkow & Barkow eds., 2011).

17 Alexander Dyck et al., *Who Blows the Whistle on Corporate Fraud*, 65 J. Fin. 2213 (2010).

18 Jonathan M. Karpoff et al., *Proxies and Databases in Financial Misconduct Research*, 92 Acc. Rev. 129 (2017).

19 *Compare* Press Release, SEC, SEC Charges Bank of America for Failing to Disclose Merrill Lynch Bonus Payments (Aug. 3, 2009), *available at* www.sec.gov/news/press/2009/2009–177.htm, *with* Susan Beck & Andrew Longstreth, *All Sides of the Fence*, 31 Am. Lawyer 13 (Apr. 2009) (summarizing the media coverage four months prior to the SEC's release).

specific control weaknesses led to the wrongdoing? Was it really just a low-level rogue employee or a more pervasive problem?

Second, the reputational impact of settlement announcements is further diluted by the SEC's tendency to target whole industries.[20] Announcing that company X allegedly engaged in wrongdoing does not really help market players if all company X's competitors face similar allegations. Stakeholders cannot take their business elsewhere – cannot dispense reputational sanctions – unless the SEC provides details that distinguish between one alleged wrongdoing and another: which are attributed to technical errors and which reflect more deep-seated issues.[21]

Third, *the SEC often lets defendants shape the content and timing of announcements.* Most of the settlements are pre-negotiated,[22] and the SEC lets big-firm defendants minimize the reputational impact in two ways. The simultaneous announcement of complaint and settlement limits the negative publicity exposure to only one event. And it allows defendants to put a "nothing to see here" spin on what could have been damning indications about their behavior. The bad news of allegations is comingled with the good news of "case closed."

Aside from timing, the pre-negotiation also allows defendants to shape the public perception of the SEC's allegations by affecting the *language* of SEC announcements. As part of the negotiations, defendants get to revise the regulator's drafts.[23] It is not just that defendants are not required to admit wrongdoing; they also get to dictate how the SEC's version of what happened will be presented. The *Citigroup* case illustrates how the SEC's public version is watered down compared to the SEC's internal version. In *Citigroup*, the same misconduct (material statement) led to two complaints: one against the company, and one against an employee (Brian Stoker). Yet for some reason the language used to describe the misconduct was different. The complaint against the company emphasizes that no bad intentions were involved, while the Stoker complaint does indicate intentionality.[24] The complaint against

20 Macey, *supra* note 12, at 225, 236.

21 *Id.* at 23–24. Jesse Eisinger, *Needed: A Cure for a Severe Case of Trialphobia*, ProPublica, Dec. 14, 2011, www.propublica.org/thetrade/item/needed-a-cure-for-a-severe-case-of-trialphobia ("[The announcement] renders the settlement little more than turning on the light in a kitchen full of roaches. . . . [T]he settlements merely show how the bad actors are scattered everywhere"); Johnson, *supra* note 14, at 674.

22 Johnson, *id*, at 665; Dreilinger, *supra* note 8, at 12–13.

23 Jason E. Siegel, *Admit It! Corporate Admissions of Wrongdoing in SEC Settlements: Evaluating Collateral Estoppel Effects*, 103 Geo. L. J. 433, 454 (2015).

24 Brief of Amicus Curiae former SEC General Counsel and Chairman Harvey Pitt in Support of Affirmance of District Court's Ruling at 26, SEC v. Citigroup Global Mkts., Inc., 673 F.3d 158 (2d Cir. 2012) (No. 11–5227) [hereinafter Harvey Pitt Brief].

Stoker mentions the gross revenues collected by Citigroup in the toxic transaction, while the complaint against Citigroup uses only the less damning net-profits figure. Both aspects – the degree of intentionality involved and harm done – are important determinants of reputational sanctions. The framing of the *Citigroup* complaint therefore limited the reputational damages to the company.

Finally, the SEC argues that settlement announcements are informative even without containing admissions, simply because defendants are barred from denying the allegations. But *in reality the "no denial" requirement is not (and perhaps cannot be) enforced.* The information contained in the SEC allegations is open to interpretation and disagreement, if only because companies find ways to implicitly contest the allegations.[25] Indeed, SEC Commissioner Luis Aguilar himself decried the common practice of "the press release issued by a defendant after a settlement explaining how the conduct was really not that bad or that the regulator overreacted."[26] Other current and former securities regulators agree that there is no such thing as a "no-spin zone": defendants find various ways to bypass the requirement.[27]

The upshot is that SEC settlements with big companies underproduce relevant information. The next question is why. SEC investigations generate internally high-quality information on how things went wrong; so why does the SEC not publicly convey information in a comprehensible and thorough way? Why does the SEC leave information on the table in settlements? The following Section locates the roots of the information-underproduction problem in the reputational incentives of both parties to SEC settlements.

4.4 EXPLAINING THE PROBLEM: WHY THE SEC TRADES INFORMATION FOR FINES

Large publicly traded companies have incentives to pay slightly higher settlement awards as long as they can prevent unfavorable information about them from

[25] SEC v. Vitesse Semiconductor Corp., 771 F. Supp. 2d 304, 308 (S.D.N.Y. 2011).

[26] Luis Aguilar, *Speech Before International Trade Center, Setting Forth Aspirations for 2011* (Feb. 4, 2011), *available at* www.sec.gov/news/speech/2011/spch020411laa.htm.

[27] *Examining the Settlement Practices of U.S. Financial Regulators: Hearing Before the Comm. on Fin. Services.* 112th Cong. 45 (2012); Bruce Carton. *Settling SEC Defendants Never "Admit" Wrongdoing But They Sometimes Later "Deny" It*, Compliance Week (Dec. 7, 2011), *available at* www.complianceweek.com/settling-sec-defendants-never-admit-wrongdoing-but-they-sometimes-later-deny-it/article/218356; *Still More on Defendants' Post SEC-Settlement Statements*, Compliance Week (Feb. 15, 2011) (providing specific examples by former SEC staffer Bruce Carton in a series of blog posts), *available at* www.complianceweek.com/still-more-on-defendants-post-sec-settlement-statements/article/196413. *But see* Johnson, *supra* note 14, at n.119.

reaching the market. This is because negative information may generate reputational ramifications,[28] which are more risky for large companies than legal sanctions. Chapter 1 showed us that the typical reputational sanction attached to revealed misconduct dwarfs the equivalent legal sanction. Moreover, many types of legal sanctions are paid by insurance companies, while reputational damages are less easily insurable. Large companies therefore typically fear an uptick in reputational sanctions more than they fear an uptick in legal sanctions.

As for the SEC's incentives, here the story gets more complicated. One could argue that the SEC decision makers' incentives are aligned with the public interest, and so whenever the SEC blocks information from getting to the market it is only because the benefits from settling early and for larger amounts outweigh the informational benefits. From that perspective information underproduction is not really a problem but rather a welfare-enhancing tradeoff. But such an argument misses how the incentives of agents work in a multitasking environment. When agents make tradeoffs between multiple tasks they tend to overemphasize the tasks that are being closely monitored by principals.[29] The SEC's constituencies – the general public and congressional overseers – evaluate the SEC mostly according to readily observable yardsticks such as the amount of fines collected or the number of cases brought.[30] The public and Congress have difficulties in observing and attributing the indirect benefits from information production to the SEC. The logic of incentives therefore suggests that the SEC will prioritize the number of cases brought and the amount of fines collected. Indeed, the SEC's own communications reflect such emphasis;[31] and former SEC staffers acknowledged that the SEC tilts the fines–information tradeoff against providing information and to the detriment of the public interest.[32]

28 Brief of Defendant-Appellee-Cross-Appellant at 6–7, SEC v. Citigroup Global Mkts., Inc. 673 F.3d 158 (2d Cir. 2012) (No. 11–5227); Becker, *supra* note 11, at 1860–61.

29 *See generally* Bengt Holmstrom & Paul Milgrom, *Multitask Principal–Agent Analyses: Incentive Contracts, Asset Ownership, and Job Design*, 7 J.L. Econ. & Org. 24 (1991). For applications to regulators' behavior, see Moshe Maor & Raanan Sulitzeanu-Kenan, *The Effect of Salient Reputational Threats on the Pace of FDA Enforcement*, 26 Governance 31, 32, 37 (2013).

30 Urska Velikonja, *Reporting Agency Performance: Behind the SEC's Enforcement Statistics*, 101 Cornell L. Rev. 901, 903, 908 (2016) (noting that the media follows closely these yardsticks).

31 See, for example, the SEC Director of Enforcement's public reaction to Judge Rakoff's decision in *Citigroup*. Jonathan Macey, *The SEC's Publicity Hounds*, Defining Ideas, July 7, 2011, *available at* www.hoover.org/publications/defining-ideas/article/84831.

32 Becker, *supra* note 11, at 1871; Brief of Amici Curiae Securities Law Scholars at 15 n.15, SEC v. Citigroup Global Mkts., Inc., 673 F.3d 158 (2d Cir. 2012) (No. 11–5227). For a thorough empirical examination, see Velikonja, *supra* note 30. Another reason for the SEC's reluctance to reveal information in settlements or to litigate stems from the tension between the SEC's two roles: preventing scandals *ex ante* and adjudicating scandals *ex post*. If the full picture of

The upshot is that even well-meaning SEC officials face reputational pressures to favor fines over information. Before we discuss how to mitigate these tendencies, let us first evaluate two recent changes that the SEC has implemented after its public battle with Judge Rakoff. The SEC has reportedly switched to requiring more admissions in settlements, and filing most of its settlements administratively instead of before federal courts. Could these changes improve information production? The next section examines.

4.5 RECENT CHANGES IN SEC PRACTICES DID NOT ALLEVIATE THE PROBLEM

4.5.1 *More Admissions*

On paper, the SEC already seems to be trending in the right direction. Under the leadership of Chairman Mary Jo White the SEC changed its settlement policy to require more admissions from certain defendants.[33] Immediately after, in September 2013, the SEC announced twenty-three neither-admit-nor-deny settlements with firms accused of short selling;[34] and two days later a settlement where JPMorgan not only paid $200 million but also admitted wrongdoing.[35] In real time, I opined that these two announcements suggest that the SEC has its priorities straight going forward, based on the type of violations and the companies involved. The alleged violation in short-selling cases does not require intent, and the firms involved are not household names. By contrast, when a giant like JPMorgan is charged with misstating financial results and lacking internal controls, it becomes essential that the public gets credible detailed information on how things went wrong.

However, in the years that have passed since, scholars who systematically examined the new admission policy found it wanting.[36] The SEC touts its new

the scope and pervasiveness of the financial sector's problems gets revealed, the SEC's reputation as protector of markets may suffer greatly.

33 James B. Stewart, *S.E.C. Has a Message for Firms Not Used to Admitting Guilt*, N.Y. TIMES (Jun. 21, 2013).

34 Press Release, SEC, *SEC Charges 23 Firms with Short Selling Violations in Crackdown on Potential Manipulation in Advance of Stock Offerings* (Sept. 17, 2013), *available at* www.sec.gov/News/PressRelease/Detail/PressRelease/1370539804376#.Uu-8ntGA3IU.

35 Press Release, SEC, JPMorgan Chase Agrees to Pay $200 Million and Admits Wrongdoing to Settle SEC Charges (Sept. 19, 2013), *available at* www.sec.gov/News/PressRelease/Detail/PressRelease/1370539819965.

36 Verity Winship & Jennifer K. Robbennolt, *An Empirical Study of Admissions in SEC Settlements*, 60 ARIZONA L. REV. 1 (2018); David Rosenfeld, *Admissions in SEC Enforcement Cases: The Revolution That Wasn't*, 103 IOWA L. REV. 113, 116 (2017).

policy as a great success, claiming that the increased number of admissions translates into greater corporate accountability. But the recent empirical studies adopt a more skeptical view. They agree that there has been an uptick in admissions, but question whether it translates into an uptick in accountability. These studies go over the underlying settlements, and suggest that the admissions are largely nominal, and the admitters are mostly small fish. Importantly for our information-production perspective, the studies document how most admissions do not pertain to the state of mind or internal checks and balances of the offenders. In other words, the offenders admit to the "what happened" question (on which the market usually already has a good grasp), but do not admit to the "how it happened" question (on which the market could have used the help from SEC investigations).

In fact, there may be reason to suspect that the SEC's need to score admissions results in a *worse* information environment. When the SEC negotiates with the misbehaving companies behind closed doors, admissions "confer a significant bargaining chip that companies can trade away in exchange for fewer incriminating disclosures."[37]

4.5.2 *Filing Administratively*

An even more dramatic change in SEC practices came in the form of shifting to file settlements in administrative proceedings, rather than in federal courts.[38] Filings administratively comes with several benefits. But from our perspective here – information production – it makes things worse. An administrative filing means that SEC's negotiations with defendants are approved internally, by a committee of SEC commissioners, without outside review.[39] The lack of third-party review means it is less likely that information will become publicly accessible (aside from the pre-negotiated SEC press release). Further, filing administratively allows the SEC to regularly open and close an enforcement action on the same day, which, we already saw, dilutes the reputational impact of what the SEC internally found out about the misbehavior.

Generally, it is not surprising that changes to SEC practices tend not to lead to better information production. The root problem is the one we discussed earlier: the SEC is not measured according to how it facilitates reputational

[37] Siegel, *supra* note 23, at 454.

[38] Urska Velikonja, *Securities Settlements in the Shadows*, YALE L. J. FORUM, 124, 133 (Sep. 7, 2016).

[39] *Id.*, at 125–26.

deterrence, but rather according to observable yardsticks, such as concrete enforcement numbers. The first step toward fixing the information-underproduction problem is therefore raising awareness to it among the SEC overseers and its own staff. The next section sketches concrete implications for judicial review and regulatory agenda-setting.

4.6 SOLVING THE PROBLEM

4.6.1 *Changes to Judicial Scrutiny*

Armed with a fresh perspective on SEC settlements, we can revisit the evergreen question of the proper scope of judicial review. As a starting point, we should switch from arguing "for or against" SEC settlements to concentrating on what type of SEC settlements we want. The solution to current problems with SEC settlements is not necessarily more litigation,[40] but rather better-designed settlements and prioritizing of cases. SEC settlements can and should provide market players with more credible information on how exactly companies misbehaved.

For SEC settlements that are still filed in federal courts, judicial review can ideally nudge SEC enforcement in the direction of better information production. To be sure, judicial review is a very imperfect method for improving SEC settlements. Judges themselves are fallible and may interfere even when the SEC makes the right considerations.[41] My point here is not to advocate for more judicial scrutiny, but rather for better judicial scrutiny, with clear guidelines for its application.[42] I offer two simple guidelines. First, judges should generally maintain deference to the SEC. Interference raises the costs of settlements and limits the range of mutually beneficial bargains between the regulator and the regulated entities. Second, the main trigger for judicial intervention in rare cases should be information production and not severity of fines. Judges should interfere whenever the settlement withholds quality information on a topic that is of wide interest to the market.[43]

40 Harvey Pitt Brief, *supra* note 24, at n.14 (claiming that for an agency that initiates hundreds of proceedings, settling most of them becomes a necessity).

41 Federal judges enjoy life tenure, but they are not immune from seeking esteem, influence, or promotions. They too may advance their own reputation at the expense of overall welfare. Fredrick Schauer, *Incentives, Reputation, and the Inglorious Determinants of Judicial Behavior*, 68 U. Cin. L. Rev. 615, 629–33 (2000).

42 Dreilinger, *supra* note 8, at 6 n.33.

43 The doctrinal hook for demanding more information production comes from the requirement to consider "the public interest" when reviewing SEC's decisions. *See* SEC v. Randolph, 736

To illustrate, consider how Judge Rakoff's war against neither-admit-nor-deny settlements played out. In 2014, the Second Circuit Court of Appeals reached a decision in the *Citigroup* case, vacating Judge Rakoff's refusal to approve the settlement.[44] Seen from the informational perspective developed here, the Court of Appeals' decision sets a bad precedent: it focuses the permissible scope of judicial review on the procedural aspects of the consent decree, and explicitly limits the judge's ability to demand more information on what and how things happened. When this judicial tendency to not interfere in information underproduction is coupled with the abovementioned regulator's tendency to file settlements administratively (which limits the scope for judicial intervention to begin with), the likely result is weaker reputational deterrence.

4.6.2 *Changes to Enforcement Policy*

If the SEC wishes to optimize information production and facilitate reputational deterrence, it should reprioritize its enforcement cases. The SEC needs to concentrate resources on cases that produce big informational benefits (disputes with giant financial firms), even at the expense of amassing complaints and litigating against smaller firms or low-level employees.

To borrow an analogy from communication science: *the SEC needs to shift to a "burglar alarm" mode of reporting*. In the past decade communication scholars have been advocating a shift from the traditional "all the news that's fit to print" mode of journalism to a burglar-alarm approach.[45] The idea is that nowadays, with the advancement of information technologies, citizens can easily access information on all issues. What citizens need is not more information but rather someone to sift the information for them: a reputable intermediary that will direct citizens' scant attention to the few pieces of information that are more relevant and critical. The same can be said with regard to SEC settlements. Nowadays market players learn about financial misconduct from multiple sources. The SEC should therefore switch from merely putting us on notice that lots of bad things are happening to flagging the more problematic cases – providing detailed information on the most

F. 2d 525 (1984). Note that any form of judicial scrutiny should consider the unintended consequences on parallel private litigation: before making settlements more informative one should consider limiting the issue preclusion and estoppel effects. Buell, *supra* note 16, at 100–01.

44 SEC v. Citigroup Global Mkts. Inc., 752 F. 3d 285 (2014).

45 John Zaller, *A New Standard of News Quality: Burglar Alarm for the Monitorial Citizen*, 20 Pol. Comm. 109, 116 (2003).

important cases and directing market players' attention to instances where they greatly under or overstated problems.

A second proposal that could mitigate the information-underproduction problem involves changing the common practice of announcing the complaint and settlement together. We saw earlier that comingling the announcements limits the media follow-up and allows companies to put a "business as usual" spin on the allegations. A straightforward solution would be to disentangle the two announcements. The SEC should not file a settlement until, say, a week has passed since it announced the filing of a complaint. Think about it as a sort of "notice and comment" period:[46] the media and other intermediaries (analysts, institutional investors) would get to devote attention to, and weigh in on, the allegations. The company will have to address them. And the SEC overseers will have an opportunity to judge whether settling the case is in the public's best interest.

4.7 PRIVATE LITIGATION VS. PUBLIC ENFORCEMENT: THE INFORMATION-PRODUCTION PERSPECTIVE

Instead of concluding by summarizing the previous sections, let us synthesize what we have learned about the reputational effects of SEC enforcement by comparing them to the reputational effects of private litigation. Which mode of enforcement injects more valuable information to the market and facilitates better reputational deterrence?

On paper, it may seem that the SEC enforcement division possesses better tools and incentives than private litigants to produce credible information. The SEC enjoys broader investigative powers compared to the ones private litigants typically enjoy in a post-PSLRA world.[47] And as for incentives, private litigants are incentivized to trade away information for money: it is not just that they settle too early and too often, but also that they settle too secretly. Almost every settlement comes with some form of a confidentiality clause.[48] By contrast, the SEC can produce press releases that detail their investigations in a fairer way than plaintiffs'-lawyer-worded complaints or media briefs. All this has led a few scholars to suggest that we can do away with private securities litigation (e.g., by allowing companies to adopt mandatory arbitration

46 *See also* Velikonja, *supra* note 30, at 134.

47 Amanda M. Rose, *Better Bounty Hunting; How the SEC's New Whistleblower Program Changes the Securities Fraud Class Action Debate*, 108 Nw. U. L. Rev. 1235, 1258 (2014). Chapter 8 elaborates.

48 Chapter 7 elaborates.

provisions with class action waivers), and instead shift more resources to SEC enforcement and whistleblowing programs.[49]

Yet the SEC enforcement-produces-better-information-environment argument applies only in a limited sense: in a specific dispute, SEC enforcement may indeed be equally/more informative than private litigation. But as far as the big picture is concerned, the overall information that comes out of SEC enforcement actions as a whole *cannot* fully substitute for the overall information that comes out due to private litigation. Private enforcement produces information in ways and on types of misconduct on which the SEC consistently underproduces information.

For one, the SEC faces budgetary constraints. It does not have the ability to pursue all investigations of misconduct that private litigators have traditionally taken on.[50] The limited resources mean that the SEC has to prioritize targets, and various empirical studies show that the SEC prioritizes in a distorted way. The SEC has historically favored going after small fish rather than big fish,[51] and provided laxer treatment for firms that are more politically connected.[52] The plaintiffs' bar, by contrast, pursues companies with much bigger market caps and without apparent political biases.[53] Private litigation is therefore likely to pursue – and flush out information on – instances of corporate misconduct that public enforcement ignores.

To reiterate: when we question the SEC's incentives, we do not need to assume a hardcore regulatory capture story. Publicly spirited SEC decision

49 Amanda M. Rose, *The Multienforcer Approach to Securities Fraud Deterrence: A Critical Analysis*, 158 U. PA. L. REV. 2173 (2010).

50 As the SEC Investor Advocate acknowledged himself. *See* Rick Fleming, Inv'r Advocate, Sec. & Exch. Comm'n, Address at PLI's the SEC Speaks in 2018, Washington, DC: Mandatory Arbitration: An Illusory Remedy for Public Companies Shareholders (Feb. 24, 2018), www.sec.gov/news/speech/fleming-sec-speaks-mandatory-arbitration. *See also* Samuel Issacharoff, *Regulating after the Fact*, 56 DEPAUL L. REV. 375, 381 (2007) (private enforcement expands the inherently limited resources of government enforcement); David H. Webber, *Shareholder Litigation without Class Actions*, 57 ARIZ. L. REV. 201, 266 (2015); James D. Cox & Randall S. Thomas, *Mapping the American Shareholder Litigation Experience: A Survey of Empirical Studies of the Enforcement of the U.S. Securities Law*, 6 EUROPEAN COMPANY & FIN. L. REV. 164, 175 (2009).

51 *Cox & Thomas, id.*, at 172–73 (summarizing studies over the years); Stavros Gadinis, *The SEC and the Financial Industry: Evidence from Enforcement against Broker-Dealers*, 67 BUS. LAW. 679 (2012).

52 Maria M. Correia, *Political Connections and SEC Enforcement*, 57 J. ACCOUNT. ECO. 241 (2014); Frank Yu & Xiaoyun Yu, 46 *Corporate Lobbying and Fraud Detection*, J. FIN. & QUANT. ANALYSIS 1864 (2011). *See generally* Jonathan R. Macey, *State–Federal Relations Post-Eliot Spitzer*, 70 BROOK. L. REV. 117, 117–18 (2004).

53 James D. Cox & Randall S. Thomas, *SEC Enforcement Heuristics: An Empirical Inquiry*, 53 DUKE L.J. 737, 779 (2003).

makers maximize what they are being measured upon. And they are being measured upon the total amount of fines it collects and the number of enforcement actions it opens. From our viewpoint, the problem is that in pursuing these numbers the SEC too often trades off information. It often lets the targets of its enforcement actions influence the language and timing of the enforcement action press release. It tends to target whole industries for minor offenses. Targeting whole industries does not affect reputations: the stakeholders of company X cannot punish the company for misbehaving if all company X's competitors face similar allegations (they cannot take their business elsewhere).

Further, targeting companies for strict liability offenses allows the SEC to investigate and prosecute quickly, but produces little reputational value.[54] Enforcement action for a strict liability offense would tell the market that something happened, but would not normally elaborate on how things happened. It would not produce internal company documents showing who knew what when.

Indeed, Choi and Pritchard provided evidence that private attorneys may be better at flushing out certain types of misconduct than the SEC.[55] Their study found that the credibility of the defendant company's disclosures takes a bigger hit following a standalone class action, than it does following a standalone SEC investigation. Institutional ownership and earnings responsiveness – both proxies for how the market perceives disclosure credibility – drop more for companies that were targeted by a class action than they do for companies that were targeted by the SEC.

To be sure, private litigants' incentives to produce information are far from perfect. Our message here is not that private litigation is categorically better than SEC enforcement in information production. In line with Chapter 2, our message here is *not* to treat private litigation and SEC enforcement as a horserace, where we need to determine who the sole winner of information production is. We can acknowledge that both systems are flawed, and still recognize that the systems' coexistence can make things better as long as each system's flaws are imperfectly correlated with the other's.[56] For example,

[54] We will come back to the reputational effects of strict liability rules in the Conclusion.

[55] Stephen J. Choi & A. C. Pritchard, *SEC Investigation and Securities Class Actions: An Empirical Comparison*, 13 J. Empirical Legal Stud. 27, 46 (2016).

[56] *See also* John C. Coffee Jr., *Rescuing the Private Attorney General: Why the Model of the Lawyer as Bounty Hunter Is Not Working*, 42 Md. L. Rev. 215. 226–27 (1983) (referring to private litigation as a failsafe mechanism that checks problems with public enforcement); William B. Rubenstein, *Why Enable Litigation: A Positive Externalities Theory of the Small Claims Class Action*, 74 UMKC L. Rev. 709, 725 (2006) (even if private litigation is flawed, the sheer diversity of enforcers is valuable).

private litigants have incentives to get damning information out early in the process, to survive the motion to dismiss and leverage their claims into a hefty settlement. The SEC, by contrast, keeps any damning information it extracts confidential until after a settlement was reached.[57] Chapter 8 comes back to this point, when discussing the mandatory arbitration revolution, which threatens to end shareholder litigation as we came to know it. In a world without private litigation, public enforcement cannot be counted on to carry the information-production load on its own.

[57] Érica Gorga & Michael Halberstam, *Litigation Discovery and Corporate Governance: The Missing Story about the "Genius of American Corporate Law,"* 63 EMORY L.J. 1383, 1428 n.236 (2014).

5

Corporate Philanthropy as Signaling and Co-optation

5.1 INTRODUCTION

Why do business companies donate to charity? Why do some companies donate more than others? The prevalent answers to these questions usually invoke reputation: companies donate in hope of securing good reputation among their stakeholders, or so the argument goes. Yet, the same problem we observed with the conventional wisdom on reputational sanctions appears here as well, with the conventional wisdom on reputational rewards: all too often legal scholars simply assume that donating to charity boosts a company's reputation, without fully examining how reputational rewards work, or how the legal regime influences companies' reputational incentives to donate.

This chapter argues that, contrary to common wisdom, corporate philanthropy is less about boosting a firm's reputation for being nice, and more about boosting a firm's reputation for being financially sound or having good products. The chapter also delineates the circumstances under which companies' donations do not result in reputational rewards, but rather destroy value and become a corporate governance problem. Finally, the chapter examines how the existing legal regime – which in the United States is virtually a regulatory vacuum – hurts the ability of reputation markets to incentivize impactful corporate prosociality.

Our starting point is the undeniable prominence of the corporate social responsibility (CSR) movement. Companies nowadays increasingly invest resources in activities that do not directly benefit the bottom line or meet legal requirements. They move to greener production, become more employee-friendly, or donate to charitable causes. The ever-growing phenomenon of corporate prosociality impacts not just social and environmental causes, but also financial allocations. Indeed, over $12 trillion are currently invested in part based on corporate social performance.[1]

Yet despite its growing importance, corporate prosociality remains an elusive phenomenon. This is especially true in the corporate law literature where, instead of understanding the causes and consequences of prosocial profit sacrificing, commentators traditionally focus their attention on the endless normative debate over whether corporations *should* engage in non-maximizing activities.[2] Even when the focus is shifted to understanding *why* companies behave prosocially, the discussion anachronistically alludes to the market forces driving corporate prosociality, without attempting to understand what affects those market forces.

Instead of grouping all CSR activities together, I focus on the subset of corporate philanthropy (CP).[3] CP is defined as corporate donations to qualified (i.e., tax-exempt) charitable organizations.[4] I focus, then, on behaviors that are more *explicitly* non-maximizing. I will not focus on behaviors like treating employees nicely, where the expenditures are on the immediate corporate realm (operational profit sacrificing), or on behaviors like cause-related marketing or corporate sponsorships of sports events, which are more akin to traditional advertising. By contrast, CP lacks expectations for an immediate, direct quid pro quo. When a New York–based investing bank donates $10 million to build a shelter home for the poor in Atlanta, the beneficiaries of the donation will likely not buy from, work for, or invest in the company. Focusing on CP allows us to resist "fighting the hypothetical," that is, evading issues arising from profit sacrificing by assuming that the behavior is really profit maximizing in disguise.[5]

1 *Report on US Sustainable, Responsible and Impact Investing Trends*, SOC. INV. FORUM 1 (2018), www.ussif.org/files/Trends/Trends%202018%20executive%20summary%20FINAL.pdf.

2 *See generally* A. A. Berle, Jr., *Corporate Powers as Powers in Trust*, 44 HARV. L. REV. 1049 (1931); E. Merrick Dodd, Jr., *For Whom Are Corporate Managers Trustees?*, 45 HARV. L. REV. 1145 (1932).

3 On the need to study individual components of CSR separately and the advantages of focusing on the CP component, *see, e.g.*, Baruch Lev et al., *Is Doing Good Good for You? How Corporate Charitable Contributions Enhance Revenue Growth*, 31 STRATEGIC MGMT. J. 182 (2010).

4 I will deal mostly with "direct" corporate giving, as opposed to giving through corporate foundations, which raises substantially different questions. Roy Shapira, *Corporate Philanthropy as Signaling and Co-optation*, 80 FORDHAM L. REV. 1889, 1894 n.9 (2012).

5 Another reason to focus on CP is that in the debate over the proper purpose of the corporation, CP is the example traditionally used in the legal literature. It is therefore fitting to revisit it by freshly examining the assumptions that commentators made in that normative debate. For the terminology I adopt here, see Einer Elhauge, *Sacrificing Corporate Profits in the Public Interest*, 80 N.Y.U. L. REV. 733 (2005).

The first contribution of this chapter comes from revising the current "profit-enhancing approach," which construes CP as buying goodwill for the company. We cannot simply assume that companies, by acting nicely, would boost their reputations. Instead, we should ask: reputation for what? To whom? And how does CP affect it – what do outsiders infer when they observe companies significantly increasing their prosocial expenditures?

The answer, I argue, lies in costly signaling. Explicit sacrifices of profits can serve as costly signals that build a firm's reputation. They reliably convey messages about attributes that are important to shareholders, consumers, and employees, who are evaluating whether to invest in, buy products from, or work for those companies. For example, CP can serve as a costly signal that builds a firm's reputation toward its investors. An increase in the level of donations could convey messages about financial strength to potential investors, who could infer that future free cash flows are perceived by insiders to be relatively high, that the company is now less financially constrained, or that the riskiness of future cash flows has decreased. Acknowledging the possibility that benefits arise from signaling also has legal implications: laws affect the flow and quality of information, as well as the choice of signals.

The second contribution comes from revisiting the "agency–costs approach," which views CP as a managerial perk. Yet even if we assume that CP decisions are driven by managerial utility, it is unclear whether they are detrimental to shareholder value or merely a value-neutral diversion (i.e., a substitute for other managerial perks within a fixed level of appropriation). The more relevant question, I claim, is whether insiders can use their discretion over corporate donations to dilute the mechanisms that are supposed to cap managerial agency costs. CP can be a co-optation mechanism, allowing insiders to escape restrictions on board independence (such as by donating to directors' pet charities), and campaign finance. The upshot is that some sort of legal intervention may be needed. Leaving agency problems totally unregulated in the CP context could create negative spillovers in other contexts.

Finally, the chapter builds on the CP as signaling/co-optation explanations to make the case for some form of mandatory disclosure. Regulating some standardized, comparable, subject-to-liability form of disclosure could facilitate a better-functioning market for reputational rewards. At the same time, exploiting the potential to use undisclosed CP to co-opt governance mechanisms stresses the importance of not leaving CP in the dark. In this respect, legal intervention should focus not only on the levels of prosociality (*how much* does the company donate), but also on its targets (*to whom* does the company donate). Mandatory disclosure could therefore also facilitate reputational sanctions for abuses of CP.

The chapter proceeds in four sections. Section 5.2 provides a critical synthesis of the existing literature. Section 5.3 introduces my signaling theory of CP. Section 5.4 clarifies whether and how CP could be a corporate governance problem. Section 5.5 sketches policy implications. Section 5.6 offers concluding thoughts by reevaluating the claim that CP serves as a reputational *buffer* against reputational sanctions.

5.2 THE EXTANT CP LITERATURE: DATA AND THEORY

5.2.1 *Existing Data*

We have a good grasp on the magnitude of corporate donations. American companies spend approximately $20.5 billion annually on philanthropy.[6] These $20.5 billion amount to 0.9 percent of corporate pre-tax profits.[7] While the absolute amounts increase over time, donations as a percentage of profits remain somewhat stable, around 1 percent. At the industry level, pharmaceutical companies give the most.[8] At the firm level, the biggest product donors (Pfizer, Merck, Google) evaluate their contributions in billions, while the biggest cash donors (Gilead Sciences, Wells Fargo, Goldman Sachs) each donate around $300 million annually.[9] Among the *Fortune* 100 companies, the median giving is around $63 million annually, and among the top quartile, that number jumps to close to $170 million.[10]

We also have a good grasp of what exactly companies donate: cash donations are clearly the most dominant form of giving, over product donations or employee release time.[11] And on the "who decides" question, it seems that despite a recent trend to put CP policy in the hands of specialized departments

[6] Giving USA Found. & Ctr. on Philanthropy at Ind. Univ., Giving USA 2018: The Annual Report On Philanthropy For The Year 2017 1 (hereinafter: Giving USA 2018). For a comparative perspective, CP in the entirety of the EU was reported as $28.33 billion in 2013 terms. The comparative numbers in this Section are based on the *Giving in Europe* project, *available at* www.dedikkeblauwe.nl/news/givingineurope, and on the *Corporate Giving by the FTSE 100* project, *available at* www.cafonline.org/about-us/publications/2018-publications/corporate-giving-by-the-ftse-100.

[7] *Id.*, at 2.

[8] Brian O'Leary et al., *Drug, Tech and Financial-Services Companies Top List of Corporate Donors*, The Chronicle of Philanthropy, Sept. 5, 2018. The pharmaceutical companies lead CP outside the United States as well.

[9] *See* the Chronicle of Philanthropy's interactive project, *America's Big Corporate Givers*, *available at* www.philanthropy.com/interactives/corporateleaders2018.

[10] For a comparative perspective, among the FTSE 100 (firms with largest market capitalization listed on the London Stock Exchange), the average giving is around $26.8 million.

[11] Giving USA 2018, at 147–66 (cash donations comprise 82 percent of total CP).

and professionals, CEOs still exert a lot of influence over these discretionary expenditures.[12]

Beyond these stylized facts, the management literature has obsessed over finding a link between CP and the financial bottom line. Does doing good lead to doing well? We can quickly summarize the overarching patterns of this voluminous literature thusly:[13] (1) there is a small but positive association between social and financial performance; (2) this association is stronger for CP than for other social performance proxies (such as corporate policies and transparency); and (3) the link from financial to social performance is at least as strong as the reverse (i.e., doing well enables doing good; companies that generate more profits can afford to sacrifice more profits in the public interest). The main lesson is that, while we cannot conclude that companies do well *by* doing good, we can conclude that companies can both do well *and* do good. In other words, there is no evident financial punishment for prosociality.

Things get murkier when we try to go beyond the "in general" question (does giving generally lead to having), and identify the conditions under which CP increases or decreases the value of a given company.[14] From a legal scholar perspective, studies linking the quality of corporate governance mechanisms and CP behavior are the most interesting. In theory, if there is a positive correlation between strong governance and CP, then the profit-enhancing approach is supported, and the need for legal intervention decreases. If there is a positive correlation between weak governance and CP, then the agency–costs approach is supported, and the need for intervention increases. Yet so far, empirical studies linking governance to CP remain largely inconclusive and open to interpretation. CP levels positively correlate with some proxies for weak monitoring (e.g., firms with low debt ratios donate more), while negatively correlating with others (firms with more independent boards donate more).[15]

[12] This is notable when considering the relatively small size of such expenditures. CEOs of large companies do not exert such influence on equivalent expenditures. Jayne W. Barnard, *Corporate Philanthropy, Executives' Pet Charities and the Agency Problem*, 41 N.Y.L. Sch. L. Rev. 1147, 1157–60 (1997).

[13] *See generally* Joshua D. Margolis et al., Does It Pay to Be Good? A Meta-Analysis and Redirection of Research on the Relationship between Corporate Social and Financial Performance 59 tbl.3 (2007) (unpublished manuscript), *available at* http://stakeholder.bu.edu/docs/walsh,%20jim%20does%20it%20pay%20to%20be%20good.pdf.

[14] David Vogel, The Market For Virtue 33 (2005).

[15] *See generally* Barbara R. Bartkus et al., *Governance and Corporate Philanthropy: Restraining Robin Hood?*, 41 Bus. & Soc'y 319 (2002); William O. Brown et al., *Corporate Philanthropic Practices*, 12 *J.* Corp. Fin. 855, 857–58 (2006).

In summary, our knowledge of CP practices remains in a high level of generality. We know that CP is neither a huge nor an insignificant corporate expenditure, that top managers exert a lot of influence over these ultra-discretionary expenditures, that there is no evidence that prosociality is being punished financially, and that conditions leading to more giving or more profit-minded giving are hard to identify. Mainly, we know that we do not know much. We need better data.[16] Importantly, we also need a better theory: better articulation of the mechanisms that might link CP to outcomes that are good or bad for the company.[17]

5.2.2 *Existing Theory*

Current theoretical accounts of CP fall under two main categories: the "profit-enhancing approach," which construes CP as buying goodwill for the company, and the "agency– costs approach," which views CP as a managerial perk. Both accounts suffer from under-articulation. They do not clearly identify the mechanisms linking CP with enhanced profits or managerial agency costs.

The profit-enhancing approach usually rests on a "delegated philanthropy" assumption: the idea that when companies sacrifice profits, they simply meet the charitable preferences of stakeholders. Stakeholders are willing to pay more for companies that donate, and so when companies donate they increase demand or reduce their operating costs. In other words, stakeholders prefer "nice" companies. When consumers purchase a product from a donating company, they get a bundle of direct utility from consuming, and "warm glow" from buying products that were manufactured by nice companies.[18]

Yet these delegated philanthropy explanations rely on too-unrealistic assumptions. First, while people are quick to profess in surveys their willingness to pay for nicer companies' products, evidence of actual buying decisions is rather tenuous.[19] Second, even if you believe that declarations in surveys do translate into actions, you cannot conclude that CP is especially effective at buying goodwill. After all, in those surveys consumers profess much stronger preferences for other prosocial expenditures, such as labor

[16] I have elaborated on limitations in data and methodology in Shapira, *supra* note 4, at 1898–99.

[17] Margolis et al., *supra* note 13, at 27.

[18] Joshua Graff Zivin & Arthur Small, *A Modigliani-Miller Theory of Altruistic Corporate Social Responsibility*, 5 Topics Econ. Anal. & Pol'y, no. 1, 2005, at 1.

[19] Vogel, *supra* note 14, at 46–47; Michael E. Porter & Mark R. Kramer, *Strategy & Society: The Link between Competitive Advantage and Corporate Social Responsibility*, Harv. Bus. Rev., Dec. 2006, at 83; David F. Larcker & Edward M. Watts, *Where's the Greenium?*, Rock Center Working Paper No. 239 (Feb. 12, 2019), https://papers.ssrn.com/sol3/papers.cfm?abstract_id=3333847 (investors are not willing to pay more for greener companies).

and environmental issues, than for cash donations.[20] Third and perhaps most pertinently, evidence shows that consumers are too often unaware of different levels of CP.[21]

Finally, even if consumers have meaningful charitable preferences, and even if they are able (i.e., aware of CP levels) to act upon them, one still needs to explain why consumers would want to delegate charity. Instead of paying more for a nice company's product, consumers can pay for a value-adjusted cheaper product of a non-sacrificing firm. Consumers can then use the cash saved to satisfy their own charitable preferences, which, in all likelihood, differ somewhat from those of the donating company's managers.[22]

The agency–costs approach, by contrast, suggests that the seemingly irrational CP phenomenon is completely rational from a corporate decision-maker standpoint. The impetus driving CP behavior is private benefits to corporate insiders. A manager donating with shareholders' money gets invitations to board seats, tickets to gala events, esteem from her peers, personal satisfaction of her own altruistic preferences, and warm glow.[23]

One problem with such managerial–utility explanations is that they do not fully explain why managers would choose CP as a channel to reap private benefits, rather than other channels such as negotiating for higher pay/perks. If the manager engages in CP to get warm glow and satisfy her own charitable preferences, she could arguably get more warm glow from negotiating higher pay and then donating the extra dollars in her own name. Indeed, existing data casts doubt on mechanisms that were traditionally offered to link CP to managerial utility. For example, one study found that firms that pay their CEOs more are not the ones donating more, and another found that replacing the CEO does not change the firm's donating policy.[24] Another problem with managerial–utility

[20] *See, e.g.*, Roland Bénabou & Jean Tirole, *Individual and Corporate Social Responsibility*, 77 ECONOMICA 1, 14 (2010); Linda Sugin, *Encouraging Corporate Charity*, 26 VA. TAX REV. 125, 127 n.5, 141 n.43 (2006).

[21] Naomi A. Gardberg et al., *The Impact of Corporate Philanthropy on Reputation for Corporate Social Performance*, 58 BUS. & SOC'Y 1177 (2019).

[22] Note the difference between operational profit sacrificing, such as spending more on a greener mode of production, and explicit profit sacrificing, such as cash donations. With the former, there is good reason to believe that the company is better positioned to bundle direct utility with warm glow. With the latter, there is not. Bénabou & Tirole, *supra* note 20, at 10–11.

[23] Faith Stevelman Kahn, *Pandora's Box: Managerial Discretion and the Problem of Corporate Philanthropy*, 44 UCLA L. REV. 579, 609–25 (1997).

[24] Peter Navarro, *Why Do Corporations Give to Charity?*, 61 J. BUS. 65 (1988); Steven C. Trost, An Examination of Corporate Charitable Contributions: Evidence from Firm, Managerial,

accounts is that they often fail to clearly answer the "so what?" question: assuming CP is indeed driven by managerial utility, is it necessarily bad for the company, the shareholders, or overall welfare?

Both the profit-enhancing and agency–costs approaches therefore suffer from serious theoretical flaws. And the existing empirical evidence on which captures reality better is inconclusive. Even findings presumed to favor one approach can be interpreted to cut both ways, at least until the mechanisms that link CP to company-level and managerial-level benefits are better articulated.[25] The next two sections attempt to do just that: provide a better explanation of the mechanisms in play.

5.3 CP AS A COSTLY SIGNALING MECHANISM

To illustrate the problem with the buying–goodwill explanation for CP, consider a puzzling pattern identified by a famous study, which tested whether and how prosociality reduces labor costs.[26] The buying–goodwill argument generates two hypotheses: (1) companies that donate more will do better at attracting potential job applicants; (2) the abovementioned effect will be mediated by the applicants' "social preferences." In other words, applicants who feel strongly about social or environmental issues will be more attracted to prosocial companies. The study's findings were consistent with the first hypothesis, but inconsistent with the second. Job applicants did consider prosocial companies as more attractive places to work. But the effect was *not* mediated by the applicants' social or environmental preferences. Job applicants considered prosocial companies as more attractive to work for, *regardless* of whether applicants cared about social issues.

This empirical pattern suggests that something else is in play here, beyond the supposed preference for nicer companies. Even strictly profit-minded stakeholders prefer companies that are nice; not because of the niceness per se, but rather because niceness is an indication of something else. The interesting questions are thus: what is prosociality indicative of, and how exactly can prosociality be credibly indicative of other traits?

and Community Factors 90–93 (May 2006) (unpublished Ph.D. dissertation, University of Virginia), *available at* www.stevenctrost.com/diss.pdf.

25 Barbara R. Bartkus et al., *Governance and Corporate Philanthropy: Restraining Robin Hood?*, 41 Bus. & Soc'y 319, 337 (2002).

26 Daniel W. Greening & Daniel B. Turban, *Corporate Social Performance as a Competitive Advantage in Attracting a Quality Workforce*, 39 Bus. & Soc'y 254 (2000).

5.3.1 *The Basic Story: Signaling Financial Strength*

Our starting premise is that there exists asymmetric information about companies' underlying attributes. Insiders know more than outsiders. Both have incentives to mitigate the asymmetry. One method for insiders to mitigate asymmetries is to communicate information to target audiences about unobservable qualities through observable activities. This is the basic background of a costly signaling story.[27] As applied here, profit sacrificing in general and CP in particular can serve as costly (thereby credible) and observable attributes, conveying messages about unobservable attributes.

Consider for example the potential of using CP to signal future free cash flows. The signaler in our informal model is the company, or, more precisely, its decision-makers (top management in widely held companies, or dominant shareholders). Receivers of the signal – the target audience – are outside investors. One important attribute for how outsiders evaluate the company is future free cash flows. Because future free cash flows are not readily observable by outsiders, they make a plausible subject for costly signaling.[28] What could constitute an observable costly attribute that credibly conveys messages about future cash flows? In the current context, big changes in cash donations could fit the bill. Cash donations are costly in an intuitive manner: insiders decide to take a dollar that they could have used to meet the demands of contractual claimants, and instead give it to unrelated third parties. Outsiders that observe a company substantially increasing its expenditures on prosocial profit sacrificing will infer that the company's insiders perceive their ability to procure future resources as better than was previously evaluated. Outsiders then update their forecasts about the company's prospects accordingly.

But for such a signal to work, it needs to be more than just costly. It has to be costlier for low-quality companies in order to avoid mimicry (the costs have to be differentiating and quality-dependent). In the current context, cash donations need to be costlier for firms with low future free cash flows than for those with high cash flows. One could argue that companies with low future cash flows can finance a high level of donations out of retained earnings or external

[27] My informal explanation builds on formal models of signaling developed in economics and sociobiology. *See, e.g.*, Herbert Gintis et al., *Costly Signaling and Cooperation*, 213J. THEORETICAL BIOLOGY 103 (2001); Alan Grafen, *Biological Signals as Handicaps*, 144 J. THEORETICAL BIOLOGY 517 (1990); Michael Spence, *Job Market Signaling*, 87 Q.J. ECON. 355 (1973). *See generally* AMOTZ ZAHAVI & AVISHAG ZAHAVI, THE HANDICAP PRINCIPLE: A MISSING PIECE OF DARWIN'S PUZZLE (1997).

[28] Accounting concepts like depreciation and capital investment bridge a gap between net profits and uncommitted cash flows. Asymmetric information only increases when the attribute in question is a perceived future ability.

finance. If insiders can simply borrow money to raise their CP levels even when times are bad, then outsiders will not change their valuations based on observing CP.

Yet empirical studies showing that corporate goodness is costlier for financially constrained firms refute this argument.[29] There are several possible reasons behind such a link between corporate goodness and financial constraints. For one, borrowing to finance the donations is costlier for companies with relatively bad future prospects because it requires them to expose themselves to unfavorable covenants or disclosure requirements.[30] Furthermore, there is evidence that managers care deeply about meeting earnings benchmarks and smoothing earnings, to the extent that they will even sacrifice projects with positive net present value to set aside buffer cash.[31] Thus, it is plausible to assume that insiders in low quality firms will find it more costly to spend ultra-discretionary dollars on CP, since they need all the cash buffers they can get. Outsiders observing a large increase in CP levels could therefore infer that insiders know they are not going to be financially constrained.[32]

Stated differently, the conditions for costly signaling are as follows. First, companies vary in their ability to generate future free cash flows. Second, outside investors cannot readily observe future free cash flows, and stand to gain from knowing more about them. Third, at the same time, outsiders cannot simply believe all direct messages from insiders about future free cash flows; insiders stand to gain from sending exaggerated signals. So, outsiders resort to making inferences based on some observable, costly behaviors of companies, and the fact that the behavior is costly assures the credibility of the signal. Low-quality signalers cannot incur the same amount of costs as high-quality signalers. Fourth, one such observable behavior is explicit profit sacrificing. Big cash donations will carry information about the prospects of the company as long as the costs of donating are negatively correlated with an ability to generate future free cash flows.

29 Harrison G. Hong et al., Financial Constraints on Corporate Goodness 31 tbl.3 (Jan. 3, 2011) (unpublished manuscript), *available at* http://ssrn.com/ abstract=1734164. Another study that could be interpreted as suggestive evidence in favor of signaling establishes that CP is a good predictor ("Granger-cause") of future financial health (revenue growth): Lev et al., *supra* note 5.

30 For a discussion of external finance as cost-differentiating, see generally Sudipto Bhattacharya, *Imperfect Information, Dividend Policy, and "The Bird in the Hand" Fallacy*, 10 Bell J. Econ. 259 (1979) (a dividend-signaling model).

31 John R. Graham et al., *The Economic Implications of Corporate Financial Reporting*, 40 J. Acct. & Econ. 3, 33 (2005).

32 Alternatively, outsiders can infer that insiders do not care so much about meeting the earnings per-share benchmarks and are not subject to short-term market pressures.

If these propositions are plausible, then we can assume that communication through profit sacrificing will be informative. Yet a fully conscious, meditated decision to sacrifice profits with a clear intent to signal financial strength is not needed. When the above propositions apply, we can assume that some "design force" – conscious decision-making, market forces selection, or imitation of successful companies – will instill in CP the tenets of a costly, informative signal of financial strength. But are all these propositions really plausible? The next section elaborates on potential limitations, in order to identify the specific circumstances under which we can expect signaling by conspicuous goodness.

5.3.2 *Refining the Basic Story: Limitations*

Before concluding that prosocial profit sacrifices bring benefits through signaling, several conditions and limitations need to be addressed. Consider the following four potential limitations.

First, CP is just one of many other signals available. If throwing cash away serves as a signal for an ability to procure resources, why should companies throw it away on charitable organizations? Why not throw it on investors, in the form of dividends?[33] Alternatively, why not throw it on conspicuous consumption, such as building luxurious headquarters, or purchasing lavish perks?[34] All it takes is for a firm to sacrifice profits, so why make the sacrifice in the public interest? The key to answering this question is acknowledging that signaling through prosocial sacrifices does not preclude the use of other signals. In real life, unlike in models, multiple messages are conveyed by multiple means.[35] The real question, then, is not choosing CP over another expenditure, but what the mix of signals chosen in the given circumstances will be.

Think about the choice between signaling through increasing dividends and signaling through increasing CP expenditures. For most firms, the choice is nonexistent, as they never pay dividends.[36] For firms that do pay dividends, and can use dividends as signaling financial strength, it still may make sense to use CP as a *backup signal*: another signaling channel to convey the same

33 For a discussion of the classical dividend-signaling models, see Bhattacharya, *supra* note 30.

34 *See generally* THORSTEIN VEBLEN, THE THEORY OF THE LEISURE CLASS (Penguin ed. 1994) (1899) (recognized as the first elaborate treatment of conspicuous consumption as signaling).

35 In finance, see Harry DeAngelo et al., *Reversal of Fortune: Dividend Signaling and the Disappearance of Sustained Earnings Growth*, 40 J. FIN. ECON. 341, 365 (1996). In sociobiology, see Eileen A. Hebets & Daniel R. Papaj, *Complex Signal Function: Developing a Framework of Testable Hypotheses*, 57 BEHAV. ECOLOGY & SOCIOBIOLOGY 197 (2005).

36 Alon Brav et al., *Payout Policy in the 21st Century*, 77 J. FIN. ECON. 483, 516 (2005).

message. Signaling through multiple channels (rather than exaggerating signals through the same channel) makes sense when receivers are prone to err in evaluating signals.[37] The corporate environment fits the conditions of an error-prone environment: noisy communications, strong incentives to cheat, widely varying perceptions and preferences of receivers, and accelerating signaling costs.[38] A corporate decision maker who wishes to signal good prospects, may supplement the increase in dividends with an increase in CP levels, to make sure that outsiders get the right message (e.g., that outsiders are not attributing an increase in dividends to bowing to pressures from shareholders eager for payouts). While this CP-as-backup-signal speculation is ultimately a matter for future pinpointed empirical research, existing evidence indicates that it is not far-fetched. Firms that pay out more also donate more.[39]

A second potential criticism is that CP is not costly enough to be a costly signal. To be sure, CP does cost something, but is it truly a handicap to big firms? After all, CP levels in many companies represent only a "modest incremental cash drain on resources available to managers,"[40] and modest costs cannot differentiate between high- and low-quality signalers. To accommodate this valid objection, we need to refine our predictions regarding benefits arising from signaling. Prosociality will convey credible messages about future financial prospects only when conducted on a large scale relative to a company's size and resources. Day-to-day marginal contributions are not likely to generate signaling benefits; big changes in CP policy are.[41] For example, in March 2008, when Goldman Sachs announced a new $100 million CP program meant to further business education of women in the developing world, outsiders took notice.[42] Outsiders were free to infer that

37 Rufus A. Johnstone, *Multiple Displays in Animal Communication: "Backup Signals" and "Multiple Messages,"* 351 PHIL. TRANSACTIONS BIOLOGICAL SCI. 329 (1996). The reason we borrow insights from models developed in the sociobiology literature is that the information economics literature focuses more on the strategic aspects of signaling (the why), while sociobiology focuses more on the efficacy of signaling (the how). Efficacy considerations cannot be ignored when analyzing corporate communications in a noisy environment filled with strong incentives to cheat.

38 For discussions on conditions for backup signaling, *see* Johnstone, *id.*; Sarah R. Partan & Peter Marler, *Issues in the Classification of Multimodal Communication Signals*, 166 AM. NATURALIST 231 (2005) (noncooperative, competitive contexts favor the evolution of conspicuous, redundant signals).

39 Navarro, *supra* note 24, at 87–88.

40 DeAngelo et al., *supra* note 35, at 343–44.

41 The emphasis is not only on "big" but also on "changes." CP policy of pursuing rigidly a rule of thumb like donating 1 percent of profits year after year will tell us less than unexpected changes.

42 10,000 *Women Brochure*, GOLDMAN SACHS, www2.goldmansachs.com/citizenship/10000women/10000-women-immersive/10000-women-brochure.pdf (last visited Apr. 15, 2019).

Goldman's top managers simply cared about the cause of women's business education, or that they were hoping to buy goodwill by appearing nice. But outsiders may also have inferred that Goldman's managers thought that the company could afford to sacrifice profits much more than it had previously because future prospects were looking brighter.[43]

A third potential criticism would point out that CP is not sticky enough to be an effective signal. If a certain expenditure is completely discretionary, then it cannot be a good signal. Signals need to have some level of stickiness to be reliable because something removable at will is not a true handicap. To accommodate this limitation, we first need to understand that the stickiness of signals is not a binary matter. While CP might be less sticky than other prosocial expenditures (such as reversing expenditures on employees' working conditions), anecdotal evidence indicates that there is a degree of asymmetric stickiness to CP. Managers enjoy much flexibility when deciding to initiate or raise CP levels, but there are costs to omitting or dropping existing levels. For example, managers fear reputational sanctions and personal pressures from NGOs or social rating indices if the company drops its support.[44]

A fourth potential limitation of the signaling theory is that prosociality is not observable to outsiders in a timely and useful manner. Although this limitation applies more strongly to operational profit sacrificing than to CP – cash donations in particular are readily communicated and quantified – this is still a strong limitation. Disclosure of CP is unregulated, and this creates an environment in which it is difficult for companies to reliably convey the relative level of their explicit prosociality.[45] Though lack of regulation is likely to reduce the benefits from signaling, it will not totally eliminate them. We should think of it as creating conditions for some *coarse* signaling story: companies wishing to distinguish themselves can voluntarily disclose their conspicuous goodness in a wide and timely manner, but outsiders will be able to distinguish between companies based on their CP levels only when the differences across companies and time are great. Again, the conclusion is that

43 In the past I suggested parameters for event-study examination of announcements of big donations. Shapira, *supra* note 4, at 1910 & n.181. New studies that came out since have elaborated. Section 5.3.5 elaborates. Note also that the optics here are bigger than the actual numbers. Managers of companies that fail to meet expectations will arguably be pressed to explain why they were so conspicuously generous with the company's dwindling resources, rather than to explain equivalent expenditures on greener modes of production or employees' conditions.

44 Interview with Bill Valentino, Vice President for CSR in China, Bayer, in Cambridge, MA (Oct. 6, 2010); Bénabou & Tirole, *supra* note 20, at 12 n.18.

45 Section 5.5.3.

the profit sacrifices most likely to generate signaling benefits are big changes, which are easily communicated to outsiders.

Having accommodated all those considerations, we are now left with a limited, refined story of corporate prosociality as a signal to outside investors. Only sacrifices that are relatively significant in size, readily observable, and not easily reversed can be expected to serve as an effective signal. Granted, these limitations confine the applicability of the signaling story to only a small number of actual CP decisions. Yet it is precisely those few large donations that are practically important; a small number of donations comprise the bulk of overall corporate giving expenditures and raise the most concerns. The signaling-to-investors story is therefore relevant to the more significant and/or controversial cases of CP, and thus merits attention.

Furthermore, even when circumstances make the signaling-to-investors story unlikely, CP can affect the company's reputation for other attributes, and among other crowds. For example, donating products or employee release-time might be ineffective as signals to investors looking for information on future financial strength, but effective as signals to employees looking for information on management's commitment to a certain corporate culture. It is these other sorts of signaling stories – signaling to nonfinancial stakeholders – to which we now turn.

5.3.3 *Other Possible Stories: Signaling Product Quality or Workplace Attractiveness*

The story of corporate donations signaling financial strength is only one of several potential signaling stories. Acts of corporate niceness can also have other informational contents (not just financial strength) and target audiences (not just investors). Consider the following three examples.

First, think about a signaling-to-customers model, where high levels of corporate donations convey information about the quality of the firm's product.[46] Such a model assumes two types of entrepreneurs. One type has other-regarding preferences, and thus cares about externalities, and the other type lacks those preferences and cares only about profits. For the other-regarding types, sacrificing profits is less costly, as they gain warm glow by refraining from externalities. By contrast, for the purely profit-motivated entrepreneurs, CP is a total sacrifice. Accordingly, the model assumes that

[46] Fisman et al., *supra* note 22 (setting out a model); Donald S. Siegel & Donald F. Vitaliano, *An Empirical Analysis of the Strategic Use of Corporate Social Responsibility*, 16 J. ECON. & MGMT STRATEGY 773 (2007) (empirical testing of the model).

when customers observe a company engaging in higher CP levels than its competitors, they infer that insiders in this company will be more averse to sacrifice unobservable qualities of products than their competitors are (because sacrificing product quality will generate externalities, which will in turn decrease the other-regarding entrepreneur's utility).

This CP-as-signaling-product-quality theory addresses some of the flaws in the delegated philanthropy accounts. It argues that CP is value-enhancing not because it satisfies customers' preferences for nice companies, but rather because it mitigates informational gaps about attributes relevant to the company's line of business. Yet the specifics of this signaling-to-customers theory still rest on some shaky assumptions. Just like delegated philanthropy explanations, the signaling-to-customers theory assumes that charitable preferences drive corporate behavior – only here, the preferences are those of entrepreneurs rather than consumers. Such an assumption might be plausible in manager-owned, small companies where the entrepreneur is tantamount to the company, but it is less plausible for large impersonal corporations. Further, the theory assumes that information on CP levels can be easily observed and compared by customers who make purchases accordingly, but academic evidence on the ground suggests that consumers' awareness of CP policies is actually low.[47]

A second possibility for prosociality to generate signaling benefits is through attracting high-quality employees. This relates to the puzzling empirical pattern discussed above: job applicants preferred prosocial companies regardless of how they felt about prosociality itself.[48] So what did the level of prosociality teach applicants about the company? Can a company's niceness boost its reputation for workplace conditions? Why would building a shelter home for the poor improve the company's reputation for how it treats its employees?

For one, prosociality could have sent a message about a "cooperative" corporate culture. Applicants may figure that top managers who commit to spend more on charity are not solely short-term-profits-hungry. These are the managers that you assume will not fire you or nickel-and-dime you in every chance they get. By explicitly sacrificing profits in the public interest, insiders can credibly and visibly commit to a certain culture, thereby attracting job applicants who will fit the culture.[49] Note that the signaling-to-workers

[47] *See, e.g.*, Sankar Sen et al., *The Role of Corporate Social Responsibility in Strengthening Multiple Stakeholder Relationships: A Field Experiment*, 34 J. ACAD. MARKETING SCI. 158, 164 (2006).

[48] Greening & Turban, *supra* note 26.

[49] The emphases are on credibility and visibility. Existing signaling-to-employees stories do not account adequately for issues such as mimicry; if management can reduce labor costs at will

hypotheses are more relevant in high-quality labor industries, and so in those industries we should expect more CP, all else being equal. Perhaps it is yet another factor explaining the dominance of pharmaceutical and technology companies among the largest corporate donors.

A third example of an alternative signaling story takes us back to investors as the intended audience, but this time with a different message: big increases in CP can convey fundamental information not only about the level of future free cash flows, but also about systematic decreases in *riskiness* of future cash flows. In other words, observing a big donation can make investors update the denominator rather than the numerator in the discounted cash flow formula. When projections of cash flows become less risky, insiders can make better assessments of their future opportunities and opportunity costs, and can thus better maximize the level of prosocial sacrifices – they need fewer cash buffers. In this respect, prosociality could mitigate asymmetric information about changes along the life cycles of organizations and managerial reactions to those changes.[50]

5.3.4 *Adding Complexity*

We have sketched the contours of basic signaling explanations to corporate prosociality. But it is important to note potential layers of complexity that can be followed through in future research, such as the choice between prosocial and wasteful signals, the possibility for errors in signaling, and costs from attracting the wrong reaction.

A necessary condition for costly signaling is that the behavior will be costly to the signaler. But nothing in the model requires the behavior to actually benefit others. The handicap can be prosocial, but it can just as well be wasteful (as in conspicuous consumption). A fuller analysis should thus account for conditions under which prosocial signals are more effective than wasteful ones. For example, if receivers have preferences for prosocial displays and if such displays receive greater attention (known as the "broadcast efficiency" of the signal), then the signaler should prefer them to wasteful

simply by denoting certain organizational values, why do we not observe every company doing so? Regarding visibility, for a corporate culture to attract outsiders, it needs to be visible to those not experiencing it; hence, there must be some observable symbols associated with certain cultures.

50 Tianjiao Zhao & Xiang Xiao, *The Impact of Corporate Social Responsibility on Financial Constraints: Does the life cycle Stage of a Firm Matter?* 63 INT. REV. ECON. FIN. 76 (2019) (finding that the association between CSR engagement and financial constraints is mediated by the firms' life cycle); Marc Orlitzky & John D. Benjamin, *Corporate Social Performance and Firm Risk: A Meta-Analytic Review*, 40 BUS. & SOC'Y 369, 376 (2001).

handicaps.[51] The choice of signals also has policy implications. Society might be better off when corporate signaling is done via prosocial handicaps, rather than wasteful ones[52] – think donations versus gold-embroidered shower curtains.

It is also important to take fuller account of errors in signaling communication. We have already mentioned that receivers are error-prone when perceiving signals in noisy environments. Signalers can be error-prone, too. For example, corporate managers are overly optimistic.[53] When deciding CP levels based on their upwardly biased perception of future prospects, managers might "advertise" too much, that is, engage in too much CP. A bias in forecasting future cash flows erodes the value of the signal and at some point the signaling stops being informative.

Finally, future research could also consider the possibility of another type of cost to the signaler – namely, attracting an unintended observer or provoking an unintended reaction from target audiences. Explicit profit sacrificing is conspicuous, and conspicuousness can attract predators who think that the signaler has too much waste. Activist hedge funds are a case in point. When activist hedge funds observe a company increasing its profit sacrificing, they may decide to target the company because of the slack it obviously possesses. Regardless of whether activist hedge funds are beneficial to overall welfare, incumbent managers usually want to avoid attracting them. Insiders worried about attracting hedge funds could be pushed to choose suboptimal signaling levels *ex ante*. Future empirical research could try to shed light on this speculation by examining, for example, whether changes in CP policies attract certain investors.

5.3.5 *Fit with Evidence*

When I started writing about CP as signaling, a decade ago, there was little firm-specific evidence that could lend credibility or discard my hypotheses. I therefore relied mostly on stylized facts and industry-level data, pointing to patterns that were inconsistent with the prevalent delegated philanthropy

51 *See* Gintis et al., *supra* note 27, at 112–15. As applied here, the choice between different signals is perhaps where the "delegated philanthropy" consideration kicks in, as (only) a second-order influence. Companies sacrifice profits to signal their ability to procure resources, and they do so by being nice, rather than being wasteful, because their audiences have a weak preference for interacting with nicer companies.

52 *Cf.* Geoffrey F. Miller, *The Handicap Principle: A Missing Piece of Darwin's Puzzle*, 19 Evolution & Hum. Behav. 343, 347 (1998).

53 J. B. Heaton, *Managerial Optimism and Corporate Finance*, 31 Fin. Mgmt. 33, 39–40 (2002).

approach, but consistent with my signaling approach. For example, a signaling-cash-flows theory predicts a higher level of CP in companies and industries where future free cash flows are less readily observable by outsiders, free cash is perceived to be good for the company,[54] and other channels for signaling cash flows are blocked or too costly. The fact that pharmaceuticals and technology companies are among the largest donors is consistent with these predictions.[55]

Another empirical pattern I pointed out that could not be reconciled with the existing approaches is that CP – the most discretionary, explicit form of profit sacrificing – has a stronger association with financial performance than other corporate social performance expenditures. The signaling story, by contrast, fits this empirical pattern. Cash donations are more effective signals than operational profit sacrifices; they are more easily communicated and quantifiable to outsiders. And the fact that they benefit unrelated third parties (i.e., are more explicit sacrifices) means that they are perceived as greater handicaps than operational sacrifices.

Relatedly, existing theories cannot explain the dominance of cash over in-kind donations. Traditional profit-enhancing theories predict that in-kind donations would yield better results than cash donations in terms of tax advantages, better bundling of warm glow with intrinsic utility, and stronger consumer preferences. Yet the opposite is observed: cash donations generate better reputational payoffs.[56] Why? I proposed that some of the value enhancement comes from signaling: cash donations are more effective signals because they are easily observable and less open to interpretation.

In recent years, several empirical studies directly tested the signaling hypothesis, and corroborated it. Large-N studies now explicitly state that the signaling hypothesis is a better fit with evidence than the buying goodwill hypothesis.[57] A couple of studies explicitly find that cash donations are more strongly related to better financial performance and firm value than in-kind donations.[58] Several of my other conjectures remain untested, though:

54 Excess cash could be evaluated positively or negatively by investors, depending on multiple factors such as the quality of corporate governance. Stewart C. Myers & Raghuram G. Rajan, *The Paradox of Liquidity*, 113 Q.J. ECON. 733 (1998).

55 For a detailed explanation, see Shapira, *supra* note 4, at 1916–17.

56 *See, e.g.*, Stephen Brammer & Andrew Millington, *Corporate Reputation and Philanthropy: An Empirical Analysis*, 61 J. BUS. ETHICS 29 (2005).

57 *See, e.g.*, Thomas Lys et al., *Signaling through Corporate Accountability Reporting*, 60 J. ACC. & ECON. 56 (2015); Kiyoung Chang et al., *Is There Informational Value in Corporate Giving?* 152 *J.* BUS. ETHICS 473 (2016); Hao Liang & Luc Renneboog, *Corporate Donations and Shareholder Value*, 33 OXFORD REV. ECON. POL'Y 278 (2017).

58 Liang & Rosenberg, *id*; Chang et al., *id*.

whether conspicuous philanthropic activity attracts hedge funds activism, whether companies operating in an environment with high levels of asymmetric information signal in multiple channels (e.g., both dividends and CP), and so on. These remain avenues for potential future research.

5.4 CP AS A CO-OPTATION MECHANISM

After examining how CP can be good for the company, let us now understand how CP can also be bad for the company. The existing accounts of the negative sides of CP usually adopt an agency–costs perspective, claiming that managers use shareholders' money to donate to their own pet charities. While it is not contested that CP is driven to some extent by managerial–utility considerations, there is still a lively debate around the extent, and the implications. We enrich this debate by introducing an oft-ignored distinction between profit-sacrificing expenditures that merely *reflect* agency costs, and those that actually *aggravate* agency costs. CP is not really bad for the company if it merely reflects existing problems. It starts being a problem once managers can use their discretion over CP money to weaken corporate governance.

5.4.1 *Motivating Examples*

It is best to start with a concrete example that illustrates the distinction between problem-reflecting and problem-generating CP: juxtaposing the infamous cases of Occidental Petroleum Co. (Oxy) and Enron. Oxy donated more than $85 million (a third of its annual profits) to a museum named after Armand Hammer, its soon-to-retire CEO. Enron was much more modest; the company donated between $1 and $2 million to a medical center headed by a member of the board audit committee, and several hundred thousand to a think tank that employed another independent director.[59] Usually, agency explanations of CP lump both instances together. In both cases, decision makers used discretion over corporate profit-sacrificing money to satisfy the preferences of top management. Seen from this angle, the Oxy case is much more detrimental to company and shareholder interests simply because the sacrifice is larger.

[59] Kahn v. Sullivan, 594 A.2d 48 (Del. 1991) (containing an analysis of the Oxy CP decision); Stuart L. Gillan & John D. Martin, *Financial Engineering, Corporate Governance, and the Collapse of Enron* 49 tbl.6 (Univ. of Del. Coll. of Bus. & Econ., Working Paper No. 2002-001, 2002), *available at* http://papers.ssrn.com/sol3/papers.cfm?abstract_id=354040 (examples of Enron's CP policy).

But is it really more problematic? In Oxy's case, the donation was disclosed, as the amount was material enough to mandate disclosure under the securities laws. No adverse impact on stock prices was observed when the sacrifice was announced,[60] perhaps because the market already anticipated that Armand Hammer controlled the board and could pass decisions on whatever other types of profit sacrificing that he pleased. Arguably, no agency costs were created because of this donation; it only reflected existing agency costs.

By contrast, Enron consistently pursued a CP policy that undermined the checks and balances on corporate governance. Perhaps not surprisingly, its donations were not disclosed. The direct hit to the financial bottom line from those donations was insignificant, but what mattered more than the levels of the donations were the targets of the donations. The choice of targets made it somewhat less likely that the CEO would be asked tough questions later. In my view, these latter types of donations represent a corporate governance problem justifying legal intervention even more than the former type of pure self-aggrandizement.

The Enron case illustrates the possibility that managers will use their discretion to sacrifice profits to entrench themselves and weaken the mechanisms that monitor them. It therefore pokes holes in the existing debate. A generic objection to the "CP-is-bad-for-the-company" arguments rests on a "fixed appropriation" logic. Say a manager used company's money to donate to her favorite charity. Such a donation does *not* hurt shareholders, as long as we assume managerial discretion is capped by market and/or contractual mechanisms. If managerial discretion is not limitless, then increased use of discretion to sacrifice profits prosocially may come at the expense of other managerial expenditures, such as executive pay and perks. Benefits that managers achieve through CP will offset other forms of managerial appropriation.[61] Scholars have attacked the fixed appropriation argument on various grounds.[62] What the Enron example illustrates is a different (nonexclusive) rebuttal: CP as co-optation, to which we turn next.

5.4.2 *Mechanisms of Co-optation*

Managerial discretion in an unregulated channel like CP can be used to co-opt those in charge of monitoring. Let us focus on three governance

60 R. Franklin Balotti & James J. Hanks, Jr., *Giving at the Office: A Reappraisal of Charitable Contributions by Corporations*, 54 Bus. Law. 965, 990 n.161 (1999).
61 *See, e.g.*, Elhauge, *supra* note 5, at 835–39.
62 Shapira, *supra* note 4, at 1920 (providing a summary).

mechanisms: using CP money to co-opt independent directors, influence politicians, and ally with activist stakeholders.

The first channel through which CP can generate agency costs is co-optation of board independence. The point here is that managers use CP not merely to donate to their own pet charities, but also to donate to the pet charities of those who are supposed to monitor the mangers. This pattern is not limited to the Enron case. Look to other postmortem analyses of failed governance mechanisms and you will find similar tactics in play. Ross Johnson did it at RJR Nabisco,[63] Conrad Black at Hollinger,[64] and Dennis Kozlowski at Tyco,[65] to name but a few. As board independence has become a governance panacea,[66] the attractiveness of CP as a backdoor channel to influence directors without losing their "independent" tag will likely only increase.[67]

A second mechanism that makes CP a corporate governance issue is the use of money designated as CP to influence politics. The ability and willingness of corporations to use CP in politics is especially relevant today. In the aftermath of the *Citizens United v. FEC*[68] decision, there has been a lively discussion in Congress, the SEC, and legal academia on the need to introduce protective mechanisms for explicit political spending. Not enough attention, however, has been directed to the possibility of bypassing protective mechanisms through corporate donations to tax-exempt "charitable" organizations that serve as conduits for political influence; that is, implicit political spending. CP is relatively unregulated, so managers have incentives to couch political spending as CP in order to evade restrictions on explicit political donations.

The means exist to effectuate this managerial will. While under IRC § 501 (c)(3) nonprofit organizations may not legally engage in political activity, there is ample room to characterize political activity as "educational," thus maintaining an organization's tax-exempt status. Two notable ways to engage in politicized CP are: first, funding think tanks that qualify as educational organizations while de facto supporting very specific policies or politicians.

63 Bryan Burrough & John Helyar, Barbarians at the Gate 82, 97 (1990).

64 Report of Investigation by the Special Committee of the Board of Directors of Hollinger International Inc. 409–25 (Aug. 30, 2004), *available at* www.sec.gov/Archives/edgar/data/868512/000095012304010413/y01437exv99w2.htm, at 419 tbl.15.

65 Michael J. Bohnen & David M. Phillips, *Corporate Gifts Should Be Disclosed*, Chron. Philanthropy, Mar. 21, 2002, at 39.

66 Yaron Nili, *Out of Sight out of Mind: The Case for Improving Director Independence Disclosure*, 43 J. Corp. Law. 35, 46 (2017).

67 *Cf.* Lucian A. Bebchuk & Jesse Fried, Pay Without Performance: The Unfulfilled Promise of Executive Compensation 29 (2004).

68 130 S. Ct. 876 (2010).

And, second, supporting classic advocacy organizations (also known as § 501 (c)(4) organizations) with CP money, through the "c3/c4 split" (i.e., lobbying organizations establishing a complementary tax-exempt entity that is heavily funded by corporations).[69] Indeed, a recent strand of empirical studies managed to spotlight the usage of covert political activities.[70] One study in particular shows that firms use charitable contributions through their foundations as a tax-exempt lobbying mechanism. The use of CP as lobbying, they conclude, amounts to over $1 billion a year – much more than lobbying through political action committees (PACs).[71]

A separate question is whether usage of CP as a covert political influence mechanism is bad for shareholders. If insiders use their clout over politicians to further favorable policies, then society as a whole may suffer, but the shareholders of a given company may actually value the purchase of political clout with CP money. Yet managers can also use political donations to further narrow, managerial interests, such as lowering investor protection. Consider the case of managerial lobbying for anti-takeover legislation. When Dayton Hudson, a Minnesota corporation, became a target for takeover in 1987, the managers convinced the state to hold a special legislative session where the company's charitable record was used as consideration for enacting a new anti-takeover bill.[72] More generally, when diversified shareholders hold the market portfolio, and managers use CP money to purchase policies that favor one company at the expense of another, then CP expenditures amount to a transfer with deadweight costs.[73]

A third, less intuitive use of CP to generate further agency costs is as a subtle anti-takeover mechanism. Managers can invest strategically in profit sacrificing in order to gain support from activists, such as consumer groups or public pension funds. Those activists are then expected to return the favor by reducing the probability of CEO turnover. Even if a potential raider can increase

[69] Frances R. Hill, *Corporate Philanthropy and Campaign Finance: Exempt Organizations as Corporate-Candidate Conduits*, 41 N.Y.L. Sch. L. Rev. 881, 908–11, 922 n.197, 928 (1997); Kahn, *supra* note 23, at 636–62.

[70] On the covert political activity literature more generally, see Timothy Werner, *Investor Reaction to Covert Corporate Political Activity*, 38 Strat. Mgmt. J. 2424 (2017).

[71] Marianne Bertrand et al., *Tax-Exempt Lobbying: Corporate Philanthropy as a Tool for Political Influence* (Mar. 14, 2018), www.nber.org/papers/w24451.

[72] For an elaborate discussion of the role Dayton Hudson's CP policy played in influencing the legislation, see Harvard Bus. Sch. Case Study No. 9-391-403, Dayton Hudson Corporation: Conscience and Control (A, B, C) (1990). For other examples, see Faith Stevelman Kahn, *Legislatures, Courts and the SEC: Reflections on Silence and Power in Corporate and Securities Law*, 41 N.Y.L. Sch. L. Rev. 1107, 1140 n.126 (1997); Kahn, *supra* note 23, at 633–34.

[73] *Cf.* Robert H. Sitkoff, *Corporate Political Speech, Political Extortion, and the Competition for Corporate Charters*, 69 U. Chi. L. Rev. 1103, 1117 (2002).

a company's value, activist stakeholders will have incentives to keep incumbent managers in place, as long as incumbents credibly commit to continue investing in specific social or environmental issues. Activists can use nonconventional "voice" mechanisms – mounting a media campaign, threatening boycotts, or using their political clout – to support incumbents and fend off takeovers.

The empirical studies that support the prosociality as entrenchment hypothesis[74] focus on operational profit sacrificing (as in moving to a greener production to appease environmental groups). For our purposes, the question is can managers gain personal favor with activists also by donating to charity? Anecdotal evidence suggests they can.[75] In the Minnesota anti-takeover bill, for example, Dayton Hudson's CP policy was not merely touted as valuable; the incumbents also called upon the company's grantees – apparently key players in the state – to help promote managerial lobbying efforts.[76] More generally, the CP-as-co-optation idea can explain why firms with independent boards donate more. If profit sacrificing is a managerial perk, then arguably managers who are monitored by independent boards should engage in it less. But if CP is not only self-aggrandizing but also entrenching, then managerial-driven CP should only increase when internal governance is stronger (e.g., when boards are more independent). Under a greater internal threat to their authority, managers need to invest more in maintaining influence (a demand-side explanation). Unregulated managerial discretion over prosocial expenditures is therefore more likely to be used in such contexts as another tool to influence key players, whose support managers need more when threatened from within.

*

Throughout this book, our analysis has followed two steps: understanding how reputation works in a given market, and then examining how the law affects reputation. This chapter has focused thus far on the first prong: how reputational incentives push companies to engage in CP. We now move to the second prong: how the law shapes both the signaling and co-optation aspects of CP behavior.

74 Giovanni Cespa & Giacinta Cestone, *Corporate Social Responsibility and Managerial Entrenchment*, 16 J. Econ. & Mgmt. Strategy 741 (2007) (setting a model); Jordi Surroca & Josep A. Tribó, *Managerial Entrenchment and Corporate Social Performance*, 35 J. Bus. Fin. & Acct. 748 (2008) (empirical testing of the model).

75 *See, e.g.*, Joseph Galaskiewicz, *An Urban Grants Economy Revisited: Corporate Charitable Contributions in the Twin Cities, 1979–81, 1987–89*, 42 Admin. Sci. Q. 445 (1997) (managers using CP money to get involved in the social circles of NGO leaders, forming a bond).

76 Jerome L. Himmelstein, Looking Good and Doing Good: Corporate Philanthropy and Corporate Power 129 (1997).

5.5 HOW THE LAW AFFECTS CP: THE CASE FOR DISCLOSURE

Legal systems across the world have afforded wide discretion to corporate managers to sacrifice profits in the public interest, while very few protective mechanisms apply. In the United States, for example, companies do not even have to disclose their CP activity. This legal treatment may have been a consequence of viewing the buying goodwill mechanism as extremely simple: companies donate because stakeholders like the fact that companies donate. Companies can increase profits by acting philanthropically, and if CP increases profits, then there is no need to intervene. Nonexistent legal regulation may also be a consequence of a simplified view of the critical accounts of CP as agency costs. The agency approach assumes that managers will always have some discretionary resources to spend as they wish, as totally eliminating agency costs is simply too costly (monitoring managers is imperfect). Given this level of discretionary resources at the managers' disposal, it should be of no consequence to shareholder value whether managers choose to spend on their preferred charity or on traveling in luxurious company jets. Moreover, the understanding goes, these expenditures are insignificant in dollar terms and thus do not merit intervention.

Yet once we introduce the CP-as-signaling and the CP-as-co-optation approaches, the case for some form of intervention – particularly, mandatory disclosure – becomes stronger. As this section shows, here as well, legal intervention can actually facilitate better reputational control of the positive and negative aspects of CP. Section 5.1.1 details the existing legal structure for regulating CP, in the United States and elsewhere. Section 5.1.2 then clarifies what we should not do, namely, ban CP. Section 5.1.3 provides the case for what we should do: implement some form of mandatory disclosure. Section 5.1.4 offers some political economy thoughts on why past efforts to legislate disclosure requirements have failed.

5.5.1 *The Existing Regime: a Regulatory Vacuum*

The reputation-through-litigation story does not apply in the corporate niceness context, simply because there is very little litigation. In most developed countries, the law grants corporations the power to engage in philanthropy, and allows managers wide discretion in exercising this power.[77] Only rarely do

[77] For the American perspective, see Elhauge, *supra* note 5, at 867–68. A notable exception comes from India, where, starting in 2014, the law mandates that companies spend above

shareholders challenge management's decision to donate. When they do, the courts are quick to assume that managers decided to donate with some long-term benefit for the company in mind.[78] And donating to charity would not constitute "waste," because managers can practically always justify profit sacrifices by alluding to some indirect benefit.

To the extent that the law affects reputational incentives to donate, it does so through a different channel: not litigation but rather disclosure rules. Some countries have installed detailed disclosure rules, requiring companies to reveal the amounts they donated, or the beneficiaries.[79] The United States, by contrast, does not subject CP to a specific disclosure requirement.[80] The only resemblance of disclosure requirements comes from private ordering: the top stock exchanges demand that a listed company that donates over a certain amount to a charity affiliated with an independent director disclose this contribution.[81] Yet such soft-law requirements are rarely enforced.

The upshot is that CP practices exist in the United States in a regulatory vacuum. The laws evolved to grant wide discretion to sacrifice profits prosocially, without affording investors the means to control this discretion, such as by mandatory disclosure or a shareholder vote.[82] Armed with insights on the circumstances under which CP can be either good or bad for the company, we can now assess whether not regulating at all is optimal. Here as well, there are two layers to the optimality question: how the law affects behavior directly, by

a certain threshold on CSR. Other countries, such as Indonesia and the Philippines, have their own versions of mandating some form of CSR. Rajat Panwar et al., *Legislated CSR: A Brief Introduction*, *in* BUSINESS AND SOCIETY 360, VOL. 2: CORPORATE SOCIAL RESPONSIBILITY 133, 134–36 (2018).

78 For the classic American cases, see Kahn v. Sullivan, 594 A.2d 48 (Del. 1991); Theodora Holding Corp. v. Henderson, 257 A.2d 398 (Del. Ch. 1969); A.P. Smith Mfg. Co. v. Barlow, 98 A.2d 581 (N.J. 1953); Union Pac. R.R. v. Trustees, Inc., 329 P.2d 398 (Utah 1958).

79 Notable examples include Denmark, France, Israel, the United Arab Emirates, Australia, and China. *See, e.g.*, Panwar, *supra* note 77, at 134–35.

80 CP is not captured by the general disclosure criteria either: because donations are almost never significant in terms of their size relative to the company's resources, they are not captured by the materiality requirements of the securities laws or accounting standards. Balotti & Hanks, *supra* note 60, at 989; Kahn, *supra* note 23, at 582–83 nn.7–8. Further, a shareholder cannot employ his right to inspect the books to learn about her company's CP practices. Narrow interpretation of such statutory rights deems them inapplicable for attaining CP information. Kahn, *Reflections*, *supra* note 72, at 1132–33.

81 NYSE, INC., LISTED COMPANY MANUAL § 303A.02(b), *available at* http://nysemanual.nyse.com/LCMTools/PlatformViewer.asp?selectednode=chp_1_4&manual=%2Flcm%2Fsections%2Flcm-sections%2F. My 2012 paper (*supra* note 4) explains at length why even this requirement is a watered-down version, and how both NYSE and NASDAQ rarely enforce these requirements.

82 Kahn, *Reflections*, *supra* note 72, at 1146.

sanctioning certain behaviors, and how the law affects behavior indirectly, by producing information.

5.5.2 *The Case against Banning CP*

Would we be better off with a legal regime that directly intervenes and bans CP? The answer is clearly no. The body of literature studying the link between CP and the financial bottom line tells us there at the minimum there is no financial penalty for CP. A blanket legal ban cannot be justified on economic grounds.

The next option to consider is a targeted ban: sanctioning certain types of CP behaviors. After all, we saw that certain CP practices do not enhance company's value but rather benefit managers at shareholders' expense. Those opposing legal intervention frequently respond that, while some donations are indeed about managerial self-aggrandizement, those are only isolated cases of relatively small magnitude that do not merit intervention. Yet, Section 5.4 shed light on the problems that arise from continuing to ignore CP. In the subset of cases in which managerial-driven CP not only reflects existing agency costs but also generates additional agency costs, the case for legal intervention is much stronger. Failure to address agency problems in CP decisions might make it more difficult to address agency problems in other corporate decisions.

But is it really feasible to target and ban those CP decisions that are bad for the company and allow all others? Probably not. Our discussion of the signaling benefits of CP highlights how a targeted ban may be impractical and unwarranted. Shareholders and courts will have a hard time distinguishing profit-enhancing from profit-reducing donations. Sacrificing profits may still be value enhancing, if it constitutes a handicap – a costly signal that mitigates asymmetric information. Attempting to eliminate bad CP decisions based on the existence of clear signs of quid pro quo, or professed insiders' motivations, is therefore futile.

Still, it is one thing to refrain from direct interference with CP decisions (as we should), and another to leave CP in a regulatory vacuum (as we should not). The optimal regulation of CP seems to be leaving profit-sacrificing discretion to managers, while helping the market check managerial discretion, by providing some form of mandatory disclosure.

5.5.3 *The Case for Disclosure*

The lack of any substantive disclosure requirement in the United States is not due to omission. Proposals for legislation have been brought up frequently in

Congress and the corporate and securities law literature starting in the 1990s.[83] Yet those proposals, even the modest ones, never made it into law.[84] By delving into the legislative history of these proposed disclosure bills, we can distill the arguments made against disclosure into three categories: (1) the direct costs of implementing disclosure; (2) the expected chilling effect on overall CP; and (3) the marginal benefits of regulated disclosure – the relevant information is already public and/or no one is interested in it. A closer look reveals that all three arguments are shaky.

The first argument invokes the costs of compiling and disseminating data. Yet in practice, introducing a new disclosure requirement will not add significantly to the mix of costs already incurred. Firms are required to report the levels and targets of certain donations to the IRS, so no compiling costs would be added.[85] Since large firms disseminate information about their prosocial behavior to the public via company websites and separate, lengthy CSR reports, no disseminating costs will be added either.

The second argument suggests that disclosure will decrease the overall levels of CP. Managers will simply steer away from the unwanted distraction that may come with disclosure, and keep their CP engagement to minimum. Any benefits that shareholders may get from sunlight disinfecting bad CP decisions will be dwarfed by the negative impact that too much sun will have on the nonprofit sector. I elaborated elsewhere on why such chilling-effect argument is inconsistent with logic.[86] Let us focus here on why it is also inconsistent with evidence. While the United States never experienced mandatory CP disclosure, other countries had, and we can tap their experience for evidence on the real-world consequences of enacting disclosure.

The Israeli experience, for example, suggests that requiring disclosure results in *ratcheting up* CP levels rather than chilling them. In 2001, the Israeli Securities Authority (ISA) introduced a new reporting requirement, requiring firms to disclose in their annual reports (in the directors' report section) the amount of money given to charities, as well as the strategy behind to whom did they donate. Following the new regulation, firms disclosed more and, importantly, actually donated more.[87] Further, media coverage of CP

83 See the representative proposal in H.R. 3745, 107th Cong. (2d Sess. 2002), which was later duplicated in subsequent Congresses. *See also* Barnard, *supra* note 12, at 1169–70.

84 For example, the House of Representatives version of the Sarbanes–Oxley Act contained a CP-disclosure requirement, but it was omitted from the final Act. *See* H.R. 3763, 107th Cong. § 7 (2d Sess. 2002).

85 Kahn, *supra* note 23, at 586 n.20.

86 Shapira, *supra* note 4, at 1929–30.

87 Yaron Elad & Nir Zichlinski, *Reporting on Donations in the Board Report – 31.12.2003 – the Beginning of a New Era* (a BDO-Haft study, 2004) [*in Hebrew*].

numbers and policies increased, and the first CSR ratings was established.[88] The head of the ISA summed its experience with CP reporting in retrospect thusly: "[mandating CP disclosure] promoted a 'competition' among publicly-traded firms, whereby they increased their social involvement."[89]

The UK experience completes the picture, by providing us with a glimpse into what happens when a country shifts from a mandatory- to a voluntary-disclosure regime. After the regulator dropped the mandatory disclosure requirement of CP in 2013, companies disclosed less, and, importantly, donated less.[90] Both the Israeli and the UK example suggest that requiring disclosure of CP actually ramps up, rather than chills, overall CP levels.

The third recurring objection to requiring disclosure of CP posits that investors simply are not interested in information about CP, and those investors who are interested can assemble the relevant pieces of public information without needing regulatory intervention. In support of this claim, opponents of disclosure invoke the relative dearth of shareholder litigation and proposals on the matter. But all we can really conclude from such evidence is that shareholders are not interested in the information currently available. Naturally, the abuse of profit-sacrificing expenditures will not be disclosed voluntarily, so shareholders and regulators cannot act upon them *ex ante*. A more relevant question is whether the managers of Enron and RJR Nabisco could have freely used CP as a co-optation device if there had been a disclosure requirement in place at the time.[91] And as for learning everything investors need to know from existing public reports, it is true that by now virtually all large companies generate detailed CSR reports, yet these reports achieve no real transparency.[92] In an uninformative "cheap talk" environment, practically all companies profess to be nice, and no manager professes to abuse CP money to entrench herself, so outsiders cannot distinguish between nice guys and pretenders.

The upshot is that some form of regulated disclosure could better align CP practices with shareholder value. Firms cannot be expected to voluntarily

88 Moshe Terry, *Public Companies and Reporting on Involvement in the Community*, Sept. 9, 2003 (An address by the head of Israel Securities Authority, detailing the experience with the new CP disclosure requirement) [*in Hebrew*].

89 Moshe Terry, *Reporting Requirements of Public Firms Regarding Environmental Issues*, Nov. 11, 2005 [*in Hebrew*].

90 Nava Cohen, How Do Firms Respond to a Shift from Mandatory to Voluntary Disclosure? Evidence from Corporate Charitable Donations Disclosures in the UK (working paper, 2018), *available at* www.semanticscholar.org/paper/How-do-firms-respond-to-a-shift-from-mandatory-to-Cohen/c812ed0f9d457fad1d759e9717375db7f38d53d8#extracted.

91 Kahn, *Reflections*, *supra* note 72, at 1123–24.

92 *Cf.* Michael E. Porter & Mark R. Kramer, *Strategy & Society: The Link between Competitive Advantage and Corporate Social Responsibility*, HARV. BUS. REV., Dec. 2006, at 81.

provide sufficient and comparable information on their prosocial activities, due to agency and coordination problems.[93]

Agency problems mean that, when left on their own, insiders will have incentives to provide biased disclosure, whether by exaggerating the positive aspects of donations or by camouflaging the negative aspects. Mandatory disclosure could serve as an early warning by flushing out cases of self-aggrandizement, as well as reducing the ability of managers to use CP as a co-optation device.

Coordination problems mean that when each firm makes its individual, voluntary disclosure decisions, it does not take into account the positive externalities that come from producing information that facilitates comparisons to other firms. Mandatory disclosure could standardize both the form and the substance of the information, thereby allowing comparing among different companies' donations, and increasing the value of information to outsiders.

For all these reasons, I do not take the direct-costs objection, the chilling-effect objection, or the no-one-cares objection seriously. Yet there is another, valid objection to requiring CP disclosure, namely, the risk of *overwhelming investors with information*. Proposing disclosure is too easy of a solution, for academics and policymakers alike, across all types of issues. As a result, the market is already bombarded with disclosure requirements of various kinds. At the same time, the attention span and cognitive capacities of intended audiences do not expand – they remain bounded. Therefore, any piece of added mandatory disclosure, even if valuable in end of itself, crowds out attention to an existing disclosure in another area, perhaps even more valuable. In other words, adding disclosure requirements come with negative externalities, which should be weighed against the presumed benefits of said disclosure.[94]

Yet, acknowledging the already-existing flow of social responsibility information discredits the "information overload" argument as well. On the contrary, because the mass of public information is currently presented in a distorted, nonstandardized, and nontransparent manner (anecdotes instead of comparable numbers, forcing readers to wind through the maze of long CSR reports), any requirement that companies publicize a standardized and concise form, such as a single number of overall donations, will not muddy the waters but rather crystallize them.

93 *Cf.* Reinier Kraakman et al., The Anatomy of Corporate Law 278–79 (2d ed. 2009).

94 *See generally* Omri Ben-Shahar & Carl E. Schneider, More Than You Wanted to Know: The Failure of Mandated Disclosure (2014).

5.5.4 *How Come Disclosure Proposals Never Made It into Law?*

Given that the commonly raised objections to disclosure do not have enough merit, why do proposals that would require disclosure of CP continue to be rejected? While this was not the original focus of my research, I came out with a surprising political economy story based on personal interviews I conducted, and reading congressional hearings: among those pushing against disclosure were the charitable organizations themselves.

While some nonprofit organizations publicly supported disclosure, leaders of the mainstream foundations and associations were vocal in their resistance. Publicly, they professed their concern that disclosure would yield a chilling effect (an objection we dismissed above). But perhaps there is a cynical flavor to their opposition: what those players care about might not be the level of overall CP, but rather the share of CP directed at their own specific nonprofits. They might fear that disclosure would hinder their advantage in influencing corporate insiders behind closed doors.

From the point of view of the third sector as a group, however, regulated disclosure would likely improve things. In the existing unregulated disclosure regime, companies that actually invest heavily in prosociality find it hard to distinguish themselves from those who merely pretend to be generous. This cheap-talk environment leads insiders to invest in marketing rather than actual philanthropic impact. In other words, prosocial activities are picked for their window-dressing value. Some form of regulated disclosure could lead to less cacophony, and less cacophony could lead to more incentives to engage in meaningful prosocial profit sacrificing.

*

Overall, the corporate governance concerns raised by CP should not be overstated. There are other agency problems more urgent than misuse of prosocial discretion. The legal system does not need to interfere too much with existing practices. At the same time, misuses of CP could be indicative of agency problems and, when used in tandem with other co-optation devices, could generate agency problems. Introducing a limited form of the less restrictive protective mechanism – mandatory disclosure – may therefore be the best option. Whatever form of regulation is introduced, careful attention has to be paid to its expressive aspects. Intervention should be couched as not interfering with voluntary sacrifices and not taming corporate prosociality, so as not to crowd out motivations and erode benefits arising from signaling.[95]

*

The argument against disclosure run into a common flaw that we have seen throughout this book in various context: not accounting enough for how laws affect reputational concerns. While corporate prosociality is very much a product of reputational incentives, these reputational forces do not operate in a vacuum. They are rather influenced by the existing legal regime. The law dictates the quantity and quality of information on CP activities. Without a background of legal standards governing prosocial disclosure, reputational forces are limited in their ability to ensure that companies engage meaningfully in prosocial activities and report accurately.[96] For reputational forces to work their magic, they need legal control of the flow of information. Particularly, they need a one-two punch: *ex ante* regulation requiring standardized reporting of form and substance, and *ex post* liability threat for falsely communicating or failing to report. Injecting some form of legal control would increase the threat of reputational sanctions for managers abusing CP expenditures, as well as the promise of reputational rewards, allowing firms to credibly commit to prosociality with real impact.[97]

5.6 FINAL THOUGHTS: CORPORATE PHILANTHROPY AS A REPUTATIONAL BUFFER

While this chapter focused on how CSR helps companies reap reputational *rewards*, much of the writing on CSR over the past decade has focused on the

[95] *Cf.* Eric A. Posner, Law and Social Norms 176 (2000) (noting that external intervention can cause unintended consequences, such as pushing signalers to signal in a worse way, or to stop signaling and pool).

[96] Similarly, intermediaries – who compile data and rank companies based on their corporate social performance – cannot be assumed to produce satisfying results on their own without standardization of metrics, credible third-party liability threat, or access to comparable information. *See* Jason Scott Johnston, *Signaling Social Responsibility: On the Law and Economics of Market Incentives for Corporate Environmental Performance* (John F. Kennedy Sch. of Gov't, Harvard Univ., Corp. Soc. Responsibility Initiative Working Paper No. 14, 2005), *available at* www.hks.harvard.edu/m-rcbg/CSRI/publications/workingpaper_14_johnston.pdf.

[97] At the risk of stating the obvious, it should be emphasized that disclosure cannot be treated as a panacea for all negative aspects of CP. I elaborated elsewhere on the remaining concerns. Shapira, *supra* note 4, at 144–45.

other side, namely, how CSR serves as a buffer against reputational *sanctions*. When stakeholders perceive company X as nice, they will give it the benefit of a doubt when bad news breaks, or so the argument goes. Recall the Odwalla contaminated juice story crisis from Chapter 2: because the company had a preexisting image of a do-gooder, stakeholders believed that top management could not have prevented the harm, and the reputational fallout was initially contained.

However, careful studies have questioned the CSR-as-buffer argument. Prior nice-guy reputation works as a buffer only in limited scenarios. It may provide you with the initial benefit of a doubt, but it only lasts that long: if credible damning information about you comes out, it will violate stakeholders' high expectations from you, and the reputational sanction will actually be bigger.[98] Further, bad news about a nice company would attract more media coverage and NGOs, because of the man-bite-dog aspect to it.[99]

From our perspective, the interesting question is how the law shapes companies' incentives to engage in CP to minimize reputation risk. We can point out three potential effects.

First, the legal system can shape the baseline tradeoffs, between investing in CP as a reputational buffer and reducing one's legal and reputational risk in other ways. To illustrate, consider the case of a chemical company that stumbles upon a profitable-yet-dangerous chemical, and faces a choice between investing in abatement measures *ex ante*, and investing in a nice-guy buffer that will supposedly limit the reputational fallout *ex post* (once bad news about the pollution breaks).[100] The higher the expected legal sanction, the more the company has incentives to invest in actual abatement of pollution instead of buffering reputational fallouts.

Second, the law can determine whether the nice-guy image serves as a buffer or more as an amplifier. When bad news breaks about a supposedly

98 Brayden G. King & Mary Hunter McDonnell, *Good Firms, Good Targets: The Relationship among Corporate Social Responsibility, Reputation, and Activist Targeting, in Corporate Social Responsibility in a Globalizing World* 430 (2015); Michael Jensen et al., *Meeting Expectations: A Role-Theoretic Perspective on Reputation, in* The Oxford Handbook of Corporate Reputation (Barnett & Pollock eds., 2012) (on violations of role expectations more generally).

99 Julian F. Kolbel, Timo Busch & Leonhardt M. Jancso, *How Media Coverage of Corporate Social Responsibility Increases Financial Risk*, 38 Strategic Mgmt. J. 2266, 2281 (2017); W. Timothy Coombs, *Situational Theory of Crisis: Situational Crisis Communication Theory and Corporate Reputation, in* The Handbook of Communication and Corporate Reputation 265 (Carroll, ed., 2014).

100 Roy Shapira & Luigi Zingales, *Is Pollution Value-Maximizing? The DuPont Case* (Nat'l Bureau of Econ. Research, Working Paper No. 23866, 2017), www.nber.org/papers/w23866.

nice company, that company can build on its preexisting reputational cache and try to convince stakeholders to give it the benefit of a doubt. Yet, the sooner litigation and regulatory investigations start producing information about what and how things happened, the less this benefit of a doubt lasts, and the more likely it is that stakeholders will view what happened as a violation of their expectations.

Finally and similarly to our analysis in Section 5.5, the legal system affects the CP-as-buffer dynamics via disclosure rules. In a country with an effective disclosure regime, which facilitates standardization and comparisons, companies have incentives to go beyond mere appearance management and truly become more socially responsible, so as not to be exposed as hypocrite and have their investment in CP turns into a double-edged sword.

You probably sense the overarching theme by now. In all three channels, when legal deterrence is nonexistent, appearance management becomes key; but when legal deterrence matters, appearance management is not enough. In other words, the more effective legal deterrence is, the less effective CSR becomes as a window-dressing reputational buffer.

6

Regulators' Reputation

6.1 INTRODUCTION

Can judicial review effectively check regulators' behaviors? The answer largely depends on how regulators behave – what motivates them. If, as in traditional economic theory, regulators mostly maximize their narrow self-interest, then there is little that judicial review can do to stop regulatory capture. Judges may invalidate specific regulatory decisions after the fact, but they cannot overcome the inherent advantages that special interests enjoy in the way of offering lucrative future business opportunities or campaign financing. If, however, regulators care not just about material incentives, but also about their reputation, then judicial review can shape regulators' behavior indirectly, by providing information on how regulators behave. Regardless of whether courts intervene and strike down specific regulatory decisions or not, the process of litigation can generate reputational pressures that propel the regulators to change their behavior. Judicial review mitigates the risks of regulatory capture not so much through modifying regulators' material incentives, but rather through *shaping the public's perceptions of regulators*.

In other words, the gist of this book's main argument applies not just in the context of corporate reputation, but also in the context of regulators' reputation. A burgeoning political science literature empirically documents that regulators care about reputation and proactively react to what the media writes about them. With this literature as our background, we can ask the prior question, of what shapes the media agenda. What regulatory issues the media will cover? How it will cover them? In the regulatory arena, much like in the business world, a large part of the answer is the legal system. Litigation produces information that shapes what we think about regulators.

The most intuitive channel for information about regulators is administrative litigation, which implicates regulatory behavior directly, as in requiring the regulator to provide detailed explanations for why she decided the way she did. A less intuitive channel is private litigation, which implicates regulatory behavior indirectly, as in when a tort law defendant raises the regulatory compliance defense, and turns the trial into a referendum on the regulator's standard-setting abilities. Information from litigation mitigates the asymmetries that usually exist between the well-informed special interest groups and the hitherto-uninformed dispersed public. It thereby helps the public shame regulators into standing up to powerful interests.

This chapter proceeds in five sections. Section 6.2 synthesizes insights from the burgeoning literature on regulators' reputation concerns. The section explains why the fact that regulators care about reputation does not necessarily mean that they will do a better job in protecting the public interest. There exists an asymmetric monitoring problem: special interest groups are better at monitoring regulators' behaviors and spotlighting mistakes against them, while the dispersed public is often unaware or unable to spotlight mistakes. As a result, counterintuitively, a regulator who cares about her reputation will tend to err on the side of the regulated industry and against the public.

Section 6.3 argues that judicial review mitigates the asymmetric monitoring problem, therefore reducing the risk of regulatory capture. The section emphasizes the importance of reason-giving requirements in facilitating bottom-up monitoring of regulators. At the same time, public litigation is more limited in its ability to affect change via reputational pressures than private litigation, for various reasons that the section details. In most circumstances, then, reputational pressures on regulators will have to come from elsewhere.

This is where Section 6.4 enters, extending the argument by focusing on how private litigation (to which the regulator is not even privy) can affect the regulator's reputation, pushing her to promote the public interest. Section 6.4 maps typical scenarios where private litigants have incentives to generate information that implicates the regulators' behavior. The section then revisits the "regulation through litigation" literature, by emphasizing the distinction between information-producing and reputation-shaping effects.

Section 6.5 sketches policy implications, such as identifying the types of cases where judicial activism makes more sense. Section 6.6 finishes with big-picture observations on the differences between the reputational effects of public law litigation and those of private law litigation.

6.2 REGULATORS' REPUTATION CONCERNS

We can define regulators' reputation in similar fashion to how we defined corporate reputation: the set of beliefs that the regulator's audiences hold regarding her capabilities, performances, and roles.[1] The political science literature examines the questions of *whether* regulators care about their reputation (they do), *why* they care about it (because it helps them secure autonomy and power), and *how* they manage it (by prioritizing salient threats). Yet we still know relatively little about the "so what" question: does the fact that regulators care about reputation mean that they will be more effective, promoting the public interest? Does reputational deterrence work in the regulatory context? This section provides reasons for skepticism. Regulators' reputations may be too noisy and detached from reality to provide optimal deterrence. A regulator who cares about her reputation will not necessarily do a better job promoting the public interest.

6.2.1 *Regulators Care about Reputation*

Answering the first question – *whether* regulators care about reputation – is straightforward: yes. Very much so. With the exception of a few public choice accounts,[2] by now most political scientists acknowledge that regulators care about more than just their narrow self-interest. Regulators want to do a good job. And they want to be *perceived* as doing a good job.[3] When deciding how to design, implement, and enforce policy, regulators frequently consider

1 Daniel P. Carpenter, Reputation and Power: Organizational Image and Pharmaceutical Regulation at the FDA 45 (2010). There are at least two related-yet-distinct notions of regulators' reputation. One is the notion of regulators' career concerns, which is oft-mentioned in the context of the "revolving doors" argument: regulators wish to maximize their future earning opportunities, and this desire affects their behavior while in the public sector. Such labor-market reputation notion is different from the one we use here, which speaks to how regulators seek the positive evaluations and esteem of various audiences, such as those who appoint them or are affected by them, beyond and regardless of future job opportunities. Another important distinction concerns the different effects of reputation at the level of the individual, and reputation at the level of the regulatory agency. We collapse this distinction for our purposes here, for considerations of scope. Brevity and scope also dictate that we lump together all types of regulators – political appointees, "lifer" bureaucrats, and so forth. In reality, reputational concerns operate differently on each type of regulator. But for our modest purposes here, namely, drawing attention to a hitherto-understudied channel of influence on regulators (information coming from the legal system), treating them as a group suffices.

2 David Zaring, *Against Being against the Revolving Door*, 2013 U. Ill. L. Rev. 507, 549 (2013).

3 Clare Leaver, *Bureaucratic Minimal Squawk Behavior: Theory and Evidence from Regulatory Agencies*, 99 Am. Econ. Rev. 572, 572 (2009).

appearances. They think strategically about how their decisions will be perceived by the politicians who appoint them, the public whose interests they are supposed to protect, the industry whom they are supposed to monitor, and so on.

A fast-emerging literature dubbed BRT (for "bureaucratic reputation theory") has shifted attention to the second question, namely, *how* regulators care about reputation. The BRT literature empirically documents how regulators proactively manage their reputations, and prioritize their responses to external signals/ criticisms.[4] For example, some studies show that regulators react differently based on the *content* of the allegations they are facing: prioritizing allegations of under-regulating over allegations of over-regulating.[5] Other studies show that regulators react differently based on the *visibility* of allegations: they prioritize addressing criticisms that make it to front-page media coverage.[6] The BRT literature also documents the arsenal that regulators employ in managing their reputation: they can react to external threats by changing their enforcement decisions, or by changing their communication strategy. Within their communication strategy, under certain conditions regulators respond to allegations by keeping silent, while under other conditions they are more likely to openly address allegations.

We can also tap the BRT literature for insights on the third question, namely, *why* exactly regulators care so much about reputation. Regulators carefully manage their reputation not just due to concerns about higher prestige and status. A good reputation provides regulators with more autonomy and discretion.[7] It buffers them from political attacks, and helps them secure higher budgets.[8] After all, politicians are more likely to vest resources and authority in regulators who are perceived to be expert and effective. Further, an agency that enjoys a good reputation can recruit and retain higher-quality

4 For an overview, *see* Moshe Maor, *Theorizing Bureaucratic Reputation, in* Organizational Reputation in the Public Sector (Waeraas & Maor eds. 2014).

5 Sharon Gilad et al., *Organizational Reputation, Regulatory Task and Strategic Silence*, 23 J. Public Adm. Res. Theory 581 (2013).

6 Daniel P. Carpenter, *Groups, the Media, Agency Waiting Costs, and FDADrug Approval*, 46 Am. J. Pol. Sci. 490 (2002) (showing that the FDA reviews new drugs quicker when the disease treated by these drugs are more commonly covered by the media); Moshe Maor & Raanan Solitzeanu-Kenan, *The Effect of Salient Reputational Threats on the Pace of FDAEnforcement*, 26 Governance 31 (2013).

7 Jason A. MacDonald & William W. Franko, Jr., *Bureaucratic Capacity and Bureaucratic Discretion: Does Congress Tie Policy Authority to Performance?* 35 Am. Pol. Res. 790 (2007) (providing statistical, large-N evidence); Daniel P. Carpenter, The Forging of Bureaucratic Autonomy: Reputations, Networks, and Policy Innovation in Executive Agencies, 1862–1928 (2001) (providing historical case studies).

8 Carpenter, *supra* note 1, at 53–56.

public servants. And an individual regulator who enjoys good reputation is more likely to secure promotions. Good reputation also helps regulators with their interactions with the industry they are supposed to regulate or the consumer groups they are meant to protect.[9]

Still, one interesting question remains understudied: what does it mean that regulators care about their reputation? How do regulators' reputation concerns affect regulatory behavior? Political scientists too often allude to regulators' reputation concerns positively, as a trump card against arguments of regulatory capture.[10] These scholars *assume* that the need to maintain a good reputation imposes discipline on regulators. A regulator who cares about her reputation would think twice before conceding to special interests, out of fear that the deal she strikes with them will be exposed and her reputation lost, or so the argument goes. Regulators are aware of the old adage: it takes years to build a strong reputation, but one revealed misbehavior to destroy it. As a result, they will be extra careful about catering to special interests, because one piece of bad news may irreversibly damage their reputation.[11]

Such reputation-concerns-cure-all argument is flawed. It is one thing to acknowledge that regulators care about reputation, and another to assume that reputational concerns push regulators toward the public interest. As the previous chapters showed, in commercial markets reputations are too often noisy and fail to deter misbehavior or reward good behavior. Similar dynamics are in play in the regulatory context, albeit with some interesting twists.

6.2.2 *Regulators' Reputations Are Noisy*

Regulators' reputations are noisy. A regulator could promote the public interest and get a bad reputation, or cater to special interests and get a good reputation. As a result, reputational concerns do not necessarily promote better regulatory behavior. A responsive regulator does not always respond to the right signals. The same basic flaws that plague the process of reputational judgments in other contexts appear in the regulatory context as well, and with a vengeance.

[9] *Id.*, at 49.

[10] *See, e.g.*, Donald Wittman, The Myth of Democracy Failure 20–21 (1995); Edward Balleisen & David Moss, *Introduction, in* Government and Markets: Toward a New Theory of Regulation 5 (Balleisen & Moss, eds. 2009).

[11] Bryan Caplan, The Myth of the Rational Voter 104 (2007).

6.2.2.1 *Players Who Dispense Reputational Sanctions*

When we think about policymakers' target audiences, we normally think about the public: the classic reputational sanction in politics would be voting you out if you did not meet expectations. On paper, the fear of not being reelected or reappointed should drive regulators to cater to voters' preferences. Yet in reality, voters often lack the information necessary to judge whether economic regulators "misbehaved."[12] Voters do not have the ability or incentives to keep themselves informed. In a modern-day economy, the apparatus of socioeconomic regulation is all encompassing, detailed, and complex. For the average citizen, remaining informed on whether regulator X did a good job or not is a Herculean task. Remaining *un*informed is actually the rational thing to do: while the public as a whole benefit if the polity is informed enough to keep decision makers honest, the private costs of becoming informed dwarf the private benefits. This is the famous *rational ignorance* problem.[13]

In fact, in political markets the problem may be more severe. In commercial markets, misjudging reputations can come back to haunt you immediately, as in buying from a shady company or not buying from a great company. In politics, by contrast, you have very little skin in the game. Each voter knows that her single vote is not likely to sway policies. To use Bryan Caplan's terminology, voters suffer not just from rational ignorance but also from rational *irrationality*.[14] That is, voters feel free to indulge their biases when collecting information and voting on policies: I can vote with my favorite team, regardless of whether this team offers the best policies. A voter would feel free to identify certain bad policy choices as praiseworthy and good policy choices as blameworthy, and not suffer the consequences of misjudging.

A different type of target audience is the elected officials who appoint regulators. Ministers are arguably much better informed than the average voter is. Yet politicians, too, often lack the proper information and expertise to judge regulators' reputation effectively. After all, informational and expertise problems push politicians to delegate policy to professional bureaucrats to begin with. The same problems would likely hinder the ability of politicians to monitor professional bureaucrats after the fact.

12 *See, e.g.*, Robert J. Blendon et al., *Bridging the Gap between the Public's and Economists' Views of the Economy*, 11 J. Econ. Perspect. 105, 107–10 (1997) (providing empirical evidence of a gap between the public's perception of economic issues and actual economic performance).

13 Anthony Downs, An Economic Theory of Democracy 207–76 (1957).

14 *Supra* note 11.

6.2.2.2 *Players Who Facilitate Reputational Sanctions (Information Intermediaries)*

In the political realm, the relevant information intermediaries (those who select, certify, and diffuse information on regulatory behavior) usually fall into two categories: mass media and interest groups. On paper, both have better access to information and more expertise than the public. Yet evidence shows that both rarely cover the meaningful aspects of regulatory behavior, or cover them in a slanted way.

Much like media coverage of big business, media scrutiny of big government is slanted due to dependence on sources and advertisers.[15] Even if journalists manage to overcome their own biases and lack of expertise, they still need to cater to their readers' (-voters) biases. Voters are interested in topics that are vivid and discernable, and opinions that fit their own priors.[16] Media scrutiny of regulatory behavior is therefore very selective – the media picks its battles according to entertainment value and not according to the issue's real impact on society.[17]

Importantly, media coverage of regulatory issues is slanted in hidden ways. The problem is not so much with how the media covers a certain regulatory issue, but with all the issues that the media does not cover.[18] Major regulatory agencies, even those that preside over huge budgets and responsibilities, often do not have any reporter assigned to their beat (i.e., no one covers them regularly).[19] This media-slant-by-omission problem represents a key weakness in the BRT literature: existing studies document how regulators react to what the media covers, but they do not (cannot) document what the media does not cover. To better understand how reputational concerns shape regulatory behavior we first need to understand who sets the media agenda: who and

[15] Government agencies spend big on advertising too. Rafael Di Tella & Ignacio Franceschelli, *Government Advertising and Media Coverage of Corruption Scandals*, 3 AM. ECON. J. APPLIED ECON. 119 (2011) (reporting that media outlets bias their scrutiny of government as a function of government advertising).

[16] Matthew Gentzkow & Jesse M. Shapiro, *What Drives Media Slant? Evidence from U.S. Daily Newspapers*, 78 ECONOMETRICA 35 (2010) (providing statistical evidence for demand-driven slant).

[17] *See, e.g.*, *Self-Censorship: How Often and Why*, Apr. 30, 2000, www.people-press.org/2000/04/30/self-censorship-how-often-and-why (providing survey evidence for journalists avoiding important-yet-boring issues).

[18] Roumeen Islam, *Overview: From Media Markets to Policy*, *in* INFORMATION AND PUBLIC CHOICE: FROM MEDIA MARKETS TO POLICY MAKING 6 (Islam, ed., 2008).

[19] Florence Graves, *Watchdog Reporting: Exploring Its Myth*, *in* 21ST CENTURY MUCKRAKERS (2008).

what makes certain regulatory behaviors more vivid and coverable for the media. (Without forecasting too much, a large part of the answer is litigation.)

The other type of information intermediary that can facilitate reputational sanctions for regulators are interest groups. Yet not all interest groups are created equal. Narrow-interest groups are better at squawking when a regulator is about to hurt their interests than public interest groups are.[20] Certain types of information on regulatory behavior tend to be more immediately and widely diffused than others.

The example of regulating rates of return illustrates.[21] When regulators wish to prevent monopolies from overpricing consumers, they sometimes set a maximum price, based on a formula of the costs to the monopolist firm. On paper, whenever the costs change, the regulator should update the allowed rate of return. In reality, there is an asymmetry: whenever the costs go up, regulated entities trigger a review, and the regulator updates the rate of return upwards. By contrast, when the costs go down, no one triggers an update of the maximum rate of return. In Israel, for example, regulators set in the mid-1990s a rate-of-return formula across sectors, at a time when the general interest rate was in double digits. When the interest rate dropped to 1 percent in the 2000s, no one triggered an update of the formula, rendering price controls completely ineffective.[22]

The upshot is that, beyond the asymmetric information problem we recognized earlier, there is also an *asymmetric monitoring* problem. Some groups monitor the regulator's behavior more diligently.

Recognizing asymmetric monitoring dynamics leads to a counterintuitive and troubling conclusion: a regulator who cares about her reputation would tend to err in favor of the industry and against the public interest. To see why, imagine that you are a publicly spirted regulator. You know that you are bound to make mistakes at some point, given the complexity and uncertainty inherent in modern markets. The question you are asking yourself is how the outside world will perceive my mistakes. Will they spotlight, remember, and hold the mistakes against me? Or will they ignore and forget them? You quickly realize that mistakes against the regulated entities are immediately noticed by an army of dedicated and expert industry people; while mistakes

[20] Ernesto Dal Bó, *Regulatory Capture: A Review*, 22 OXFORD REV. ECON. POL'Y 203, 212 (2006); *Leaver*, *supra* note 3.

[21] Paul L. Joskow, *Inflation and Environmental Concern: Structural Change in the Process of Public Utility Price Regulation* 17 J. L. & ECON. 291 (1974). Leaver, *id.*, provides corroborating empirical data.

[22] Meirav Arlosoroff, *Milking Israeli Consumers with Dairy Price Controls*, HA'ARETZ, Jul. 8, 2014, www.haaretz.com/business/1.603609.

against the public seldom get noticed.[23] To paraphrase the philosophical question about a tree falling in the forest when no one is around (did it really make a sound?): if a regulator makes a mistake at the expense of the diffuse public, did she really hurt her reputation? Erring in favor of the regulated industry minimizes the chances that people will notice your (real or perceived) mistakes, saving you from criticism.[24]

6.2.2.3 *Players Who Suffer Reputational Sanctions (the Regulators)*

The BRT literature shows that regulators do not take expected reputational sanctions as given. They rather proactively manage the information environment to make themselves appear better than they truly are. For instance, one study shows that regulators prioritize responding to the more *visible* criticisms. A regulator will prioritize responding to a marginal issue covered in the front pages, even at the expense of more important issue covered only at the back pages.[25] Another study finds that regulators fight off reputational threats with communication strategies (what they say) rather than with actions (what they actually do). They would rather talk their way out of criticism. Yet another study shows that regulators who face reputational pressures simply choose less visible ways to concede to special interests (but concede nevertheless).[26] In other words, regulators take care of what is risky for regulators; not necessarily what is risky for society.[27] Regulators' ability to manage the information environment reduces the effectiveness of reputational deterrence.

*

[23] Michael A. Livemore & Richard L. Revesz, *Regulatory Review, Capture, and Agency Inaction* 101 Georgetown L. J. 1337, 1352 (2013) ("Agencies may also be more averse to negative publicity or congressional pressure concerning the costs of regulation than to failures to regulate: costs are often immediate and felt by an identifiable and concentrated group, whereas the benefits of regulating often address latent, long-term risks experienced by a diffuse population").

[24] The desire to minimize criticism taps into more than just regulators' reputational concerns. Regardless of how much a regulator cares about her reputation, she may wish to minimize criticism simply because of her "conflict avoidance" tendency, or her preference for the "quiet life." Ian Ayers & John Braithwaite, *Tripartism: Regulatory Capture and Empowerment*, 16 L. & Soc. Inq. 435, 471 (1991); Matthew D. Zinn, *Policing Environmental Regulatory Enforcement: Cooperation, Capture, and Citizen Suits*, 21 Stan. Environ. L. J. 81, 111 n.108 (2002) (compiling references).

[25] Maor & Solitzeanu-Kenan, *supra* note 6.

[26] *Id*; Gilad et al., *supra* note 5.

[27] Sharon Gilad & Tamar Yogev, *How Reputation Regulates Regulators: Illustrations from the Regulation of Retail Finance*, in The Oxford handbook of corporate reputation 320 (2012).

The bottom line will sound familiar to readers of the previous chapters: when left on its own, the market for regulators' reputation is too flawed to consistently deter misbehavior. Yet in reality, the market for regulators' reputation is rarely left alone. Litigation – both public and private – generates credible information on how regulators behave. The next two sections elaborate.

6.3 HOW JUDICIAL REVIEW IMPACTS REGULATORS' REPUTATION

The administrative law literature tends to focus on what courts do – whether they interfere with regulatory decisions or not – rather than on how regulators react.[28] To answer how regulators react, one needs a developed theory of how regulators behave, including how reputational concerns affect regulators. If we merge the insights from the BRT literature (on how reputation matters for regulators), with the insights developed thus far in this book (on how litigation affects reputation), we get a part of the answer: regulators anticipate that being challenged in court, regardless of the legal outcome, may alter what their audiences think about them. Judicial review therefore affects regulators not just by modifying their material incentives (as in conventional economic analysis), but also by shaping the public's perceptions of them.

6.3.1 *The Basic Story*

Judicial review can mitigate several of the problems that plague the market for regulators' reputation: it can provide the public with information on regulatory decision-making to which they were not privy; level the playing field between public-interest groups and narrow-interest groups; and reset the media agenda, facilitating coverage of meaningful issues.

At the most basic level, judicial review helps mitigating the asymmetric information problem. Nowhere is this more evident than with *reason-giving requirements*. These requirements force regulators to reveal what exactly they decided, and why they decided that way. Indeed, judicial review has become "the principal tool for prompting agencies to undertake reason-giving."[29] Courts shifted over the years from merely requiring regulators to provide reasons for the record, to giving the provided reasons a *hard look*: digging

28 Jerry L. Mashaw, Agency-Centered or Court-Centered Administrative Law? A Dialogue with Richard Pierce on Agency Statutory Interpretation, 59 ADMIN. L. REV. 889, 891–3 (2007).

29 Lisa Schultz Bressman, *Judicial Review of Agency Inaction: An Arbitrariness Approach*, 79 N.Y. U. L. REV. 1657, 1691 (2004).

into whether the reasons are adequate, whether the methods used to acquire evidence are reliable, whether agencies dully considered all contrary evidence, and so on.[30] As a byproduct, the public gets an expert opinion on whether regulators are doing their job properly.[31]

The existing literature emphasizes three types of justifications for reason-giving requirements:[32] (1) bolstering "the legitimacy of government action"; (2) facilitating legal review of the decision after the fact; and (3) promoting internal reflection by the decision maker before the fact. We can now add another, nonexclusive, justification: (4) reason giving facilitates bottom-up, *reputational* monitoring of regulators.

By making regulators publicize their reasoning in detail, courts make it easier for civic society to assess, debate, and hold regulators accountable.[33] A good example comes from judicial review of national security decisions. There, the court forced regulators to spell out in public the criteria for when and how they decide to transfer detainees to other countries, or target US citizens overseas.[34] Court-imposed disclosure made these decisions explicit and accessible, providing "a baseline against which ... the public may evaluate future executive behavior and challenge that behavior when it appears to countermand the stated policy."[35]

Judicial review also mitigates the *asymmetric monitoring* problem. That is, judicial review allows public-interest groups to more readily mobilize the masses against bad regulation. Public-interest groups can more easily spot damning information about regulatory behavior through the litigation process, than they can through the political process.[36] As one staff attorney in an

30 Motor Vehicle Manufacturers Association v. State Farm Mutual Automobile Insurance 463 U.S. 29, 43 (1983). For a quick summary of the historical evolution of reason-giving requirements, see Sidney A. Shapiro & Richard E. Levy, *Heightened Scrutiny of the Fourth Branch: Separation of Powers and the Requirement of Adequate Reasons for Agency Decisions*, 1987 Duke L.J. 387, 414–19 (1987).

31 Emily Hammond Meazell, *Dialogue, Deferred and Differentiated*, 112 Colum. L. Rev. Sidebar 185, 191 (2012).

32 Glen Staszewski, *Reason-Giving and Accountability*, 93 Minn. L. Rev. 1253, 1281–89 (2009); *Id.*, at 188.

33 *Cf.* Louis J. III Virelli, *Deconstructing Arbitrary and Capricious Review*, 92 N.C. L. Rev. 721, 743 (2014) ("One way to protect against irrational, unchecked agency action is to require that the agency explain itself. While the simple existence of reasons cannot ensure that an agency reached a rational conclusion, it can ensure that irrational or unsupported conclusions will be more readily identified and addressed by all three branches of government *and the public*") [emphasis added].

34 Ashley S. Deeks, *The Observer Effect: National Security Litigation, Executive Policy Changes, and Judicial Deference*, 82 Fordham L. Rev. 827, 851–53 (2013).

35 *Id.*

36 Gerald Rosenberg, The Hollow Hope 24 (2008).

environmentalist NGO told me: "so much of what the EPA does is opaque. So, even though [you can see that the] outcomes favor industry, the process of the EPA looks reasonable. Only litigation can pull out [and help you identify] the unreasonable aspects of regulator behavior."[37] Further, if a regulator ignores input from public-interest groups during the political process, the court will force her to explain why she did so after the fact.[38]

In that way, judicial review makes the regulator's favoritism more visible. The increased visibility, in turn, makes it easier for public-interest groups to enlist the help of donors, volunteers, and citizens who are normally disengaged. We have seen this story in previous chapters, in the commercial context: litigation does not just reveal new information, but also increases the saliency and shapes the framing of existing pieces of information. As one commentator noted in the context of judicial review of school segregation policies: "The courts have helped politicize issues that otherwise might have remained unattended."[39]

To appreciate the reputational impact of judicial review, we can follow the path of previous chapters, and look at how litigation shapes media coverage of regulators. Judicial review provides journalists information subsidies, as in ready-made versions of why the regulator took a certain decision, or detailed assessments of how that decision should affect the readers. Judicial review thereby reduces the costs for journalists of covering bad aspects of regulators' behavior. It puts hitherto-ignored regulatory issues on the media and public agendas.

To illustrate, consider the 1995 Pulitzer-winning story of disability pension abuse by the Long Island police. There, the abuse of disability pension benefits has been going on for decades, while the political establishment was "unwilling to clash with the well-organized and well-financed police-union lobby, which pushes for more generous policy benefits while helping to finance politicians' campaigns and delivering coveted endorsements."[40] To use a famous political economy typology, the problem was of the concentrated-benefits, dispersed-costs kind:[41] A powerful interest group enjoyed benefits at the expense of taxpayers. Those with the power to monitor and stop the abuse had no interest in fighting the powerful group on an issue that is far from the public's eye. As an insider later confessed: "I think the big problem with the system is there's not

37 Telephone interview with James Pew, staff attorney for Earthjustice (Jun. 4, 2019).

38 Wendy Wagner, *Revisiting the Impact of Judicial Review on Agency Rulemakings: An Empirical Investigation*, 53 Wm. & Mary L. Rev. 1717, 1720 n.4 (2012).

39 Daniel J. Monti, *Administrative Foxes in Educational Chicken Coops: An Examination of the Critique of Judicial Activism in School Desegregation Cases*, 2 Law & Pol'y Q. 233, 237 (1980).

40 Brian Donovan & Stephanie Saul, *The Road to Reform: Proposals Abound to Stop Those Who Abuse System*, Newsday, Jul. 2, 1994.

41 James Q. Wilson, The Politics of Regulation 357–94 (1980).

always someone on the other side."[42] Then, investigative reporters from *Newsday* exposed the abuse, and their story reverberated. The increased saliency immediately pushed the regulators to step up and stop the abuse.

The most important part in this story, at least from our perspective, is what facilitated the journalistic exposé. The *Newsday* reporters could not have generated such an impactful story without having access to information form litigation. They culled court documents from tort litigation involving the supposed victims, showing that they were undeserving of the benefits they extracted. The causal chain worked thusly: litigation produces (as a byproduct) information on a neglected regulatory issue; the media picks up the information, packages it compellingly, and diffuses it widely, thereby putting the issue on the public agenda; and regulators react to the potential public backlash by taking care of the hitherto-neglected problem. "Where the public is ignorant of certain conditions, and political elites do not want to deal with them" the litigation process can change the political agenda, prioritizing hitherto unattended topics.[43]

Beyond increasing the saliency of a given issue, judicial review can also *reduce the complexity* of the issue at hand. As Emily Hammond Meazell suggested in the context of regulatory scientific determinations, a key function of judicial review is translating highly specialized information into a generalist account that even nonprofessionals can follow.[44] Judicial review thereby makes a complex issue more understandable and coverable by the media. Political scientists have long recognized that regulatory enforcement tends to drift away from the public interest in issues with low saliency and high complexity.[45] When courts increase the saliency and reduce the complexity, they therefore reduce the risk of regulatory capture.

6.3.2 *Refining the Basic Story: Limitations*

Thus far, we have kept the story neat: public litigation produces information on how regulators behave, and the information translates into reputational pressures that push regulators to behave better. Yet in reality, the reputation-through-litigation dynamics are limited in the public litigation arena much

42 Brian Donovan & Stephanie Saul, *For Some LI Cops . . . Lucrative Disability*, NEWSDAY, Jun. 25, 1994.

43 *Cf.* Rosenberg, *supra* note 36, at 25.

44 Emily Hammond Meazell, *Super Deference, the Science Obsession, and Judicial Review as Translation of Agency Science*, 109 MICH. L. REV. 733, 778 (2011).

45 William T. Gormley, Jr., *Regulatory Issue Networks in a Federal System*, 18 POLITY 595 (1986); Wagner, *supra* note 38, at 1724.

more than they are in private litigation. This section elaborates on the unique limitations of public litigation, and then points to alternative channels, such as torts against the government.

Several of the limitations we covered in earlier chapters, in the context of corporate litigation, apply also here. Take for instance the *time lag* problem: If a regulator's tenure is three years and the judicial process takes four years to get going, then the threat of reputation-through-litigation is not as deterring. Similarly, just like private litigation, there are types of biases that public litigation simply cannot fix, such as voters' irrationality, or the media's dependence on advertising dollars. We will not rehash the similar limitations here, but instead focus on three limitations that are unique to public law litigation: the ideological bent of judges, the ability of regulators to sidestep court-induced reputational pressures, and the ability of the industry to use court-induced reputational pressures as an influence mechanism.

First, the *politicization of judicial review muddles the signal* it sends. One well-established empirical pattern of judicial review is its ideological bent.[46] When judges decide whether to interfere with agency action, they are affected by their own personal political preferences. A conservative judge is more likely to vote down liberal agency actions, and vice versa.

The politicization of judicial review presents a challenge to our reputational argument, because politicization muddles the signal that litigation generates. If audiences observe a judge criticizing and overturning a regulator's decision, they would not necessarily view it as indicative of the regulator being incompetent or captured. They could instead attribute the criticism to the judge's own political preferences. Perhaps the regulator was promoting what she believes is the public interest, and it just happens to be the opposite of what the judge believes the public interest is. Private litigation can facilitate reputational control even when judges are biased, simply because the main impact comes from the process itself rather than the final verdict. In other words, the process of (private) litigation tends to generate relative objective documentation, regardless of the judge's subjectively tilted

[46] *See, e.g.*, Richard J. Pierce, Jr., *What Do the Studies of Judicial Review of Agency Actions Mean?* 63 ADM. L. REV. 77, 88–89 (2011); Frank B. Cross, *Decision-making in the U.S. Court of Appeal*, 91 CAL. L. REV. 1457, 1471 (2003); Richard J. Pierce, Jr., *Two Problems in Administrative Law: Political Polarity on the District of Columbia Circuit and Judicial Deterrence of Agency Rulemaking*, 1988 DUKE L.J. 300. *But see* Harry T. Edwards & Michael A. Livermore, *Pitfalls of Empirical Studies That Attempt to Understand the Factors Affecting Appellate Decisionmaking*, 58 DUKE L.J. 1895 (2009).

interpretations. Yet public litigants do not enjoy the same information-extracting powers.

A second problem with reputation-through-*public*-litigation is that *regulators may respond only symbolically or too aggressively*. The BRT literature has established that regulators proactively manage their reputation. It is therefore safe to assume that when faced with court-generated reputational pressures, regulators will not stand idle but rather attempt to dilute the expected reputational sanction. Regulators may choose courses of action that are less likely to be reviewed in court to begin with.[47] In cases where they are nevertheless challenged in court, regulators may engage in damage control by responding in a symbolic manner, weathering the storm without making substantive changes.[48]

To illustrate, let us recast the example of criticism directed at the SEC in the wake of the 2008 financial crisis. You may recall from Chapter 4 that the SEC responded to the public backlash by announcing a change in policy, committing to demanding more admissions in future settlements. Initially, it seemed that the court-generated reputational pressures worked. Then evidence started surfacing, suggesting that the new policy did not substantively address the criticism. In other words, the professed change of policy could have very well quieted down the public outcry without meaningfully improving the actual outcomes of SEC enforcement.

At the same time, I do not wish to overstate the co-opting-reputational-pressures limitation. Even symbolic responses and "cheap talk" commitments may represent a step in the right direction. They "shape citizens' expectations from government and expose bureaucracies to external scrutiny when their performance falls short of expectations."[49] To go back to our example: while it is true that the SEC can ramp up the number of admissions in small cases, we saw in Chapter 4 that its commitment to change has also generated meaningful admissions in several impactful cases.

Another possibility that may limit the positive reputational effects of litigation is that regulators will *over*react to court-generated reputational pressures. The logic here is intuitive: once bad news breaks, media coverage tends to gravitate toward the sensational and negative, looking for a villain. Such coverage may push regulators to engage in overkill. A good illustration comes from the breast implants litigation. There, litigation had the media pointing fingers at the FDA, which reacted by banning breast implants

47 *Cf*. Meazell, *supra* note 31, at 189–90.

48 *See, e.g.*, Saar Alon-Barkat & Sharon Gilad, *Political Control or Legitimacy Deficit? Bureaucracies' Symbolic Responses to Bottom-Up Public Pressures*, 44 POLICY & POLITICS 41, 42 (2016).

49 *Id.*, at 42.

altogether. Many critics suggested that the FDA's decision, at the time, was bad science (based on one piece of unsubstantiated evidence that surfaced in litigation) and bad policy, driven by the regulator's desire to appease raging media scrutiny and public opinion.[50]

Here as well, I do not wish to overstate the point. Yes, the risk of litigation-driven media coverage pushing regulators to overreact is real. But when all things are considered, it seems that instances where regulators over-regulate due to media scrutiny balance out with many cases where the watchdog did not bark, and regulators ended up under-regulating because the issue remained under the public's radar. To go back to the breast implants example, litigation helped breaking a decade-plus cycle of regulatory inaction. Before litigation-driven pressures pushed the FDA to err on the side of aggressively regulating breast implants, the FDA had been erring for more than a decade on the side of regulating too laxly, not pushing the industry to test the safety of their products as required.[51]

Finally, another problem with reputation-through-*public*-litigation is that *the regulated industry itself often uses litigation as a lever*. Challenging regulatory action in courts requires resources: time, money, and expertise. Special interest groups usually have more of these resources, and are therefore better at employing the judicial review channel in their favor, relative to the dispersed public.[52] Applied here, one could argue that court-generated reputational pressures are simply another mechanism used by special interest to capture regulators. A part of the problem, rather than the solution. To recast the tobacco litigation example: there, the industry sued the EPA, arguing that the regulator relied on junk science and became too trigger-happy.[53] A recent (rare) empirical study of the reputational effects of judicial review indeed focuses on how the regulated industry in Spain and in the UK uses legal challenges as a strategic resource, to gain favorable policies.[54]

50 Joni Hersch, *Breast Implants: Regulation, Litigation, and Science, in* REGULATION THROUGH LITIGATION 177 (Viscusi, ed., 2002). *See also* MARCIA ANGELL, SCIENCE ON TRIAL: THE CLASH OF MEDICAL EVIDENCE AND THE LAW IN THE BREAST IMPLANT CASE (1997).

51 Wendy Wagner, *When All Else Fails: Regulating Risky Products through Tort Litigation*, 95 GEO. L.J. 693, 718 (2007). Wagner sums it up nicely: "without an institutional 'check' on preexisting regulatory commitments to force the production of … information, regulators themselves may be more lax in insisting on the information, especially given the vigorous participation of regulated industry in agency decision-making." *Id.*, at 720.

52 Wagner, *supra* note 38, at 1732–33; Nicholas Bagley & Richard L. Revesz, *Centralized Oversight of the Regulatory State*, 106 COLUM. L. REV. 1260, 1284–85 (2006).

53 Wagner, *supra* note 51, at 730.

54 Luis E. Mejia, *Judicial Review of Regulatory Decisions: Decoding the Contents of Appeals against Agencies in Spain and the United Kingdom*, Reg. & Gov. (forthcoming, 2020).

The main premise of this argument is valid: the regulated industry is, indeed, likely to try to use judicial review as a lever. But it does not follow that our point is mute: judicial review will, nevertheless, generate positive reputational momentum. To understand why, consider another stylized fact from the BRT literature: it is better for regulators' reputation to be perceived as over-regulating, than to be perceived as under-regulating. Once a certain regulatory issue becomes salient, the regulators will be less worried about appearing to be populists on the issue (over-regulating), and more worried about appearing to be in the industry's pocket (under-regulating). Applied here, we can assume that the reputational vector generated by industry-driven judicial review would be weaker than the reputational vector generated by public-interest-group-driven judicial review.

6.3.3 *Torts against the Government*

Torts against the government are another type of litigation that produces quality information on regulators' behavior, and actually avoids some of the abovementioned limitations of administrative litigation. A good starting point to illustrate would be Daryl Levinson's skepticism regarding constitutional torts.[55] Levinson maintains that deterrence does not work in tort claims against the government, because those who ultimately pay damages are us taxpayers, rather than the negligent regulators themselves. What Levinson misses is that making someone pay legal sanctions out of pocket is not the only way to deter. Litigation can deter regulators also by making them suffer *non*legal sanctions. Myriam Gilles's account of the information-producing function of municipal liability suits provides a case in point, and maps nicely into our argument here.[56]

Constitutional tort victims wishing to hold municipalities liable cannot rely on vicarious liability, but rather have to show a consistent policy or custom, Gilles shows.[57] As a result, constitutional tort victims usually try to unearth evidence of deliberate indifference, repeat offending, or a general problematic attitude on part of the municipal police force. This is exactly the type of information that is relevant to reputation judgments: it speaks to the intentionality and preventability of past behavior and is indicative of future behavior. Such claims are also likely to attract media attention, as they typically

55 Daryl J. Levinson, *Making Government Pay: Markets, Politics and the Allocation of Constitutional Costs*, 67 U. Chi. L. Rev. 345 (2000).

56 Myriam E. Gilles, *In Defense of Making Government Pay: The Deterrent Effect of Constitutional Tort Remedies*, 35 Ga. L. Rev. 845 (2001).

57 *Id.*, at 863.

implicate high-profile social issues such as police brutality or government cover-ups.[58]

In all, if we map Gilles's analysis of municipal liability suits onto Chapter 1's analysis of how information translates into reputation, we can conclude that torts against the government often increase the likelihood that information will be properly attributed and widely diffused, thereby increasing the effectiveness of reputational deterrence.

*

The main gist of the reputation-through-litigation argument applies in public litigation as well. At the same time, the reputational dynamics seem to be less powerful here, compared to private litigation. Reason-giving requirements hold the promise of increasing the saliency and reducing the complexity of certain regulatory issues. But the availability and scope of discovery is limited. When a public-interest group brings a record-review litigation, or attempts to compel the regulator to act, very little new information comes out. Another problem with administrative litigation is that it is often less attractive for journalists to cover. Not newsworthy enough, in their eyes. We saw in Chapter 2 that part of the reason that journalists troll court documents is that they can often find there the materials for a good story, in particular identifiable victims and villains. Record-review litigation, by comparison, is dull. As a result, the reputational effects frequently come not necessarily from administrative litigation, but from other channels. One such channel is the aforementioned torts against the government. Another is litigation between two private parties that indirectly implicates the regulator's behavior.

6.4 HOW PRIVATE LITIGATION IMPACTS REGULATORS' REPUTATION

It is intuitive to think that judicial review of regulatory behavior would affect what we think about the regulator. Less intuitively, but sometimes more importantly, even litigation between two private parties can affect regulators' reputation. Section 6.4.1 sheds light on common scenarios in private litigation where the regulator's behavior is implicated. Section 6.4.2 distinguishes between our reputation-through-litigation argument and the extant regulation-through-litigation literature.

[58] *Id.*, at 860.

6.4.1 *The Basic Story*

Litigation can make us reevaluate what we think about a regulator, even when the regulator is not a side to it. Think about a scenario of mass tort litigation between a polluting plant and victims who live in proximity to the plant. Such litigation may reveal information on how the defendant company skirted environmental regulation and got away with it. The litigation may thus affect not just the defendant company's reputation, but also the regulator's reputation, raising questions about how the regulator let the pollution happen under her not-so-watchful eye.[59]

To use a concreate example, consider the 2008 Pulitzer-winning project on faulty regulation of baby products.[60] There, the investigative journalists drew heavily from documents produced in litigation between victims of product defects and manufacturers of said products. Yet the journalists did not make it a story about a specific defected car seat or harmed baby. They rather pieced together the evidence into a big-picture story about systematic failures in regulating baby products, pointing fingers at the "captive," "myopic," and "docile" Consumer Product Safety Commission (CSPC). The private lawsuits therefore helped implicating the CSPC's reputation, without the CSPC being a side in litigation. Following the journalistic exposé and ensuing public backlash, the CSPC changed its ways and acted more aggressively, as in making more sweeping recall demands. The reputational pressure seemingly worked. Another example comes from the tobacco litigation. There, the judge's 1,742-page verdict was a "ringing denunciation" of the defendant tobacco companies.[61] More pertinently, however, is that press coverage of the verdict did not stop at criticizing the tobacco companies, but pointed fingers at the regulators, for not having enough gumption to rein in the powerful industry.[62]

The mechanisms through which private litigation typically affects regulators' reputation differ from the ones we highlighted in the previous section, when discussing judicial review. Unlike judicial review, judges presiding over private litigation would not require the regulator to provide detailed reasoning, or directly evaluate the adequacy of regulators' reasoning. Yet in private

59 For a real-world case that fits the hypothetical, see Roy Shapira & Luigi Zingales, *Is Pollution Value-Maximizing? The* DuPont *Case* 25 (Nat'l Bureau of Econ. Research, Working Paper No. 23866, 2017), www.nber.org/ papers/w23866.

60 The full project is available at www.pulitzer.org/winners/staff-67.

61 United States v. Philip Morris USA Inc., 9F. Supp. 2d 1 (D.D.C. 2006).

62 *See, e.g.*, *Tobacco Racketeers Get off Easy*, N.Y. TIMES, Aug. 20, 2006, at WK9.

litigation the parties themselves have strong incentives to use their fact-finding powers to extract information that indirectly implicates regulators' behavior.

To illustrate, consider the frequent usage of two tort law doctrines, namely, *regulatory compliance defense* and *negligence per se*. Defendants are the ones raising the regulatory compliance defense, arguing that their behavior cannot be negligent if they complied with existing statutory/regulatory standards; or that their product cannot be defective if it meets the relevant regulatory requirements.[63] Yet the law treats regulatory compliance only as a partial defense. It is therefore not enough for defendants to show evidence of their compliance with the standard; they also have to convince the court that the standard is worthy. In other words, the regulatory compliance defense "rests on a factual presumption regarding the regulatory process."[64] In deciding whether to accept the defense, courts would typically evaluate the regulatory process: how deliberative, fair, thorough, and sound it was; whether the regulators have been updating the standard to keep with evolving knowledge of the risk in question; and so on.[65] It is not hard to envision such private litigation turning into a referendum on how competent and public serving the regulator has been.

There is a broader point at play here, about the complementarities between regulation and litigation. Many commentators have called on courts to adopt a stronger version of the regulatory compliance defense.[66] These commentators usually invoke an institutional competence argument: regulators develop expertise, and so generalist courts should defer to them more.[67] Yet the proponents of stronger regulatory compliance defense miss a crucial aspect, namely, information problems. Regulators often rely on information from the regulated industry itself when setting standards *ex ante*.[68] As a result, regulators may set the standards suboptimally to begin with, and fail to update it over time when a more stringent standard is called for. Remember the regulating rates of return example: the regulator depends on the industry to trigger an

63 Restatement (Third) of Torts: Prods. Liab. § 4(b) (1998); Restatement (Second) of Torts § 288C (1963–64).

64 Mark A. Geistfeld, *Tort Law in the Age of Statutes*, 99 Iowa L. Rev. 957, 1003 (2014). Note that "because regulatory compliance is an affirmative defense, the burden of proof is borne by the defendant." *Id.*

65 *Id.*, at 998; Restatement (Third) Of Torts: Prods. Liab. § 4 cmt. e (1998).

66 Richard C. Ausness, *The Case for a "Strong" Regulatory Compliance Defense*, 55 Md. L. Rev. 1210, 1212 n.13 (1996) (compiling references).

67 *See, e.g.*, James A. Henderson, Jr. & Aaron D. Twerski, *Doctrinal Collapse in Products Liability: The Empty Shell of Failure to Warn*, 65 N.Y.U. L. Rev. 265, 321 (1990); *Id.*, at 1219.

68 Teresa M. Schwartz, *The Role of Federal Safety Regulations in Products Liability Actions*, 41 Vand. L. Rev. 1121, 1147 (1988).

update, yet the industry has no incentives to trigger an update that makes things worse for them. Litigation serves a key function here: extracting valuable information on whether the standard is adequate or needs updating. Once the information surfaces, regulators may be compelled to protect their reputation by updating the standard. And the mere background threat of litigation deters regulators *ex ante*.

While the regulatory compliance defense often implicates the regulator's *standard-setting* prowess, the negligence per se doctrine typically implicates the regulator's *enforcement* efforts. Plaintiffs are the ones raising the negligence per se claim: if you manage to show that defendants routinely skirted regulation, you can establish negligence.[69] The prospect of securing *punitive damages* especially incentivizes plaintiffs to not limit themselves to bringing evidence about the particular harm done to them, but rather produce evidence on defendant misconduct more broadly, such as showing how defendants have been suppressing information on adverse health effects.[70] When the media follows up on such evidence, they often do not limit themselves to the "big bad polluting company" framing, but also adopt a "regulators were asleep at the helm!" angle, suggesting to their readers that a lax regulatory enforcement let the industry off the hook.[71]

6.4.2 *Refining the Basic Story: Information Production vs. Reputation-Shaping*

I am hardly the first one that argues that private litigation can lead to changes in regulation. A sizable literature – grouped together for our purposes under the "regulation through litigation" moniker – looks at how litigation is not only about settling past disputes, but also about bringing sweeping changes to defendants' future behavior.[72] The main difference between my argument and that literature lies in the mechanism of influence. Each account answers the "*how* litigation brings about societal change" question differently. The extant accounts suggest that policy changes come from judicial rulings, directly: judges are acting as de

69 RESTATEMENT (THIRD) OF TORTS: PRODS. LIAB. § 4(a) (1998).

70 Michael Rustad, *In Defense of Punitive Damages in Products Liability: Testing Tort Anecdotes with Empirical Data*, 78 IOWA L. REV. 1, 41 (1992) (in the context of the asbestos litigation).

71 For notable examples, see *id.* (the asbestos litigation); Shapira & Zingales, *supra* note 59 (the *DuPont* litigation); *supra* note 62 (the tobacco litigation).

72 Daniel P. Kessler, *Introduction, in* REGULATION VS. LITIGATION 3 (2011). *See also* Abram Chayes, *The Role of the Judge in Public Law Litigation*, 89 HARV. L. REV. 128 (1976) (on "public law litigation"); Lesley K. McAllister, *Revisiting a "Promising Institution": Public Law Litigation in the Civil Law World*, 24 GA. ST. U. L. REV. 694 (2012) (on "structural reform litigation").

facto legislators/regulators, filling gaps in statutory frameworks, and forcing defendant companies to accept new regulations outside the normal political process.[73] I, by contrast, suggest that the process of litigation propels the regulators to act on their own, because it threatens their reputations.

If private litigation indeed influences regulation only *indirectly*, it takes the sting away from the most common criticism of regulatory litigation, namely, the criticism of unaccountability. Many scholars have used the "regulation through litigation" moniker in a negative connotation, claiming that unaccountable judges and plaintiffs' lawyers make broad societal changes without input from the public.[74] Yet if the main effect of litigation is reputational, then input from the public plays a key role. When litigation generates information and raises public awareness to regulatory behavior, it arguably *increases* public accountability and facilitates meaningful participation.

In that regard, my account of private litigation is closest to Wendy Wagner's version, which emphasizes the information-extracting qualities of litigation.[75] Litigation helps regulators regulate better, Wagner claims, by providing them information. Litigation unlocks "stubborn information": information that regulators have a hard time extracting from the regulated industry on their own.[76] Normally, the regulated industry can use their superior access to information and expertise, as well as other influence tactics, to keep crucial information away from regulators. Litigation disrupts these dynamics: when regulated companies face resourceful plaintiff lawyers armed with court junctions, they reluctantly provide the needed information.

Where my argument differs from Wagner's is in the difference between producing information and affecting reputations. In my version, litigation propels regulators to act not solely by surfacing information, but also by facilitating wide *diffusion* (typically through media coverage) and proper *attribution* (making sure the regulator's overseers understand the regulator's role in the debacle) of that information.

The BRT literature teaches us that to it is not so much the availability, but rather the visibility of information that propels regulators to act.[77] Producing

73 Kessler, *id.*, at 3; Timothy D. Lytton, *Using Tort Litigation to Enhance Regulatory Policy Making: Evaluating Climate-Change Litigation of Lessons from Gun-Industry and Clergy-Sexual-Abuse Lawsuits*, 86 Tex. L. Rev. 1837, 1847–89 (2008).

74 Lytton, *id.*, at 1839; W. Kip Viscusi, Smoke-Filled Rooms 5–7 (2002); Peter H. Schuck, *Why Regulating Guns through Litigation Won't Work, in* Suing the Gun Industry 225, 236–38 (Lytton ed., 2005).

75 Wagner, *supra* note 51.

76 *Id.*; Wendy Wagner, *Stubborn Information Problems & the Regulatory Benefits of Gun Litigation, in* Suing the Gun Industry, *supra* note 74.

77 *See, e.g.*, Maor & Sulitzeanu-Kenan, *supra* note 6, at 52.

new information is therefore neither a necessary nor a sufficient condition for litigation to bring about regulatory changes.[78] A deeper look at many paradigmatic examples of regulatory litigation reveals that the regulators already enjoyed access to the information in question, or could have easily accessed it.[79] To borrow Wagner's term, the information in question in these cases was hardly "stubborn." The real impact of litigation came not from producing new information but rather from lighting a fire underneath the regulators' feet. I observed similar dynamics in my study of the 1995–2015 Pulitzer-winning investigations: more often than not, the problem was not that regulators could not access information, but rather that regulators were too reluctant to act against powerful players (and then started acting once the issue gained saliency).

In the clergy–sexual abuse scandal, for example, litigation made it "politically less costly" to take action against the powerful Catholic Church.[80] Along similar lines, Ida Tarbell's muckraking project on the Standard Oil Company relied on information from law enforcement actions that was already available to the public, and certainly to regulators. Yet it was only after Tarbell published her stories that the attorney general mustered courage to break the monopoly.

Litigation brings about regulatory change when it manages to make the costs of regulatory failures obtrusive to the regulators' overseers in the public and congress. It pushes an issue to the top of the media, public, and regulatory agendas.[81] In communication scientists' lingo, this is the difference between "framing" and "priming."[82] Existing accounts of regulation through litigation focus on *framing* effects, suggesting that litigation shapes how a certain situation (e.g., the dangers of smoking) is presented to the public. I, by contrast, focus on *priming* effects, suggesting that litigation directs the public's attention to certain attributes of the regulator, making us evaluate the regulator on the

78 *Cf.* Gilles, *supra* note 56, at 861.

79 *See, e.g.*, Hersch, *supra* note 50 (noting that with breast implants, the FDA could have easily asked for the relevant information in real time; and what propelled the FDA to act was not the litigation per se but rather the widespread media scrutiny); Jeffrey S. Quinn, *Does Mass Product Tort Litigation Facilitate or Hinder Social Legislative Reform – A Comparative Study of Tobacco Regulation*, 9 Rutgers J. L. & Pub. Pol'y 106, 152 (2012) (noting that with tobacco, "[i]t was not the case that the legislative bodies were unable to discover information ... Congress did not possess the information because it willingly chose not to research tobacco or create an agency to monitor tobacco").

80 Lytton, *supra* note 73, at 1864.

81 *Id.*, at 1841 ("Tort litigation also attracts press coverage that mobilizes and shapes public opinion, which in turn creates pressure for reform").

82 Shanto Iyengar & Donald R. Kinder, News that Matters: Television and American Opinion 63 (1987).

basis of these traits (e.g., not being diligent enough in demanding information from the tobacco industry).

6.5 IMPLICATIONS

Recognizing that judicial review affects regulators not just directly, by striking down their decisions, but also indirectly, by producing information that shapes their reputations, opens up space to reassessing the extant literature on judicial review and its policy implications. If litigation indeed generates information and affects the reputation of regulators, then the main thrust of the implications we have sketched in previous chapters, for doctrines of corporate and securities laws, apply also here, for doctrines of administrative and constitutional law. This section applies the reputational perspective to reevaluate longstanding debates over the hard look doctrine, standing limitations, confidential settlements, and judicial activism.

6.5.1 *Standards of Review*

The extent literature on judicial review endlessly debates whether courts should interfere with regulators' decisions. One camp argues that judges interfere too much. Nonelected, generalist judges should not interfere with the decisions of elected and professional regulators, or so the argument goes.[83] Yet, if judicial review can make public officials change their behavior not necessarily by striking down their decisions, but rather by making them face public pressure, then judicial review arguably makes the political system *more* representative of citizens' preferences.[84]

The other camp argues that judges defer too much. Courts employ abstention doctrines and rarely intervene in regulatory decisions. Further, in the rare events where courts do not abstain, they limit their review to the process, rather than the merits, of the decision in question.[85] Yet from an information-production perspective, it matters less if courts ultimately decide to defer to the regulator's judgment, as long as the *process* of litigation flushes out information about how the regulators behaved.

83 *See generally* Alexander M. Bickel, The Least Dangerous Branch: The Supreme Court at the Bar of Politics 16–18 (1962).

84 *Cf.* Joseph L. Sax, Defending the Environment: A Strategy for Citizen Action (1971) (noting that litigation can serve "as a catalyst, not a usurper, of the legislative process").

85 *See* Deeks, *supra* note 34, at 829 (compiling references); M. Elisabeth Magill, *Courts and Regulatory Capture*, *in* Preventing Regulatory Capture 399–400 (Carpenter & Moss, eds., 2014).

Abstention doctrines and lax standards of review would hurt information production only to the extent that they serve as pleading hurdles of sorts, killing any challenge in its infancy (or discouraging public-interest groups from filing in court *ex ante*). If, on the other hand, Justice Scalia was right in saying that deference does not mean "anything more than considering [the views of the other branches] with attentiveness and profound respect" before the court rejects them, then there is little reason to worry about information production.[86] In other words, we should not evaluate the effectiveness of judicial review merely through the legal bottom line. Much like with in discussion of corporate law litigation and the deferential business judgment rule, the legal outcomes of administrative litigation may skew toward respondents, yet the process itself can shed light on how problematic respondents' behavior has been, thereby propelling them to change their behavior *ex ante*.[87]

To illustrate, consider the extensive debate over the hard look doctrine.[88] Several scholars have suggested that the hard look doctrine must be inconsequential, not guiding actual judicial review, because the empirical evidence shows that agencies enjoy a very high win rate in courts.[89] Scholars also point out that regardless of the standard that courts apply (e.g., *Chevron*[90] vs. *Skidmore*),[91] agencies' win rates remain roughly the same.[92] Yet to fully evaluate the hard look doctrine, we cannot limit ourselves to the "legal" results of cases (i.e., how courts decide, as illustrated by agencies' win rates). We also need to take into account the ultimate results, that is, how regulators changed their behavior following litigation. The hard look doctrine affects the quantity and quality of information production during litigation. A regulator that needs to explain herself to the court under the hard look doctrine will have to produce granular information on what, why, and how she decided. And courts are more likely, under the hard look doctrine, to provide a detailed, relatively accessible account on how the regulator behaved. In other words, to evaluate

86 Antonin Scalia, *Judicial Deference to Administrative Interpretations of Law*, 3 DUKE L.J. 511, 514 (1989).

87 In general, we should not be surprised that the reputational dynamics described here bear similarity to the ones existing in corporate law. Corporate law and administrative law rely on several similar pillars, meant to organize large bureaucracies, which in turn lead to similar reputational effects. *Cf.* Gerlad E. Frug, *The Ideology of Bureaucracy in American Law* 97 HARV. L. REV. 1277, 1277 (1984).

88 *State Farm*, *supra* note 30.

89 Jacob Gersen & Adrian Vermeule, *Thin Rationality Review*, 114 MICH. L. REV. 1355, 1362–64 (2016) (providing evidence of a 92 percent win rate of agencies under hard look reviews).

90 Chevron U.S.A. Inc. v. Natural Resources Defense Council, Inc., 467 U.S. 837 (1984).

91 Skidmore v. Swift & Co., 323 U.S. 134, 140 (1944).

92 *See, e.g.*, David Zaring, *Reasonable Agencies*, 96 VA. L. REV. 135, 169 (2010); Pierce, *supra* note 46, at 85.

the hard look doctrine we cannot satisfy ourselves with evidence about who wins in court; we rather need to look at how media coverage of the regulatory issue changed during and after litigation, and how the regulator reacted. The doctrine may not matter much for the legal results, but it matters for the reputational results.

A concrete example comes from our Chapter 4 story of judicial review of the SEC. After Judge Rakoff started raising questions vocally, the SEC settlement practices had become the center of national attention. The SEC had eventually won the legal battle, as the Second Circuit Court of Appeals has reemphasized the need to defer to the regulators' discretion. Yet by then the SEC had already lost the battle in the court of public opinion, and had to react by publicly changing their enforcement policies to require more admissions going forward.

6.5.2 *Standing and Redressability*

If courts indeed affect the reputational pressures that operate on regulators, then access to courts dictates the vector of such reputational pressures. To fulfill its potential and combat the asymmetries in monitoring abilities, access to court itself has to be symmetric – available to public-interest groups as it is to special-interest groups. Yet in reality, even after the 1970s wave of liberalizing standing requirements,[93] there remain great asymmetries: the regulated industry establishes standing much easier than the supposed beneficiaries of regulation (the public, via public-interest groups) do. First, there is the "injury-in-fact" requirement: courts normally do not allow standings in issues of wide grievance, insisting that the plaintiff shows that she was specifically injured.[94] Then, there is the "redressability" requirement: plaintiffs have to show that the remedies they seek are capable of redressing the supposed harms.[95]

The one-two punch of injury in fact and redressability has significantly limited the ability of public-interest groups to challenge in courts – and thereby draw attention to – certain types of regulatory misbehavior.[96] While I am hardly the first to point out the asymmetries in standing between special-interest- and public-interest groups,[97] the reputational angle does add a new

93 Wagner, *supra* note 38, at 1726.

94 Lujan v. Defenders of Wildlife, 504 U.S. 555, 560–61 (1992); Adam Shinar, *Enabling Resistance: How Courts Facilitate Departures from the Law, and Why This May Not Be a Bad Thing*, 17 N.Y.U. J. LEGIS. & PUB. POL'Y 989, 1001 (2014) (compiling references).

95 *Lujan*, *id.*

96 *Cf.* Daniel A. Farber, *Politics and Procedure in Environmental Law*, 8 J. L. ECON. & ORG. 59, 77 (1992).

97 *See, e.g.*, Thomas O. Sargentich, *The Critique of Active Judicial Review of Administrative Agencies: A Reevaluation*, 49 ADMIN. L. REV. 599, 615 (1997).

twist to the debate: spotlighting an underappreciated benefit of symmetric access to courts. Access to courts leads to access to the media agenda. And access to media agenda leads to influence on regulatory agenda.

This is more than just a semantic exercise. Recognizing the links between judicial review to media agenda, and between media agenda to regulatory behavior, has implications for how courts should apply the redressability requirement. When evaluating redressability, courts inevitably engage in some kind of forecasting: deciphering whether the remedies sought can redress the harm. Recognizing that judicial review generates reputational pressures should affect the forecasting. Even in cases where judicial review is not likely to provide compensation to a specific past injury, it may nevertheless generate reputational pressures that will deter future harms. Pertinently, court-induced reputational pressures are likely to reduce the probabilities of future harms to the group that the plaintiffs represent.[98]

6.5.3 *Confidential Settlements*

We saw that an important channel of reputation-relevant information on regulators are torts against the government. This type of litigation escapes many of the limitations of administrative litigation: it features more extensive discovery and is relatively immune to politicization of judges; it comes with strong monetary incentives for plaintiffs and their lawyers to extract damning information; and so on. Yet torts against the government have one problematic feature, namely, the tendency of parties to the dispute to agree to keep the information exchanged during litigation confidential, in exchange for higher/earlier settlements. Chapter 7 will elaborate on the divergence between private and public incentives: both parties have incentives to agree to confidentiality, while the public interest would benefit from openness. The same dynamics may apply even more strongly in the context of torts against the government, due to the agency problem: taxpayers who are not privy to litigation are the ones paying for settlements, while the defendant regulators are the ones enjoying the benefits of confidentiality.[99] The upshot is that we should consider imposing limitations on the ability of regulators to settle, and to settle confidentially. Such limitations already exist in certain regulatory

98 *Cf.* Cass R. Sunstein, *What's Standing after Lujan – Of Citizen Suits, Injuries, and Article III*, 91 MICH. L. REV. 163, 207 (1992).

99 Giuseppe Dari-Mattiacci et al., *State Liability*, 18 EUR. REV. PRIVATE L. 773, 792 (2010).

areas in the United States and elsewhere in the world,[100] and we should aim to expand that blueprint.

6.5.4 *The Role of Judicial Review in Mitigating Regulatory Capture*

The final implication is the most general one: applying the reputational perspective to reassess the debate over the proper role of judicial review in mitigating regulatory capture. Proponents of judicial review claim that it is an important check on regulatory capture.[101] By adding another veto point, judicial review increases the costs of capturing the system, or so the argument goes.[102] And it is an especially effective veto point, proponents claim: judges enjoy tenure and so are less amenable to capture by career concerns, and are, in general, more neutral and less politically involved.[103] Other scholars dismiss this optimistic account. They emphasize how only a subset of regulatory behaviors are reviewable, as courts tend to avoid second-guessing regulatory decisions.[104]

To judge which claim is more convincing, we need to make some assumptions about what drives regulators. If, as in traditional public choice theory, you believe that regulators mostly maximize their narrow self-interest, then you have to acknowledge that there is little that judicial review can do. Judges may invalidate specific captured regulatory decisions after the fact, but they cannot overcome the inherent advantages that special interests enjoy in the way of offering lucrative future business opportunities or campaign financing. Judicial review is limited in dealing with the basic incentive problems that public choice highlights, for various reasons. Special-interest groups employ their better resources to use the judicial review channel in their favor. The same veto point meant to fight off attempts to capture the system, is in reality often used to fight off and delay public-interest reforms.[105]

100 In the United States, the EPA's Superfund (Comprehensive Environmental Response, Compensation, and Liability Act) prohibits confidentially. Many European legal systems also impose "severe restrictions" on regulatory settlements. *Id.*, at 809–10.

101 Cass R. Sunstein, *Interest Groups in American Public Law*, 38 STAN. L. REV. 29 (1985).

102 Magill, *supra* note 85, at 406; Jonathan R. Macey, *Promoting Public-Regarding Legislation Through Statutory Interpretation: An Interest Group Model*, 86 COLUM. L. REV. 223 (1986).

103 Jerry L. Mashaw, GREED, CHAOS AND GOVERNANCE: USING PUBLIC CHOICE TO IMPROVE PUBLIC LAW (1997) (the insights of public choice call for a more aggressive judicial review, as judges adhere to some concept of the public interest more than regulators do); Susan Rose-Ackerman, *Law and Regulation*, *in* THE OXFORD HANDBOOK OF LAW AND POLITICS 577 (Caldeira et al., eds., 2008); Magill, *id*, at 407. *But see* Einer R. Elhague, *Does Interest Group Theory Justify More Intrusive Judicial Review?* 101 YALE L. J. 31 (1991).

104 Magill, *id.*

105 Elhague, *supra* note 103.

If, on the other hand, you think that regulators care about reputation and that judicial review may affect regulators' reputation, then you are more likely to view judicial review as part of the solution to regulatory capture. We can couch the argument similarly to how we did in the corporate context: it is well accepted that media scrutiny, when done effectively, is a great antidote to regulatory capture.[106] Now the question becomes what determines the effectiveness of media scrutiny. If one recognizes that judicial review can increase the saliency and reduce the complexity of a given regulatory issue, then the evidence we discussed in Chapter 2 suggests that such judicial review would greatly increase the effectiveness of media scrutiny of said issue. Once an issue gains saliency, and becomes more understandable and coverable by the media, the threat of public backlash reverses the special-interest group politics dynamics. Judicial review can therefore have a salutary effect on regulatory behavior in ways that were hitherto underappreciated.

Viewing judicial review from such reputational perspective provides some clues as to when courts should be more or less active when reviewing regulators' decisions: the key is in saliency and complexity. Judicial review would be most desirable in cases where the costs and benefits of regulation are less salient to the public.[107]

6.6 FINAL THOUGHTS: PUBLIC LITIGATION'S RELATIVE IMPACT ON REPUTATION

We saw throughout this chapter that the reputation-through-litigation argument works differently in public litigation than it does in private litigation. Part of the difference is due to legal doctrines, such as lack of far-reaching

[106] *See, e.g.*, Alexander Dyck et al., *Media versus Special Interests*, 56 J. L. & ECON. 521 (2013).

[107] If this observation seems trivial, consider how it represents a twist on some well-known public-choice-guided proposals. William Eskridge, for example, suggests a set of cases in which judges engaging in statutory interpretation should give little weight to legislative history/intent and be less inclined to defer: regulatory issues that involve a "concentrated-benefits; dispersed-costs" structure. In such a framework, judicial review should apply more forcefully in areas where asymmetries in information and coordination abilities are the strongest. William N. Eskridge, Jr., *Politics without Romance: Implications of Public Choice Theory for Statutory Interpretation*, 74 VA. L. REV. 275 (1988). In our framework, by contrast, judicial review should focus on areas where the asymmetries in *monitoring* abilities are the strongest. To be sure, there is a sizable overlap: many regulations that confer benefits on a powerful, concentrated group at the expense of the public are ones with low visibility and high complexity. Still, there exist ample examples of mismatches, such as when a regulatory issue imposes costs on the dispersed public, yet enjoys high visibility. In these types of cases, judicial activism is needed less: the public awareness may be enough to hold regulators to account and mitigate the risk of capture.

discovery in public litigation. Another part of the difference is due to the alternatives – the non-litigation sources of information in play. Litigation is not the only channel through which the legal system shapes regulators' reputation. Nonjudicial channels, such as freedom of information (FOI) requests or congressional oversight hearings, also play a role.

FOI is not available for private entities but is in play for public entities, facilitating bottom-up monitoring of regulators. The more the media and the public can rely on non-litigation information, the less the (relative) reputational impact of litigation would be. Indeed, this difference between public and private litigation came up in each method I used in my "law-as-source" study detailed in Chapter 2. The investigative reporters I interviewed frequently cited the ability to rely on FOI laws as one reason for why it is relatively easier to hold big government to account than to hold big business to account. The reporters' tip sheets on how to scrutinize the government make less frequent references to court documents than tip sheets on how to scrutinize private businesses. And the content analysis of prizewinning investigative projects reveals a recurring theme: a journalist submitting a FOI request to extract information from regulators, and then using it to show her readers how the regulator has been sitting on the information without acting on it.

To illustrate, consider the 2015 Pulitzer-winning story on healthcare providers milking Medicare at the expense of taxpayers. *Wall Street Journal* reporters submitted FOIA requests that forced to government to release Medicare data kept secret for decades. The reporters then sifted through the data and packaged it into a compelling story, showing for example how doctors are routinely testing the elderly for drugs such as heroin and "angel dust." The reporters also made the costs of Medicare abuse clear, indicating that taxpayers are on the hook for nearly $60 billion on bogus payments each year.[108] The *Journal*'s story ignited a public outcry. And the public outcry propelled regulators to act: the relevant federal agency started denying industry's requests to cover even more questionable tests, the FBI started investigating medical providers who collected alarmingly high amounts of Medicare money, and so on.[109] Note how this newfound regulatory action was due not to new information but rather to increased saliency: the *Journal*'s FOIA request simply surfaced (and highlighted, and widely diffused) data that was available to regulators but kept secret from the public since 1979.

108 Christopher Weaver & Anna Wilde Mathews, *Doctors Cash in on Drug Tests for Seniors*, WALL ST. J., *Nov.* 10, 2014.

109 *See* the Pulitzer Prize cover letter at www.pulitzer.org/winners/wall-street-journal-staff.

Yet another channel that implicates regulators' reputation is *nonjudicial reviews*. Think for example about the regulation czar – the Office of Information and Regulatory Affairs (OIRA) – reviewing the work of a specific regulator, or of a congressional oversight hearing where the regulator is "grilled."[110] Here as well, the list of Pulitzer-winning investigations provides cases in point. In 2003, the *New York Times* exposed the abuse of the mentally ill in state-regulated homes. The *Times*' reporter culled more than 5,000 pages of annual state inspection records, using them to draw attention to longstanding disorder in state-run homes.[111] The reporting prompted a class-action lawsuit, which later translated into New York State's Department of Health gradually moving many of the mentally ill residents to better locations and treatment.[112] Again it was not new information but rather the journalistic spotlight that propelled action: the state itself had been issuing damning reports for decades, but chose to ignore them.

Similar dynamics were in play a year earlier, with the 2002 Pulitzer-winning investigation of neglect of kids in foster homes. There, the *Washington Post* obtained records of a Child Fatality Review Committee. The Committee consistently detailed the neglect and deaths of many kids put in protective care, yet its conclusions were heard only in closed-doors government meetings, and its recommendations were constantly buried.[113] Once the *Post* journalists spotlighted and packaged the data into a compelling story, the regulator stepped in, overhauling the child welfare system.

On paper, then, FOIA and nonjudicial reviews should provide ample information for journalists to hold regulators to account. Yet as Chapter 2 alluded to, these channels are too often lacking. The implementation of FOIA is dysfunctional, fraught with delays and denials. And congress convenes special hearings usually only on issues that already gained saliency. Congressional hearings normally do not spotlight an ignored issue – they amplify an issue that has already reached the spotlight.

The upshot is that while non-litigation channels play a more prominent role in holding regulators to account (relative to holding businesses to account),

110 Ian R. Turner, Reviewing Procedure vs. Judging Substance: The Scope of Review and Bureaucratic Policymaking n.4 (2018) (unpublished manuscript), *available at* www.ianrturner.com/procedure-substance-5–2018.pdf; Meazell, *supra* note 31, at 192.

111 See, *e.g.*, Clifford J. Levy, *Broken Homes; A Final Destination: For Mentally Ill, Death and Misery*, N.Y. TIMES, Apr. 27, 2002.

112 *But see* Joaquin Sapien, *Independent Monitor Faults New York State for Delays in Aiding Mentally Ill*, PROPUBLICA, Apr. 28, 2017 (reporting that the state is behind schedule in its efforts to rectify the issue).

113 *See, e.g.*, Sari Horwitz et al., *"Protected" Children Died as Government Did Little*, WASH. POST, Sep. 8, 2001.

they still cannot fully substitute litigation-generated reputational pressures. In the regulatory arena, much like in the business arena, litigation is needed to supplement the information environment and facilitate reputational control.

A promising venue for future research would be identifying the regulatory areas in which litigation plays a bigger/smaller role in inducing reputational pressures. In some areas, the market for regulators' reputation works fine even without litigation. Think for example of regulatory areas where the feedback is immediate and clear, as in when under-regulation brings about catastrophes that cause acute identifiable harms to victims. In other regulatory areas, reputational concerns would not work without litigation. Think about areas where the harms are more latent, opaque, and disperse, as in toxic pollution that increases the probability of future latent diseases. In these areas, the implications we noted earlier (such as the case against confidential settlements, or for liberal standing) apply more forcefully.

PART III

IMPLICATIONS

7

The Case for Openness

7.1 INTRODUCTION

Throughout this book we have looked at examples from prizewinning journalistic stories that were told with the help of legal sources. But we have not looked at stories that were *not* told. What about stories that were not told because the legal system held information back, stonewalling journalists? We usually get a peek at such counterfactuals in cases where the information eventually gets out, after being buried for a while.

Such was the case with the cover-up of child abuse in the Catholic Church. Elsewhere I used the clergy sexual-abuse litigation as an example of a success story in which the interactions between the media and the courts helped hold the powerful to account.[1] Law created reputational pressures that pushed the powerful organization to admit mistakes and change its ways. Yet one could also view the example as illustrating a failure to warn.[2] The legal system had produced the damning information on the cover-up of child abuse many years before it became available to journalists. Only after a fortuitous turn of events – and a media outlet financially strong enough to fight a lengthy legal battle to unseal documents – did the information turn into a journalistic source. Had the information become available earlier, one could argue, many cases of child abuse could have been avoided. The reputational sanction came too late.

That was a recurring theme in my interviews with reporters. Right after they told me how instrumental legal sources are for them, reporters would usually continue to voice frustration with a legal system that produces information yet keeps it away from them, sealing documents and redacting details. This frustration touches upon a long-standing debate in the legal literature over

[1] Roy Shapira, *Law as Source: How the Legal System Facilitates Investigative Journalism*, 37 YALE L. & POL'Y REV. 153 (2018). We come back to this example in the Conclusion.

[2] ALEXANDRA LAHAV, IN PRAISE OF LITIGATION 76 (2016).

how publicly available law enforcement records should be.[3] The debate spans multiple applications: settlement versus trial, openness of proceedings, and so on.

This chapter applies the law-as-source framework to contribute to the openness-versus-secrecy debate along three key dimensions. Section 7.2 injects a real-life implications perspective into a too-often abstracted debate. Section 7.3 disentangles the normally comingled facets of the openness-versus-secrecy debate.[4] Law-as-source dynamics play out differently in questions such as whether to keep the amount of a settlement secret or whether to seal documents already submitted to the court. Section 7.4 provides a road map for concrete steps that can facilitate more law-as-source benefits. Section 7.5 concludes on a different, big-picture note, calling for more cautious approach when advocating for nonintervention.

7.2 REAL-LIFE IMPLICATIONS OF SECRECY

The argument for and against secrecy follows a similar formula across a wide array of applications. Those in favor of openness usually summon considerations of increased accountability and accuracy of judicial decision-making.[5] Those in favor of confidentiality cite the need to respect the parties' autonomy and to conserve public and private resources.[6] What both camps agree on, however, is the need to inject some evidence into the debate.[7] Specifically, both camps agree that we do not know much about how openness-versus-secrecy affects third parties.

Take, for concreteness, the debate over secret settlements.[8] Those against secret settlements argue that keeping the details about underlying misbehavior

3 Jon Bauer, *Buying Witness Silence: Evidence-Suppressing Settlements and Lawyers' Ethics*, 87 Or. L. Rev. 481, 493 (2008) (compiling references); Jack H. Friedenthal, *Secrecy in Civil Litigation: Discovery and Party Agreements*, 9 J. L. & Pol'y 67, 67–68 (2000) (same).

4 Laurie K. Doré, *Secrecy by Consent: The Use and Limits of Confidentiality in the Pursuit of Settlement*, 74 Notre Dame L. Rev. 283, 317 (1999) (showing that different facets of the debate are unjustifiably intertwined).

5 *See, e.g.*, Nebraska Press Ass'n v. Stuart, 427 U.S. 539, 587 (1976).

6 *See, e.g.*, Friedenthal, *supra* note 3. *Cf.* Steven Shavell, *The Fundamental Divergence between the Private and the Social Motive to Use the Legal System*, 26 J. Legal Stud. 575, 606–07 (1997).

7 *See, e.g.*, Alexandra D. Lahav, *The Roles of Litigation in American Democracy*, 65 Emory L. J. 1657, 1690 (2016) (calls for evidence from a public dispute resolution supporter); Carrie Menkel-Meadow, *Whose Dispute Is It Anyway? A Philosophical and Democratic Defense of Settlement (in Some Cases)*, 83 Geo. L. J. 2663, 2671 (1995) (calls for evidence from a confidentiality supporter).

8 A "secret settlement" is a settlement agreement that contains a provision whereby the parties promise to keep aspects of the dispute secret.

secret endangers public safety, as it fails to warn third parties.[9] Those favoring secret settlements retort that the public-safety argument rests on shaky grounds.[10] Most of the time, they claim, settlements contain information already available to regulators or to anyone who reads the initial complaint. If the public really wants to avoid a certain defendant, they can do so even without reading the settlement. Further, the public would not know what to do with information coming from open settlements. Settlement is not adjudication, and the public "cannot reliably evaluate what settlement information means."[11]

The evidence presented in Chapter 2 helps us remove some of the skepticism over the ability of open settlements to warn the public. The clergy sexual-abuse litigation illustrates. The *Boston Globe* had documented proof of the church's cover-up only because one plaintiff's lawyer (you might recall him from the *Spotlight* movie as the eccentric Mitchell Garabedian) insisted on fighting the church, one trial at a time, without signing secret settlements. Chapter 2 establishes a prima facie case to consider seriously the ability of the media to turn open settlements into watchdog journalism with teeth.

Relatedly, the law-as-source study illustrates what is wrong with the argument that the public would not know what to do with open settlements. In reality, the public does not sift through court records and settlement agreements. Information intermediaries do: stock analysts, institutional investors, consumer organizations, and, notably, investigative reporters. Investigative reporters test the reliability of raw data they get from court documents, and triangulate it with other sources. They use details from scattered settlements to identify and describe a pervasive pattern of institutional misconduct. Unlike beat reporters or news reporters, investigative reporters are less interested in the color and more interested in the pattern. That is, they do not read a single settlement in isolation, but rather view it as a lead that can help them find patterns of recurring misconduct.

The upshot for our purposes is that information intermediaries will make it easier for the public to make sense of the limited information contained in a settlement and to react accordingly.[12] Confidentiality provisions that hide

9 *See, e.g.*, David Luban, *Settlements and the Erosion of the Public Realm*, 83 GEO. L. REV. 2619, 2649–50 (1995).

10 Doré, *supra* note 4, at 301 (recognizing that the argument lacks empirical backing while arguing for openness); Friedenthal, *supra* note 3; Erik S. Knutsen, *Keeping Settlements Secret*, 37 FLA. ST. U. L. REV. 1, 27 n.60 (2010).

11 Friedenthal, *id.*, at 88 (maintaining that all the public learns from one settlement is that the defendant made a single mistake – but that in itself does not reveal a danger); Knutsen, *id.*, at 27–28.

12 As one journalist noted, journalists may not be good at creating their own databases, but when they stumble upon raw data from legal documents, they are good at sifting through it and "packaging it beautifully." Shapira, *supra* note 1, at 194 n.205.

even the basic details of the dispute hurt the ability of the media to effectively inform the public.[13]

7.3 DISENTANGLING THE ISSUES

The evidence on how journalists use information from the legal system to promote accountability allows us to unpack the different confidentiality doctrines that the literature has traditionally failed to distinguish.[14] There exist important differences, for example, between the desirability of keeping the amount of a settlement confidential and protecting all discovery-exchanged documents. This section applies the law-as-source angle to reassess and distinguish between documents filed with the court, such as expert opinions and documents exchanged among litigants but not filed with the court, such as discovery. The section then flags up a separate category, of one-sided arbitration clauses with class action waivers (which has become so crucial and timely that it gets its own chapter later), and resituates our earlier discussion of pleading standards.

7.3.1 *Judicial Information*

The category of "judicial information" encompasses information that has a direct connection to the process of judicial decision-making: trial transcripts, docket sheets, settlement agreements that are filed with the court, the right to attend trial, and so on.[15] On paper, this type of information can make a great source for investigative reporting, as the law presumes full public access to such documents.[16] Yet in reality, parties often stipulate to keep major aspects of judicial information private and judges are quick to approve.[17]

The problem is that both parties have incentives to handle their disputes in ways that limit public access to judicial information.[18] Take the issue of secret

[13] *Cf.* Jennifer LaFleur, *The Lost Stories*, Rep. Committee for Freedom Press (Nov. 2003), www.rcfp.org/rcfp/orders/docs/LOSTSTORIES.pdf.

[14] Doré, *supra* note 4, at 317 (explaining how arguments in the openness-versus-secrecy debate are often unjustifiably rehashed in different contexts).

[15] Andrew D. Goldstein, *Sealing and Revealing: Rethinking the Rules Governing Public Access to Information Generated through Litigation*, 81 Chi.-Kent. L. Rev. 375, 385 n.58 (2006).

[16] Nixon v. Warner Commc'ns, 435 U.S. 589, 597 (1978).

[17] Starting in the 1990s, there have been constant efforts by legislators to ban confidentiality agreements, yet the proposed sunshine-in-litigation reforms either do not get passed or get passed but do not pass muster. Doré, *supra* note 4, at section II.C.2.

[18] Shavell, *supra* note 6, at 605; Wendy Wagner, *When All Else Fails: Regulating Risky Products through Tort Litigation*, 95 Geo. L.J. 693, nn.71–74 (2007).

settlements. While the fact that most cases settle has become a truism,[19] more relevant for our purposes is the fact that most cases settle secretly: the parties often stipulate to keep details of the dispute private.[20] Defendants are willing to pay more for a confidentiality provision, to save themselves the risk of adverse publicity. Plaintiffs anticipate defendants' willingness to pay for secrecy, and use it as a bargaining chip. A plaintiff who receives a generous offer may not care about the positive externality; that is, she may not care whether relevant information gets out to third parties.

Judges have discretion and can ignore the parties' will and keep judicial information open. Yet judges too face skewed incentives: they are measured by caseload management, and not by the amorphous (and hitherto understudied) concept of how they contribute to information production.[21] The framework developed here would urge judges to overcome pressures to clear the docket and consider, among other factors, the law-as-source benefits emanating from openness. To be sure, not all cases implicate law-as-source considerations. As Chapter 2 noted, the nominal majority of legal disputes do not interest third parties. Yet in disputes involving large manufacturers or employers, whose behavior affects many, information production should factor in.

When factoring in information production, judges should be wary of the context. Not all disputes are created equal from an information-production perspective, and certain types of information are more likely to facilitate accountability journalism than others. In the secret settlements context, for instance, the problem is less about settlements that keep the amount paid secret, and more about settlements that erase all evidence of the dispute (including the parties' names), or contain provisions requiring the destruction of information obtained during the dispute.[22] The amount agreed upon may be of interest to other potential legal claimants, or to a journalist on the beat looking for color, but it is less helpful to an investigative reporter looking for a pattern of recurring misbehavior or trying to understand what and how things happened. To establish a pattern and dig deeper into the behavior in question the media will need the basic details – the fact of the dispute and the names of the parties – to remain open to the public.

[19] J. J. Prescott & Kathryn E. Spier, *A Comprehensive Theory of Civil Settlement*, 91 N.Y. U. L. REV. 59, 61 n.2 (2016).

[20] Bauer, *supra* note 3, at 491 nn.16–19 (compiling references); Knutsen, *supra* note 10, at 945, 946 n.1 (same).

[21] Goldstein, *supra* note 15, at 388, 435.

[22] Bauer, *supra* note 3, at 492 n.22 (compiling references for how common such provisions are).

7.3.2 *Litigant-Centered Information*

A second major category of openness-versus-secrecy debates concerns litigant-centered information, such as pre-trial discovery documents, or settlement agreements that are not filed with the court. The law regarding such information is different: the strong presumption of openness that applies to judicial information does not apply here.[23] The rationale behind the different legal treatment is the link to judicial accountability: since documents not filed with the court are not part of judicial decision-making, there is less of a need to keep them open to allow monitoring of judicial decision-making, or so the argument goes.[24]

Yet from a pure reputational perspective, discovery materials can be just as valuable as judicial information in facilitating media-driven accountability. In today's world, trials are vanishing,[25] and the overwhelming majority of information being produced during legal disputes is not filed with the court. To ban openness of litigant-exchanged information is therefore to undermine the ability of the media to hold the powerful to account.

From an investigative reporter's perspective, the main role of discovery materials is less about understanding what happened (you can tell that from the complaint) and more about understanding *how* things happened. Think about our oft-used example of internal company emails indicating what top management knew, when they knew it, and what they did or did not do to stop the misbehavior in question. Here, too, the Spotlight story is a case in point. The *Boston Globe*'s investigative team sat on a child abuse story for many months, because they were searching for the bigger story on the cover-up of child abuse by higher-ups in the church. The reporters got their proof – and made an impact – only after getting access to internal church documents produced during discovery, showing who knew what and when.

7.3.3 *Mandatory Arbitration Clauses*

Nowhere is the openness-versus-secrecy debate more consequential and timelier than in our third category, of one-sided arbitration clauses. Two Supreme

[23] Goldstein, *supra* note 15, at 376.

[24] *See, e.g.*, United States v. El-Sayegh, 131 F.3d 158, 163 (D.C. Cir. 1997). For an illustration of how blanket protective orders are normally given by the courts, even against public safety concerns, see Goldstein, *id.*, at 375–78.

[25] Marc Galanter, *The Vanishing Trial: An Examination of Trials and Related Matters in Federal and State Courts*, 1 J. Empirical Legal Stud. 459 (2004) (coining the "vanishing trials" moniker); Judith Resnik, *Diffusing Disputes: The Public in the Private of Arbitration, the Private in Courts, and the Erasure of Rights*, 124 Yale L. J. 2804, 2935 (2015) (stating that in 2010, civil trials began in about one case out of 100 filed in federal courts).

Court decisions in 2011 and 2013 – *AT&T Mobility LLC v. Concepcion*[26] and *American Express Co. v. Italian Colors Restaurant*[27] – expanded the scope of arbitration by enforcing unavoidable arbitration clauses that ban collective action.[28] The use of such arbitration clauses is constantly on the rise. As of 2017, 80 percent of the 100 largest companies use mandatory arbitration clauses in employment contracts,[29] and over sixty million Americans have signed such arbitration clauses.[30] Such arbitration clauses represent the biggest threat to law-as-source benefits. When a judge seals documents or issues protective orders, the given legal dispute may nevertheless serve as a valuable source for investigative reporting, because journalists are able to cull the docket sheets, motions, and complaints.[31] By contrast, when disputes are increasingly "diffused"[32] – funneled to private arbitration or not pursued to begin with (because collective action is banned) – journalists are much less able to dig into the misbehavior in question.[33]

To illustrate, consider the case of misconduct in foster homes for kids or nursing homes for the elderly. Investigative reports revealing such misconduct historically relied heavily on information from litigation. Take for example the 2002 Pulitzer-winning investigative report detailing the neglect of children placed in foster homes in the District of Columbia. Chapter 6 relayed the story of how following the journalistic report, the city overhauled its child welfare program.[34] It is unclear whether such an investigative report could be written in today's environment. Had the same type of misconduct occurred in the 2010s, it would probably have never reached the courts. A *New York Times* exposé found that over 100 cases of wrongful death and other misconduct at

26 563 U.S. 333 (2011).

27 570 U.S. 228 (2013).

28 As the court held in *Italian Colors*, "Courts must 'rigorously enforce' arbitration agreements according to their terms." *Id.* at 233.

29 Imre S. Szalai, *The Widespread Use of Workplace Arbitration among America's Top 100 Companies*, EMP. RTS. ADVOC. INST. FOR L. & POL'Y (Sept. 27, 2017), http://employeerightsadvocacy.org/wp-content/uploads/2017/09/Insitute-2017-Report-Widespread-Use-Of-Workplace-Arbitration.pdf.

30 Alexander J.S. Colvin, *The Growing Use of Mandatory Arbitration*, ECON. POL'Y INST. (Sept. 27, 2017), www.epi.org/publication/the-growing-use-of-mandatory-arbitration.

31 *Cf.* Stephanie Brenowitz, *Deadly Secrecy: The Erosion of Public Information under Private Justice*, 19 OHIO ST. J. ON DISP. RESOL. 679, 699 (2004); Lahav, *supra* note 2, at 73 ("arbitrated disputes do not produce a public record and cannot . . . bring wrongdoing to light").

32 Resnik, *supra* note 25, at 2807 (coining the terminology).

33 Brenowitz, *supra* note 31, at 696; Lahav, *supra* note 2, at 27.

34 See the Pulitzer Prize committee's explanation. *Sari Horwitz, Scott Higham and Sarah Cohen of* the Washington Post, THE PULITZER PRIZES (2002), www.pulitzer.org/winners/sari-horwitz-scott-higham-and-sarah-cohen.

nursing homes were pushed to private arbitration between 2010 and 2014.[35] When the federal regulator in charge of Medicare and Medicaid funding proposed a rule barring nursing homes from funneling all residents' claims to arbitration, the Trump administration stepped in and scrapped it.[36] And because such disputes are not aired in the court anymore, information about the underlying misbehavior is more likely to remain out of the media's reach

Those in favor of the ever-proliferating arbitration clauses refer to the cost-saving attributes of arbitration relative to litigation. As one spokesperson puts it, "Arbitration provides a way for people to hold companies accountable without spending a lot of money."[37] Even if we assume that such an assertion is empirically valid – that is, that individual consumers who are harmed get their money back effectively in arbitration[38] – the law-as-source perspective exposes two flaws in the spokesperson's argument. First, when we evaluate the efficacy of dispute resolution channels, we should consider not just the costs and benefits to the parties to a specific dispute, but also the costs and benefits to society. Arbitration clauses with class waivers come with a set of societal costs in the form of reducing the effectiveness of media scrutiny. We will elaborate on this point in Chapter 8, coming next.

Second, and relatedly, even if we assume that companies pay full damages in individual arbitrations, such payments hardly translate into public accountability. They are more like the small costs of doing business. When a cellular company overcharges its customers on a monthly basis, and then is dragged into an individual arbitration and pays back the full amount, this $30-sized sanction does not qualify as deterrence. To hold large companies truly accountable for their misbehavior, we should expose and diffuse information on their misbehavior. Reputational deterrence is a necessary tool for achieving corporate accountability. Yet reputational deterrence only works when information on corporate misconduct is publicly available.

To be sure, applying the reputational perspective to argue against mandatory arbitration is less automatic than we have portrayed here thus far. This is why Chapter 8 below delves into the issue in depth, with a special emphasis on mandatory arbitration of shareholder claims.

35 Jessica Silver-Greenberg & Michael Corkery, *In Arbitration, "A Privatization of the Justice System,"* N.Y. TIMES, Nov. 1, 2015.

36 Jessica Silver-Greenberg & Michael Corkery, *U.S. Agency Move to Allow Class Action Lawsuits against Financial Firms*, N.Y. TIMES, Jul. 10, 2017.

37 Jessica Silver-Greenberg & Michael Corkery, *Arbitration Everywhere, Stacking the Deck of Justice*, N.Y. TIMES, Oct. 31, 2015.

38 Such assertions are deeply contested. *See, e.g.*, Resnik, *supra* note 25.

7.3.4 *Pleading Standards*

In Chapter 3 we discussed the function of pleading standards in the specific context of corporate law litigation. But the pleading standard issue is much broader: following the Supreme Court decisions in *Twombly* and *Iqbal*, the heightened-versus-liberal-pleading-standards debate has become one of the most practical and heated in the legal world today.[39] The debate revolves around arguments such as conserving judicial resources, protecting defendants from frivolous lawsuits, and allowing access to justice.[40] This book suggests one more important factor to consider: heightened pleading standards affect information production negatively, thus indirectly hurting reputational deterrence.

To understand why, recall Chapter 2's discussion about how the earlier stages in the process often produce most of the reputation-relevant information. In large-scale disputes – where the misconduct is already revealed prior to litigation – the legal system's comparative advantage (i.e., the chance that litigation will teach market players something they do not already know) comes from discovery. Heightened pleading standards reduce the chances that these cases will reach discovery, thus reducing the chances that new light will be shed on the misconduct.

A modification and clarification are in order. In most cases the reputational considerations are irrelevant (outside observers do not monitor them), and so my argument for liberal pleading standards does not apply. Nor do I suggest that screening frivolous lawsuits is unimportant. All I am suggesting is to include an overlooked factor in the cost–benefit analysis, namely, the benefit of producing information that helps market players assess companies (a positive externality). Concretely, a potential solution is to tailor different pleading standards based on the dispute's impact on third parties. On paper, we can identify a subset of cases – say, well-publicized cases with large companies – where it is best to screen suits at a later stage (not at the motion to dismiss but rather at the summary judgment stage). We saw in Chapter 3 that Delaware's corporate law has indeed developed in ways that reflect this optimum: while Delaware courts eventually screen many lawsuits and rarely interfere with managers' decisions, they do so only after providing plaintiffs with access to information-extracting tools in the early stages of the process.

39 Bell Atl. Corp. v. Twombly, 550 U.S. 544 (2007); Ashcroft v. Iqbal, 556 U.S. 662 (2009); Jonah B. Gelbach, *Locking the Doors to Discovery? Assessing the Effects of* Twombly *and* Iqbal *on Access to Discovery*, 121 YALE L.J. 2270, 2274 (2011).

40 Daphna Kapeliuk & Alon Klement, *Contracting Around* Twombly, 60 DEPAUL L. REV. 1, 1 (2010).

7.4 HOW TO SOLVE THE INFORMATION-UNDERPRODUCTION PROBLEM?

Let us be clear on what we can or cannot infer from the reputation-through-litigation argument. The fact that the law can serve as a valuable source of media coverage does *not* mean that we should outright ban secret settlements or make all discovery materials and arbitrations public. Discovery is so far-reaching in scope, and settlements so prevalent, that they beg discretion to allow confidentiality under certain conditions. Further, banning confidentiality may come with unintended effects of reducing the available flow of information *ex ante*, for example, by pushing parties to settle out of court.[41] Nor can the reputation-through-litigation argument help us weigh considerations of privacy and proprietary or embarrassing information.

What the reputational perspective does offer is a more informed background against which judges and policymakers can balance the costs and benefits of confidentiality. Consider the following concrete proposals.

7.4.1 *Lessons for Judges: Altering the Weighing of Public Interest and the Language Used*

Do not rubber-stump parties' requests to seal information. First and most basically, the reputational framework invites judges' attention to an under-appreciated set of benefits – informational benefits. Open dispute resolution facilitates reputational deterrence and accountability journalism, which in turn facilitates greater accountability in society. The sealing of documents is usually governed by judicial doctrine, and in many states the doctrine includes weighing in the public interest in access to information versus considerations such as privacy and caseload management.[42] The law-as-source argument may tilt the scale in favor of the public interest in access, at least in cases that involve large manufacturers or employers whose behavior affect many third parties.

Alter the language used to describe behavior. The reputational framework should also make judges consider altering the language they use to condemn wrongdoing. The legal system's ability to produce valuable information to

[41] I elaborated on the selection-effects caveat in Roy Shapira, *Reputation through Litigation: How the Legal System Shapes Behavior by Producing Information*, 91 WASH. L. REV. 1193, 1242 (2016). *See also* Scott Moss, *Illuminating Secrecy: A New Economic Analysis of Confidential Settlements*, 105 MICH. L. REV. 867 (2007) (arguing that there is a lot of uncertainty regarding the consequences of tinkering with secret settlements).

[42] *See, e.g.*, Goldstein, *supra* note 15, at 387.

third parties depends not just on the documents that private parties extract but also on the language that judges use. In order for the information to affect third-parties' beliefs, it has to be not just available and accurate, but also accessible and comprehensible.[43] Adherence to rigid doctrines and technical language will hurt the potential to influence reputation. In areas where the demand for reputation-correcting is great, judges should therefore consider calibrating the legal language in a manner that is more relevant to market players. Think for example of moving from "liable/not liable" dichotomy to a "liability disproved"/"liability unproved"/"liability proved" system.[44]

7.4.2 *Lessons for Policymakers: Creating Databases and Information Safety Valves*

Create open databases. Beyond inviting judges' attention and providing them with a road map to weigh law-as-source benefits, the reputational framework can also inform policymaking efforts. For example, our framework lends credence to, and underlines the importance of, existing proposals to create databases of lawsuits that were filed but settled and databases of arbitrated disputes.[45] We learned from interviews, tip sheets, and successful investigative projects, that pattern-identifying is perhaps the most important way in which the legal system helps investigative reporters. Accordingly, if we allow large companies to seal documents or use mandatory arbitration clauses, we should at least assure the documentation of the type and number of issues that were funneled to arbitration. Having a public record of the dispute would allow watchdogs to identify behavior that goes against the norms.

Install an openness safety valve. Once databases of disputes are put in place, we can establish a mechanism or institution that will release further information about certain disputes. Think of it as analogous to an information escrow/safety valve: a mechanism that is in charge of releasing information that should not remain private.[46] Say a toddler car-seat manufacturer is being sued for product defects. The victims and the manufacturer then reach a secret settlement and keep information about the dispute private. Then, a second family sues the manufacturer over the same issue. Then a third. And so on. Under existing laws, chances are that each family would be unaware of the others, and that a journalist digging into the issue would not be able to grasp the scope

43 David S. Law, A *Theory of Judicial Power and Judicial Review*, 97 GEO. L.J. 723, 749 (2009).
44 Robert Cooter & Ariel Porat, *Should Courts Deduct Non-Legal Sanctions from Damages?*, 30 J. LEGAL STUD. 401, 420 n.22 (2001).
45 Lahav, *supra* note 2, at 79.
46 *Cf.* Ian Ayres & Cait Unkovich, *Information Escrows*, 111 MICH. L. REV. 145 (2012).

and details – simply because information from each separate lawsuit remains hidden. Such was the case in the sexual-abuse cases in the Catholic Church. A way to mitigate the existing failure-to-warn problem without overburdening courts would be to pre-specify criteria under which the filing of additional disputes would trigger a mechanism that makes information about previous disputes publicly available.

For the sake of illustration, assume that the fifth family filing a complaint over the same issue would trigger a release of the basic details of the previous four legal disputes involving the same defendant manufacturer over the same alleged product defect. Without getting into specific design details, the criteria for releasing information should be specified according to industry benchmarks: how many lawsuits are being filed on average against a physician in a given practice; how many lawsuits are usually filed against a manufacturer of a given product; and so on.[47] That way, reporters or future victims would be able to search for a pattern of recurring misbehavior and expose it.[48] The increased threat of being exposed as a low-quality manufacturer would incentivize manufacturers to invest in the safety of their products *ex ante*.

Make FOIA great again. Finally, while our focus throughout this book has been on indirect channels of information production (i.e., law enforcement), we would be remiss if we did not discuss the most obvious way to improve information production, namely, revamping the direct sourcing channels. One could think, for example, about invigorating FOIA to make it easier on reporters and public-interest organizations to extract damning information about politicians. Yet, themes from the law-as-source study dovetail with others' observation that FOIA, even when executed properly, is an inherently problematic tool for promoting accountability.[49] Proposals for remedies should therefore not limit themselves to FOIA, but rather should extend to bolstering other sourcing channels, such as whistleblowing laws, or the indirect sourcing channels we have been discussing, such as openness of litigation. Concretely, this book suggests that the most important implication regarding FOIA is that if we are to promote accountability, we should reign the exemption for law enforcement records.[50]

[47] For relevant data, *see, e.g.*, Anupam B. Jena, *Malpractice Risk According to Physician Specialty*, 365 New Eng. J. Med. 629 (2011).

[48] As Ayres and Unkovich note, a somewhat similar mechanism is already in place in criminal law: a "commitment escrow" of sorts, whereby criminal records remain under seal, unless the defendant recidivates within a given period. Ayres & Unkovich, *supra* note 46, at 152.

[49] David Pozen, *Freedom of Information beyond the Freedom of Information Act*, 165 U. Pa. L. Rev. 1097 (2017).

[50] David E. McCraw, *The "Freedom from Information" Act: A Look Back at Nader, FOIA, and What Went Wrong*, 126 YALE L.J. F. 232, 239–40 (2016).

7.5 REPUTATION IS NOT A JUSTIFICATION FOR NONINTERVENTION

The most basic policy implication stemming from recognizing the role of the law in facilitating reputational control is to adopt a more cautious approach to advocating for nonintervention. We noted this from the very first paragraph of the book: A strong strand of the economic analysis of law literature treats reputation as justification for nonintervention. Such analysis rests on the assumption that law and reputation are independent of and substitutes for each other. And so when we recognize an area with strong reputational forces, we can scale back legal intervention, or so the argument goes. Manufacturers already have incentives to invest optimally in the safety of their products, because they wish to avoid the risk of losing their reputation if bad news about their products breaks.[51] Maintaining a costly system of litigation is superfluous in an already existing market system of control.

Yet if this book has taught us anything, it is that strong reputational forces are largely a *result* of product liability litigation and regulatory investigations. Virtually all investigative reporters' tip sheets on how to cover faulty products include explicit orders to look for information from litigation. If we abolish litigation, we take away a large part of the media's ability to scrutinize faulty products. Journalists rely on court documents to spot patterns that enable them to differentiate between one-off mistakes and systematic breakdowns or between genuine incompetence and clear disregard for consumers' safety. The strength of market forces, at least in the area of product safety, is very much a result of the existing legal system.[52]

There is a broader point here. When we think of the design of legal institutions, we usually have in mind goals such as assuring compensation for victims or punishing wrongdoers to deter them. Yet in some contexts, we also need to take into account the indirect deterrence function of providing information that facilitates better reputational control. Those who allude to market forces when recommending policy solutions need to be aware of the role that media scrutiny plays in market discipline, and the role that the law plays in media scrutiny.

[51] Mitchell Polinsky & Steven Shavell, *The Uneasy Case for Product Liability*, 123 HARV. L. REV. 1437 (2010). For a concise description of their (much more nuanced) argument, and a qualifier, see Shapira, *supra* note 41, at 1197.

[52] As one Pulitzer winner relayed, "To operate in a private world, without [legal intervention], would leave us [investigative reporters] with almost nothing. Would shut down a valuable source for us." *See* Appendix B (Table A1, St. John interview).

8

The Case against Mandatory Arbitration

8.1 INTRODUCTION

Throughout the 2010s, the Supreme Court of the United States has enforced contractual provisions that force arbitration of disputes and ban class actions.[1] Unsurprisingly, companies quickly went on to instill these mandatory arbitration provisions in their contracts with consumers, employees, and suppliers.[2] A heated debate ensued, bursting out of academic circles and into popular media, over the desirability of such mandatory arbitration revolution. Proponents argued it will improve efficiency, by streamlining dispute resolution and reducing lawyer fees. Opponents argued it will be unfair for the already disadvantaged workers, consumers, and suppliers, depriving them of their day in court. Yet the existing debate too often misses the forest for the trees. Instead of analyzing fairness and efficiency toward parties to a given dispute, we should focus on effects on the market overall. Even if shifting from litigation to arbitration would be good for a specific company *and* its consumers/workers/investors,[3] such shift may prove detrimental to the market overall, because we would lose the positive externalities (in the form of quality information on corporate behavior) that come with litigation.

We saw in previous chapters that litigation facilitates market discipline. Litigation provides market players with information on corporate misconduct, thereby helping them avoid doing business with shady companies and

[1] Epic Sys. Corp. v. Lewis, 138 S. Ct. 1612, 1632 (2018); Am. Express Co. v. Italian Colors Rest., 570 U.S. 228, 233 (2013); AT&T Mobility LLC v. Concepcion, 563 U.S. 333, 352 (2011). I use the (common) term "*mandatory* arbitration" here to refer to non-negotiated, take-it-or-leave-it provisions.

[2] Brian Fitzpatrick, *The End of Class Actions?*, 57 ARIZ. L. REV. 161, 164 & n.10 (2015) (compiling references).

[3] A big "if." *See* Judith Resnik, *Diffusing Disputes: The Public in the Private of Arbitration, the Private in Courts, and the Erasure of Rights*, 124 YALE L.J. 2804 (2015).

businesspersons. But in a world where disputes are either diffused (because class action is banned) or funneled to behind-closed-doors arbitration, the flow of information is severally curtailed, and reputational deterrence loses its power.

To be sure, transforming our reputation-through-litigation argument into a case against mandatory arbitration is far from automatic. Before making the reputational case against mandatory arbitration, one needs to consider both the *context* and the *counterfactual*. In some areas, most of the law-as-source benefits come from direct channels such as FOIA or disclosure laws, rather than from litigation. In these contexts, moving away from litigation will not hurt reputational deterrence much. In other areas, FOIA or disclosure laws do not produce valuable information, but neither does litigation. Some types of litigation are simply not geared toward information production: think for example about certain doctrines that make plaintiffs less likely to survive the pleading stage and reach discovery.

And even if litigation in a given context does produce valuable information, we still need to consider the counterfactual: the possibility that, once we move away from litigation, other institutions would emerge to produce valuable information. For example, ramped-up public enforcement, or individual arbitration, may substitute the informational benefits we currently get from litigation, and at lower costs.

The reputational case against mandatory arbitration is therefore highly context-specific. Accordingly, this chapter evaluates the desirability of mandatory arbitration in a specific context: shareholder claims in corporate and securities laws. As of this writing, corporate and securities litigation remain the last bastion where class actions still reign. But commentators, practitioners, and policymakers have suggested that the mandatory arbitration revolution can, and should, apply to shareholder litigation as well.[4] The idea is that companies could amend their charters or bylaws to include such a provision, or go public with it, thereby forcing shareholders to arbitrate their claims individually, putting an end to shareholder litigation as we have come to know it. By delving into the details of such proposal in the shareholder litigation context, we get to extract more generalizable lessons to other contexts as well.

Those in favor of market arbitration often base their argument on the notion that ending shareholder litigation as we came to know it is not a bad thing. They cite evidence on how shareholder litigation fares badly in compensating victims and amounts to little more than a transfer of wealth from investors to

[4] *See, e.g.*, Hal S. Scott & Leslie N. Silverman, *Stockholder Adoption of Mandatory Individual Arbitration for Stockholder Disputes*, 36 Harv. J.L. & Pub. Pol'y 1187 (2013).

lawyers. Yet compensation is not the only measuring stick, or even the most important one. When evaluating a proposed shift from litigation to arbitration, we should also consider deterrence. The critical question is whether litigation has a salutary effect on corporate behavior. Litigation will have such a salutary effect whenever it makes defendants internalize the costs of their misbehavior. Importantly, litigation can make defendants behave better not just by threatening them with legal sanctions, but also indirectly, by threatening them with nonlegal sanctions. Litigation can exact (noninsurable) emotional costs. And it can facilitate reputational penalties: the risk of having damning information about how you behaved become public, thereby reducing the willingness of outside observers to trust and do business with you going forward. Allowing companies to force arbitration without class action in such a context would be a mistake.

The chapter proceeds in five sections. Section 8.2 maps the contours of the existing mandatory arbitration debate. Section 8.3 approaches the debate from a different angle, namely our reputation-through-litigation perspective. The section highlights how shareholder litigation, specifically, is more front-loaded than other types of litigation. The main event always comes early: think about the demand requirement in derivative actions or the pleading stage in securities class actions. As a result, plaintiffs in shareholder litigation find it harder to survive motions to dismiss and reach discovery. Yet, counter-intuitively, that does not mean that shareholder litigation is less informative. Plaintiffs have developed prediscovery investigatory tools, such as requesting to inspect the company's books and records or locating current or former employees willing to share damning information. These tools allow not just for better pleading but also for production of reputation-relevant information. Section 8.3 also breaks down the differential reputational impact of various types of shareholder litigation: derivate actions, securities class actions, and deal litigation.

Section 8.4 considers the counterfactual: in a world with mandatory arbitration of shareholder claims, could other institutions substitute litigation's informational benefits? This section assesses the information-production potential of enforcement by the Securities and Exchange Commission (SEC), individual arbitration by institutional investors, and standalone requests to inspect a company's books and records, and finds them all wanting. SEC enforcement is geared toward maximizing enforcement numbers rather than information (as Chapter 4 showed). Individual arbitration is geared toward confidentiality rather than openness. And any information gleaned from requests to inspect the company's books has to remain confidential unless it is filed in conjunction with litigation. The upshot is that a shift to arbitration is bound to result in loss of informational benefits.

Section 8.5 sketches policy implications. Recognizing the informational role of litigation puts a thumb on the scales against importing mandatory arbitration provisions to corporate and securities laws. If courts and regulators nevertheless decide to enforce such provisions, we should at a minimum set basic rules ensuring that shareholder arbitration would produce meaningful information. For example, we can mandate "explained awards," whereby the arbitrator provides a short, publicly available factual description of what happened, as well as reasoning for her decision.

Section 8.6 offers concluding thoughts on the applicability of the reputational case against mandatory arbitration more generally, beyond the shareholder litigation context. The section uses specific examples from labor law, which illustrate how a shift to arbitration would have different effects on different markets. I then use examples spurred by the #MeToo movement to highlight the other side: instead of looking at how a shift to arbitration will affect reputation, looking at how reputational concerns affect firms' decisions to adopt mandatory arbitration provisions to begin with.

8.2 THE EXISTING DEBATE

Mandatory arbitration of shareholder claims is hardly a new topic. But the contours of the debate have recently changed. The existing literature has focused on whether arbitration provisions are consistent with state and federal laws.[5] Historically, companies considering adopting such provisions had to anticipate facing opposition from the courts and, notably, the SEC. But the line of Supreme Court pro-arbitration decisions, coupled with the Trump administration pressuring the SEC to change its anti-arbitration stance, now signal to companies wishing to adopt such provisions that any remaining legal hurdles will be cleared.[6] Section 8.2.1 elaborates.

Assuming the legal hurdles are cleared, should companies adopt arbitration provisions? Should the SEC give in to pressures and approve them? Section 8.2.2 details the existing policy arguments. The extant debate evaluates the desirability of arbitration by reference to the benchmark – the current state of shareholder litigation. Proponents of the shift to arbitration suggest it will leave

[5] For a recent, concise summary, see generally Zachary D. Clopton & Verity Winship, *A Cooperative Federalism Approach to Shareholder Arbitration*, 128 YALE L.J. FORUM 169 (2018).

[6] David H. Webber, *Shareholder Litigation without Class Actions*, 57 ARIZ. L. REV. 201, 205 (2015).

investors better off, simply because litigation currently offers them very little compensation with very high fees. Notably missing from the debate, however, is a full account of litigation's deterrence benefits.

8.2.1 *Is Mandatory Arbitration Good Law?*

Historically, companies wishing to adopt mandatory arbitration provisions for shareholder claims anticipated facing a slew of legal hurdles. The SEC had steadfastly opposed such provisions, viewing them as a violation of the securities laws' "anti-waiver" provisions.[7] In 2012, for example, the SEC pressured private-equity giant Carlyle to drop a mandatory arbitration provision before it signed off on the company's IPO plans and allowed companies to exclude from their proxy materials shareholder proposals to adopt such provisions.[8]

Getting courts to sign off on arbitration provisions was also far from given. The Federal Arbitration Act (FAA) enforces arbitration provisions among contractual parties. It was not clear whether corporate governance documents would be considered contracts for FAA purposes, if only because they lack the key feature of bargaining between arm's-length counterparties.[9] A more recent challenge came in 2015, when the Delaware legislature amended its corporate law to allow forum-exclusion bylaws only if they do not exclude Delaware's courts.[10] A sweeping arbitration provision would run against such law.

In recent years, however, the legal hurdles started clearing. In 2011, the Supreme Court handed down its *AT&T Mobility LLC v. Concepcion*[11] decision, enforcing an arbitration provision with a class action waiver, while ruling that the FAA trumps state contract law. Contract law, like corporate law, is considered the domain of the states, but that did not stop the Court.[12] Then in 2013, the *American Express Co. v. Italian Colors*

7 The anti-waiver provisions are Securities Act of 1933 § 14, 15 U.S.C. § 77n (2012), and Securities Exchange Act of 1934 § 29(a), 15 U.S.C. § 78cc(a). They disallow waiving compliance with securities laws. On their applicability to arbitration provisions, see Barbara Black, *Arbitration of Investors' Claims against Issuers: An Idea of Whose Time Has Come?*, 75 Law & Contemp. Probs. 107, 115 (2012); Webber, *id.*, at 209–10.

8 Pfizer Inc., SEC No-Action Letter, 2012 WL 587597, at *13 (Feb. 22, 2012); Gannett Co., SEC No-Action Letter, 2011 WL 6859124, at *1 (Feb. 22, 2012); *see also* Clopton & Winship, *supra* note 5, at 178 n.42.

9 Ann M. Lipton, *Manufactured Consent: The Problem of Arbitration Clauses in Corporate Charters and Bylaws*, 104 Geo. L.J. 583, 629 (2016). Within this line of argument, there is a distinction between charter and bylaw amendments: the former entail explicit shareholder consent and so they fit better under the FAA. Fitzpatrick, *supra* note 2, at 178.

10 Del. Code Ann. tit. 8, § 115 (2019).

11 563 U.S. 333 (2011).

12 Fitzpatrick, *supra* note 2, at 187.

Restaurant[13] decision upheld *Concepcion* and further expanded the FAA's scope by enforcing the arbitration clause even when it renders a *federal* law (the Sherman Act) ineffective. In both decisions the issue of consent seems to take a backseat to a more policy-oriented approach. Consumers of cell phone plans cannot bargain their way out of take-it-or-leave-it arbitration provisions, yet the Court enforced these provisions on them, suggesting that arbitration is the more effective procedure to handle their disputes.

The *Concepcion* and *Italian Colors Restaurant* decisions did more than just signal the lowering of legal hurdles. They also significantly increased the benefits of fighting any remaining legal uncertainties for companies; the real innovation was not in respecting arbitration provisions, but rather in enforcing the class action waivers in these provisions.[14]

A similar pro-arbitration turn may be taking place inside the SEC, with nudges from the Trump administration.[15] In 2017, the US Treasury prepared a report (in response to Executive Order 13,772) on how to relax regulations that stymie activity in capital markets.[16] The Treasury report identified reducing the costs of litigation as a key step toward reinvigorating US stock listings and recommended that the SEC investigate a shift to arbitration. The media has since reported that the Trump administration keeps pushing the SEC to reverse its anti-arbitration stance and that the SEC now privately signals to companies its willingness to change course.[17] In July 2017, then-SEC Commissioner Michael Piwowar floated the idea in a public speech[18]: "For shareholder lawsuits, companies can come to us to ask for relief to put in mandatory arbitration into their charter . . . I would encourage companies to come and talk to us about that."[19]

13 228 U.S. 228 (2013).

14 Black, *supra* note 7, at 118. Recall the evidence Chapter 7 presented, on how 80 percent of the big 100 companies use mandatory arbitration clauses in their employment contracts.

15 Chapter 7 showed the Trump administration's pro-arbitration bent in other areas of law.

16 Steven T. Mnuchin & Craig S. Phillips, U.S. Dep't of the Treasury, A Financial System that Creates Economic Opportunities: Capital Markets: Report to President Donald J. Trump (2017) [hereinafter The Treasury Report].

17 Benjamin Bain, *SEC Weighs a Big Gift to Companies: Blocking Investor Lawsuits*, Bloomberg (Jan. 26, 2018, 4:00 AM), www.bloomberg.com/news/articles/2018–01–26/trump-s-sec-mulls-big-gift-to-companies-blocking-investor-suits.

18 Sarah N. Lynch, *U.S. SEC's Piwowar Urges Companies to Pursue Mandatory Arbitration Clauses*, Reuters (July 17, 2017, 3:14 PM), www.reuters.com/article/us-usa-sec-arbitration-idUSKBN1A221Y.

19 Bain, *supra* note 17. When commissioner Piwowar stepped down, newly appointed commissioner Peirce stepped up to the plate of advocating for mandatory arbitration. *See, e.g.*, Hester M Peirce, *Speech: Festivus, Fortnite, and Focus: Remarks before the Council of Institutional Investors Spring Conference*, Mar. 5, 2019, www.sec.gov/news/speech/speech-peirce-030519.

Given this evident pro-arbitration bent, mandatory arbitration provisions are now much more likely to be considered consistent with state and federal laws. Why have we yet to see companies rushing to adopt them? We can conjecture that there is a first-mover disadvantage that companies fear. The first company that adopts such a provision will expose itself to the costs associated with defending its stance in the courtroom and the court of public opinion.[20] However, once the first test case proves successful, there is reason to expect many other companies to follow.[21] Is that a good thing?

8.2.2 *Is Mandatory Arbitration Good Policy?*

Those in favor of shifting to mandatory arbitration usually make their case by criticizing the existing state of shareholder litigation. Shareholder litigation has two main rationales: compensation and deterrence.[22] By now there is wide agreement that shareholder litigation fares badly on the first prong: compensation.[23] The recoveries that shareholder plaintiffs get are nominal.[24] And in the rare cases where compensation is not nominal, critiques continue, it is circular.[25] That is, because the company itself (directly or through insurance) is the one often compensating the plaintiffs, the costs are borne by the company's existing shareholders. Diversified investors are therefore as likely to receive payment as plaintiffs, as they are to pay as defendants. Once you factor in the transaction costs of litigation (notably, lawyers' fees), many scholars conclude that shareholder litigation merely transfers wealth from investors to lawyers.[26] Against this background, mandatory-arbitration proponents claim that a shift to arbitration will actually improve things for consumers/investors. Arbitration will generate higher monetary reliefs with lower transaction costs (a quicker, more cost-effective procedure).

[20] Claudia H. Allen, *Bylaws Mandating Arbitration of Stockholder Disputes?*, 39 DEL. J. CORP. L. 751, 809 (2015).

[21] Bain, *supra* note 17; Fitzpatrick, *supra* note 2, at 191.

[22] *See, e.g.*, John C. Coffee, Jr., *Reforming the Securities Class Action: An Essay on Deterrence and Its Implementation*, 106 COLUM. L. REV. 1534, 1538 (2006).

[23] Scott & Silverman, *supra* note 4, at 1192; Webber, *supra* note 6, at 214.

[24] On securities class actions, see James D. Cox & Randall S. Thomas, *Letting Billions Slip Through Your Fingers: Empirical Evidence and Legal Implications of the Failure of Financial Institutions to Participate in Securities Class Action Settlements*, 58 STAN. L. REV. 411, 421–24 (2005). On derivative suits, see Jessica Erickson, *Corporate Governance in the Courtroom: An Empirical Analysis*, 51 WM. & MARY L. REV. 1749, 1749 (2010).

[25] Coffee, Jr., *supra* note 22, at 1556–58.

[26] Jill E. Fisch, *Confronting the Circularity Problem in Private Securities Litigation*, 2009 WIS. L. REV. 333, 337.

A glaring weakness in the existing arguments for arbitration and against litigation is the lack of attention to the other social goal of litigation, namely, deterrence.[27] This is a broader issue: most empirical work on shareholder litigation focuses on compensation, leaving deterrence understudied.[28] In the arbitration versus litigation debate, those favoring arbitration bypass the lack of evidence by assuming that little compensation translates into weak deterrence.[29] A perfect illustration comes from the abovementioned Treasury report: the report mentions the possibility that securities class actions contribute to deterrence, only to quickly dismiss it by invoking the low-and-circular compensation point, and then calls for considering a shift to arbitration.[30] While it is understandable that difficulties in measuring deterrence make it much less amenable to empirical work, deterrence is simply too important to be ignored or lumped together with compensation.[31]

Deterrence does not hinge solely on compensation. Litigation can impose costs on defendants – making them internalize the social costs of their misconduct – even without compensating plaintiffs. Pertinently, litigation can expose defendants to nonlegal (and uninsurable) sanctions. It can impose emotional costs on defendants.[32] And it can hurt their reputations. In other words, when assessing deterrence, we need to consider both direct- and indirect-deterrence effects of facilitating nonlegal sanctions.

The existing arguments *against* mandatory arbitration tend to ignore the indirect-deterrence angle. One common type of criticism emphasizes the adverse effects of arbitration on plaintiffs in specific disputes. The arbitration

27 Myriam Gilles & Gary Friedman, *Exploding the Class Action Agency Costs Myth: The Social Utility of Entrepreneurial Lawyers*, 155 U. PA. L. REV. 103, 107 (2006) (noting and criticizing literature's "compensationalist" approach).

28 James D. Cox & Randall S. Thomas, *Mapping the American Shareholder Litigation Experience: A Survey of Empirical Studies of the Enforcement of the U.S. Securities Law*, 6 EUROPEAN COMPANY & FIN. L. REV. 164, 182 (2009) ("Compensation and deterrence frequently are joined together in debates over the social value of securities class actions. Much of the empirical research . . . bears directly on the former, but as seen here there is very little on the latter").

29 *See, e.g.*, Urska Velikonja, *The Cost of Securities Fraud*, 54 WM. & MARY L. REV. 1887, 1956 (2013) (arguing that shareholder class actions "fail to deter the wrongdoer managers, as they virtually never pay out of pocket").

30 THE TREASURY REPORT, *supra* note 16, at 33–34.

31 Elizabeth Chamblee Burch, *Securities Class Actions as Pragmatic Ex Post Regulation*, 43 GA. L. REV. 63, 92–93 (2008); Cox & Thomas, *supra* note 28, at 183 (noting that deterrence remains an "extremely important area for future research").

32 *See, e.g.*, Tom Baker & Sean J. Griffith, *Predicting Corporate Governance Risk: Evidence from the Directors' & Officers' Liability Insurance Market*, 74 U. CHI. L. REV. 487, 489 n.7 (2007) (discussing how emotional and reputational impact of shareholder litigation will affect directors and officers directly).

procedure is tilted in favor of defendants, who get to pick their favorite arbitrators and curtail discovery, the argument goes.[33] Shifting to arbitration may result in more meritorious claims getting barred to begin with or in a transfer from small to large shareholders.[34] These criticisms are mostly generic and well debated, and I have little to add.

This book raises another type of concern, namely, the adverse effects of arbitration on third parties. There exist ample accounts that highlight the positive externalities of litigation that will be lost if we shift to mandatory arbitration. Yet most of these arguments emphasize "legal" externalities. That is, they claim that litigation cultivates a vibrant, constantly evolving law that can instruct corporate behavior.[35] This book spotlights a different version of positive externalities: nonlegal externalities. Litigation, in our version, does not just help potential defendants plan ahead and avoid legal landmines; it does not just help regulators prioritize better; it also helps market players – consumers, suppliers, and investors – make better decisions regarding with whom to keep doing business.[36] The next section elaborates.

8.3 HOW SHIFTING TO ARBITRATION AFFECTS THE MARKET FOR REPUTATION

Applying the reputational framework to the issue of mandatory arbitration is not automatic, and requires context-specific examination. This section hones in on the context: we start by asking to what extent does media scrutiny matter for corporate governance issues? If it matters greatly, to what extent does shareholder litigation affect said media scrutiny? How does specific doctrines of corporate and securities laws affect information production in litigation? And how do specific types of shareholder litigation differ from each other in terms of information production?

33 Lipton, *supra* note 9, at 120 n.93.

34 Webber, *supra* note 6, at 258 (suggesting that in a world where compensation is paid only to big institutional investors, a semi-circularity problem will arise, with small investors paying for big investors).

35 Robert J. Jackson, Jr., *SEC Commissioner Jackson Talks Mandatory Arbitration*, CLS Blue Sky Blog (Feb. 28, 2018), http://clsbluesky.law.columbia.edu/2018/02/28/sec-commissioner-jackson-talks-mandatory-arbitration. *See also* Burch, *supra* note 31, at 117–18; Lipton, *supra* note 9, at 637; Webber, *supra* note 6, at 229; G. Richard Shell, *Arbitration and Corporate Governance*, 67 N.C. L. Rev. 517, 561–62 (1989).

36 For a quick round-up of existing accounts that allude to the informational benefits of litigation, and how my account differs from theirs, see Roy Shapira, *Mandatory Arbitration and the Market for Reputation*, 99 B.U.L. Rev. 873, 884 n.58 (2019).

8.3.1 *Media Scrutiny Matters for Corporate Governance*

Commercial legal scholars have traditionally understudied issues of how information is diffused, and what role the media plays in corporate governance.[37] Yet a nascent-but-burgeoning literature in other fields keeps producing evidence on the effects of agenda-setting, framing, and diffusion by the media. That literature highlights just how significant the role of the media is.

Communication scholars categorize the media's impact into capital-markets effects and corporate-governance effects.[38] Within the former category, financial economists have shown that the scope and tone of media coverage moves stock market prices even when the media reports contain no new information. One classic study found that a front-page *New York Times* article about a biotech company caused the stock prices to skyrocket, even though the article contained no new information and was actually repeating information that the *Times* had previously published in a back-page story.[39] More broadly, the intensity of media coverage was found to be conducive to the quality of financial markets.[40]

Within the latter category – corporate-governance effects – studies find that media scrutiny increases the responsiveness of corporate decision makers to shareholders,[41] as well as to salient outside groups, such as environmentalists.[42] Survey-based evidence shows that top managers view negative media coverage as the biggest threat to corporate reputation.[43] Pertinently, a recent study found that media coverage of corporate misconduct creates financial risk: one negative article brings with it an increase in credit risk in the magnitude

37 Alexander Dyck & Luigi Zingales, *The Corporate Governance Role of the Media*, *in* The Right to Tell: The Role of Mass Media in Economic Development 107, 108–09 (2002).

38 Damian Tambini, *What Are Financial Journalists for?*, 11 Journalism Stud. 158, 161–62 (2010).

39 Gur Huberman & Tomer Regev, *Contagious Speculation and a Cure for Cancer: A Nonevent that Made Stock Prices Soar*, 56 J. Fin. 387, 387–90 (2001). *See also* Brian J. Bushee et al., *The Role of the Business Press as an Information Intermediary*, J. Acct. Res., Mar. 2010, at 12–13.

40 Dyck & Zingales, *supra* note 37, at 107–11.

41 Jennifer R. Joe, Henock Lewis, & Dahlia Robinson, *Managers' and Investors' Responses to Media Exposure of Board Ineffectiveness*, 44 J. Fin. & Quantitative Analysis 579, 588–92 (2009) (discussing how media scrutiny of board effectiveness pushes scrutinized company to adopt more shareholder-value-enhancing behaviors); Kobi Kastiel, *Against All Odds: Hedge Fund Activism in Controlled Companies*, 2016 Colum. Bus. L. Rev. 60, 104–12 (discussing how media coverage of shareholder activism in controlled companies increases likelihood of accepting the advocated change).

42 Dyck & Zingales, *supra* note 37, at 105–07.

43 Joe, Lewis & Robinson, *supra* note 41, at 580; Tambini, *supra* note 38, at 160.

of about $1.3 million in additional servicing of debt.[44] In fact, the law itself acknowledges the key role of the media in disciplining corporate behavior. The doctrine developed in *Caremark*, for example, treats prior media coverage as a red flag that should propel directors to act or indicate that their internal monitoring channels were not functioning.[45]

Once we recognize the salutary effect of media scrutiny on corporate behavior, the question becomes what determines media scrutiny. In particular, we are interested in the link between corporate litigation and media coverage.

8.3.2 *Corporate Litigation Matters for Media Scrutiny*

Before we can apply the law-as-source insights from Chapter 2 to our topic here, we need to answer two questions. First, to what extent do law-as-source benefits stem from the specific channel of litigation, rather than from other legal sources such as disclosure requirements or regulatory enforcement? After all, we are interested in the desirability of shifting to mandatory arbitration, and disclosure or public enforcement will supposedly remain intact even if such a shift occurs. Second, to what extent are the law-as-source benefits of litigation relevant to our particular type, namely, shareholder litigation?

The law-as-source study detailed in Chapter 2 above provides a clear answer to the first question: litigation plays a key role in holding business companies and businesspersons to account, often more important than other types of legal sources. Granted, some media probes rely heavily on "direct" legal sources, such as companies' public filings with the SEC. But a lot of times, the smoking gun comes rather from "indirect" legal sources, such as law enforcement actions. As Chapter 2 elaborated, the reason is that litigation does not rely on powerful players volunteering damning information about themselves – it forces damning information out of powerful players.

The second question – whether shareholder litigation is as informative as other types of litigation – is harder to answer. The law-as-source study does not answer it directly, if only because Pulitzer prizes are rarely awarded for covering corporate governance issues, and so the content analysis of prizewinning projects does not provide many relevant data points. What the law-as-source study does offer in that regard are more general observations regarding how the

[44] Julian F. Kolbel, Timo Busch, & Leonhardt M. Jancso, *How Media Coverage of Corporate Social Responsibility Increases Financial Risk*, 38 Strategic Mgmt. J. 2266, 2281 (2017).

[45] 698 A.2d 959, 964 (Del. Ch. 1999); Michael J. Borden, *Of Outside Monitors and Inside Monitors: The Role of Journalists in* Caremark *Litigation*, 15 U. Pa. J. Bus. L. 921, 935 (2013).

media relies on information from litigation when it investigates companies.[46] It seems that litigation's role is actually more pronounced in investigative reporting on corporate behavior, as opposed to investigative reporting on the public sector or the third sector. Virtually every reporters' tip sheet or course syllabus that deals with how to investigate businesses mentions searching court documents. When I asked investigative reporters why this is so, they suggested a straightforward answer: business journalists rely more heavily on court documents because they have a hard time sourcing stories on business companies in other ways.[47] A journalist trying to hold big government to account will have a much easier time getting, for example, tips from the politician's rivals or relying on FOIA requests or public-records laws.[48]

The added difficulty of getting information on private businesses seems to increase the demand for getting information from litigation. And, in the words of the Dean of Columbia Journalism School, the supply tends to meet the demand: "[T]here's hardly a company in this world that is not being sued, and this is where you get a window [into what is going on in the company]."[49] A great illustration comes from a study that documented the lack of watchdog journalism by the financial media leading up to the 2008 financial crisis. That study singled out four counterexamples of great investigative pieces.[50] When I took a closer look at these projects – the rare pieces that did spotlight the shady Wall Street practices that contributed to the crisis – I learned that all of them relied heavily on court documents.[51]

46 Shapira, *supra* note 15, at 194–97.

47 In general, communication scholars have long recognized that holding big business accountable is actually tougher than holding big government accountable. *See, e.g.*, JAMES T. HAMILTON, DEMOCRACY'S DETECTIVES: THE ECONOMICS OF INVESTIGATIVE JOURNALISM 151 (2016); MICHAEL SCHUDSON, THE SOCIOLOGY OF NEWS 140 (2003).

48 As prizewinning business journalist Jesse Eisinger noted, "The structure of business news . . . is that the businesses control the news to a much greater degree than in any other area of the media. In politics, you have a built-in adversarial system." Asher Schechter, *Business Journalism Fails Spectacularly in Holding the Powerful to Account*, PROMARKET (May 30, 2017), https://promarket.org/business-journalism-fails-spectacularly-holding-powerful-account.

49 Shapira, *supra* note 15.

50 Dean Starkman, *Power Problem*, COLUM. JOURNALISM REV., May–June 2009.

51 *Id.* A 2000 story that spotlighted the Wall Street-subprime connection relied on litigation in California that found the Lehman Brothers responsible for practices of lender clients. Diana B. Henriques & Lowell Bergman, *Mortgaged Lives: A Special Report; Profiting from Fine Print with Wall Street's Help*, N.Y. TIMES, Mar. 15, 2000, at A1. A 2005 story relied on court documents to show how financial companies pushed for bad loans. Mike Hudson & E. Scott Reckard, *Workers Say Lender Ran "Boiler Rooms,"* L.A. TIMES, Feb. 4, 2005, at A1. A 2007 story did the same by collecting information from fifteen separate lawsuits against the Lehman Brothers. Michael Hudson, *How Wall Street Stoked the Mortgage Meltdown*, WALL STREET J., June 27, 2007, at A1. A 2009 post-mortem analysis relied on court documents to

Without litigation, media scrutiny of corporate behavior would lose most of its already-diminished effectiveness.

Up to this point, we have broadly discussed litigation against businesses. Yet different types of litigation produce information of different quantities and qualities. Shareholder litigation works differently than, say, product liability litigation. And within shareholder litigation, derivative suits work differently than securities class actions. It is time to delve into specifics and introduce the unique nuances of information production in shareholder litigation.

8.3.3 *Front-Loaded Information Production*

Shareholder litigation is more front-loaded than other types of litigation. Since the mid-1990s, a series of legislative and judicial reforms have severely curtailed a plaintiff's ability to survive the motion to dismiss stage, let alone reach full-blown discovery.[52] One could claim that this feature makes it less likely that shareholder litigation would produce valuable information. How can we expect useful information to come out from litigation if only a few complaints reach discovery, and even fewer lead to published judicial opinions? Without the benefit of discovery, how can litigators add information that other market players do not already know?

The answer is straightforward: Reforms that made it tougher to survive earlier stages in litigation did not eliminate the information production, but merely *front-loaded* it. Plaintiffs in shareholder litigation conduct much more prefiling, prediscovery investigations, and file more fact-rich, detailed initial complaints.[53] As a result, information about defendants' behavior is generated at much earlier stages of the litigation process. Shareholder litigation affects the market for reputation even in its infancy.

The front-loaded information production takes different degrees and forms, as a function of the forum and type of claim. With corporate governance matters settled in state courts, the main prediscovery investigatory tool is requesting to inspect the defendant company's books and records ("section 220 requests," to use the Delaware jargon).[54] With securities claims settled in federal courts, section 220 requests are unavailable, and so plaintiffs frequently resort to soliciting inside informants, who confidentially provide damning information about their current or former employers.

show how wholesalers bent the rules in every way. David Segal, *Financial Fraud Is Focus of Attack by Prosecutors*, N.Y. Times, Mar. 12, 2009, at A1.

52 Cox & Thomas, *supra* note 28, at 169.

53 Geoffrey P. Miller, *Pleading after* Tellabs, 2009 Wis. L. Rev. 507, 532.

54 Del. Code Ann. tit. 8, § 220 (2019).

8.3.3.1 Corporate Claims in State Courts: Section 220 Requests

In derivative actions, the main event comes before the suit even starts: the demand requirement.[55] To survive the demand-requirement stage, plaintiffs practically need to convince the courts that demand is futile because the company's board is too self-interested to make the right decision.[56] To do that, plaintiffs need to meet a heightened pleading standard and show that a majority of the board is implicated in the alleged wrongdoing.[57] And they need to clear those hurdles without having the benefits of discovery.[58] The solution to this pleading challenge came from the Delaware courts, which started imploring plaintiffs to use all "tools at hand" to generate information pre-suit, particularly their right to inspect the company's books.[59] Plaintiffs heeded the call and started filing section 220 requests more frequently and more broadly.[60]

Granted, section 220 requests do not generate the same quantity and quality of information as full discovery does.[61] But the practice of section 220 requests has developed such that shareholders now use them not just to get technical information such as stock-list materials, but also to extract all internal company documents related to the alleged wrongdoing, such as board minutes, internal memos, and spreadsheets. Forcing companies to volunteer such information can affect reputations, both directly and indirectly. Directly, section 220 requests that produce internal corporate communications give the market a peek behind the corporate curtain, with answers to reputation-relevant questions such as "who knew what when." Indirectly, section 220 requests allow better pleading and so increase the chances of reaching full discovery, where more relevant information is likely to come out.

To illustrate, we need simply recast the *Disney* case. There, the initial complaint was dismissed for failure to meet the demand requirement.[62] The plaintiffs regrouped and submitted a section 220 request, which generated internal company documents: letters, emails, memoranda, and board minutes. Armed with the information, the plaintiffs amended their complaint, and

55 To bring a claim, the plaintiff has to first make a demand on the company's board to pursue that claim.

56 Aronson v. Lewis, 473 A.2d 805, 811 (Del. 1984).

57 FED. R. CIV. P. 23.1(b)(3); Stone v. Ritter, 911 A.2d 362, 366–71 (Del. 2006).

58 *See* Brehm v. Eisner, 746 A.2d 244, 254 (Del. 2000); Stephen A. Radin, *The New Stage of Corporate Governance Litigation: Section 220 Demands – Reprise*, 28 CARDOZO L. REV. 1287, 1293 (2006).

59 Grimes v. Donald, 673 A.2d 1207, 1216 (Del. 1996).

60 Roy Shapira, *Corporate Law, Retooled: How Books and Records Revamped Judicial Oversight*, 42 CARDOZO L. REV. (forthcoming, 2020).

61 Saito v. McKesson HBOC, Inc., 806 A.2d 113, 114 (Del. 2002).

62 *In re* Walt Disney Co. Derivative Litig., 731 A.2d 342, 342 (Del. Ch. 1998).

this time survived the motion to dismiss, proceeded to discovery and then a full trial.[63] Chapter 3 showed how earlier stages in the *Disney* litigation shaped the frequency and tenor of media coverage of the Disney–Ovitz debacle. Now we can add the important detail of how: it was the prediscovery, section 220 requests that facilitated the reputational effects.

8.3.3.2 Securities Claims in Federal Courts: Soliciting Whistleblowers

With securities class actions, the main event similarly comes early: the motion to dismiss.[64] Out of the many challenges that securities class actions faced over the recent decades, most relevant for our purposes is the combination of heightened pleading standards with a stay on discovery.[65] The 1995 Private Securities Litigation Reform Act (PSLRA) requires that plaintiffs plead facts with particularity, showing a strong inference of scienter.[66] Such facts about the defendant's state of mind must be pled without the benefit of discovery, as the PSLRA also stayed discovery until after the motion to dismiss is decided. As a result, virtually all defendants file motions to dismiss, and plaintiffs have a tough time surviving such motions.[67]

The combination of heightened pleading standards and stayed discovery seems at first glance like a death knell to information production. Yet here as well, a closer look reveals a different, more dynamic story. Plaintiffs' lawyers who faced mounting hurdles had to raise their game and conduct more pre-complaint and prediscovery investigations.[68] They are now said to possess much more information in the motion to dismiss stage, relative to plaintiffs in other cases, and are more likely to plead their allegations in an "awesomely detailed" way.[69]

Unlike in corporate litigation, section 220 requests were not available to plaintiffs, since the law blocks their usage in securities litigation.[70] Plaintiffs

[63] *See In re* Walt Disney Co. Derivative Litig., 825 A.2d 275 (Del. Ch. 2003).

[64] Stephen J. Choi & Adam C. Pritchard, *The Supreme Court's Impact on Securities Class Actions: An Empirical Assessment of* Tellabs, 28 J.L. ECON. & ORG. 850, 851 (2012).

[65] 15 U.S.C. §§ 77z-l(b), 78u-4(b)(3)(B) (2012).

[66] The Supreme Court later clarified that "a strong inference" means pleading facts that would make "a reasonable person . . . deem the inference of scienter cogent and at least as compelling as any opposing inference one could draw from the facts alleged." Tellabs, Inc. v. Makor Issues & Rights, Ltd., 551 U.S. 308, 314, 324 (2007).

[67] Indeed, following the one-two punch of heightened pleading standards and a stay on discovery, dismissal rates in securities class actions doubled. Cox & Thomas, *supra* note 28, at 169.

[68] Michael A. Perino, *Did the Private Securities Litigation Reform Act Work?*, 2003 U. ILL. L. REV. 913, 929.

[69] Miller, *supra* note 53, at 532.

[70] For an elaboration, see Shapira, *supra* note 36, at 897 n.136.

had to resort to alternative investigatory tools. Among them, the most common and effective seems to be soliciting whistleblowing: finding current and former employees willing to share damning inside information on the behavior of defendants.[71] Indeed, reliance on "information provided by confidential witnesses" has become almost universal in securities class actions.[72]

These inside informants frequently provide information that outside observers are not privy to, regarding what and how things happened. To illustrate:[73] In *Tsirekidze v. Syntax-Brillian Corp.*,[74] a former top officer provided details on how defendants cooked the books. In *Silverman v. Motorola, Inc.*,[75] eight former employees explained how the company knowingly omitted facts about technological difficulties. In *Hubbard v. BankAtlantic Bancorp, Inc.*,[76] former bank employees fleshed out claims about shady lending practices. As with section 220 requests, the usage of such insider informants affects the market for reputation both indirectly by increasing the chances that complaints reach full discovery, and directly by providing information that can be picked up by the media even at a preliminary stage.

Another element that makes the preliminary stages in securities class actions informative is that the judges themselves are more proactive in generating information. Because the motion to dismiss effectively turned into something akin to a summary judgment, judges examine the pleading with much more rigor. And because courts in securities class actions must investigate all sources of competing inferences of scienter, they often probe even information that was not included in the initial complaint.[77]

8.4 CAN OTHER INSTITUTIONS SUBSTITUTE LITIGATION'S INFORMATIONAL BENEFITS?

To fully examine the desirability of shifting to mandatory arbitration, we need to consider not just the informational benefits of litigation in its current state, but also the counterfactual: in a world without shareholder litigation, will

71 *See, e.g.*, Michael J. Kaufman & John M. Wunderlich, *Resolving the Continuing Controversy Regarding Confidential Informants in Private Securities Fraud Litigation*, 19 Cornell J.L. Pub. Pol'y. 637, 639–40 (2010).

72 Gideon Mark, *Confidential Witnesses in Securities Litigation*, 36 J. Corp. L. 551, 554 & n.15 (2011).

73 For many examples, see Kaufman & Wunderlich, *supra* note 71, at 640 n.3; Miller, *supra* note 53.

74 No. CV-07–2204-PHX-FJM, 2009 WL 275405 (D. Ariz. Feb. 4, 2009).

75 No. 07 C 4507, 2008 WL 4360648 (N.D. Ill. Sept. 23, 2008).

76 625 F. Supp. 2d 1267 (S.D. Fla. 2008).

77 Miller, *supra* note 53, at 533.

other enforcement mechanisms step up and provide similar informational benefits to the ones we currently get from litigation? This section considers three such alternatives for information production: public enforcement headed by the SEC, individual arbitration headed by big institutional investors, and section 220 requests or whistleblowing by aggrieved shareholders and employees. The bottom line is the same: none of these institutions would be able to meaningfully substitute the information that would be lost if we switch from litigation to arbitration.

8.4.1 *SEC Enforcement*

One could argue that in a world where private enforcement happens behind closed doors, public enforcement can still produce enough information to facilitate proper reputational deterrence. The SEC's enforcement division arguably possesses better tools and incentives than private litigants to produce credible information. The SEC enjoys broader investigative powers compared to the ones private litigants typically enjoy in a post-PSLRA world.[78] Private litigants, as the previous chapter detailed, are incentivized to trade away information for money: it is not just that they settle too early and often, but also that they settle too secretly. Almost every settlement comes with some form of a confidentiality clause. By contrast, the SEC can produce press releases that detail their investigations in a fairer way than plaintiffs'-lawyer-worded complaints or media briefs. A shift from litigation to arbitration would therefore only crystalize the waters, as the information environment would be dominated by the better-informed and more credible SEC's enforcement division.

Yet we have already rebutted the argument that SEC enforcement can fully substitute for the information that comes out of private litigation, in Chapter 4 above. We discussed there why the argument may hold only in a limited sense: in a specific dispute, SEC enforcement may indeed be equally or more informative than private litigation. But from a big-picture perspective, private enforcement produces information in ways and on types of misconduct on which the SEC consistently underproduces information.

A quick recap of the factors we detailed in Chapter 4: First, the SEC faces budgetary constraints, and simply cannot pursue all instances of misconduct. Second, when the SEC prioritizes targets for enforcement, it tends to go after the small fish, less politically connected firms. Third, the SEC maximizes the observable yardsticks of the total amount of fines it collects and the number of

78 Amanda M. Rose, *Better Bounty Hunting: How the SEC's New Whistleblower Program Changes the Securities Fraud Class Action Debate*, 108 Nw. U. L. Rev. 1235, 1258 (2014).

enforcement actions it opens, which leads the agency to leave information on the table, in various ways. For example, the SEC lets defendants who are willing to settle early and for nice sums dictate the language and timing of the enforcement action press release. And it targets whole industries for minor, strict-liability-type offenses, which typically do not extract relevant internal documents from the defendant-companies. All these practices, Chapter 4 showed, limit the reputational value of SEC enforcement. It is telling that even SEC commissioners and staffers have long acknowledged that private litigation guards against selective enforcement and inaction on part of the SEC.[79] In a world without private litigation, defendants would have stronger incentives to dilute SEC enforcement efforts.[80] This will dilute not just legal deterrence but also reputational deterrence.

8.4.2 *Individual Arbitration*

One common criticism of mandatory arbitration provisions with class action waivers goes as follows: these provisions do not merely change the procedure for settling disputes, but rather effectively eliminate disputes, since victims who suffered small damages will not pursue their claims individually.[81] At first glance, such criticism applies less forcefully in our context, where there are big institutional investors that may have a large enough stake to vigorously pursue individual claims in arbitration. In a world without class actions, institutional investors may even have a legal duty to monitor and follow through on potential misconduct by companies they invest in.[82] The question for our purposes is not whether individual arbitration by institutional investors would generate enough compensation, but rather whether it would generate enough information. I tend to answer in the negative, for the following reasons.

For one, fewer instances of corporate misconduct will get flushed out. The whole impetus behind the arbitration-provisions wave is wanting to *avoid* the need to resolve certain disputes.[83] Even in cases where the individual harm is

79 *See, e.g.*, Burch, *supra* note 31, at 101–02.

80 *Cf.* John C. Coffee, Jr., *Rescuing the Private Attorney General: Why the Model of the Lawyer as Bounty Hunter Is Not Working*, 42 MD. L. REV. 215, 227.

81 As Professor Resnik notes, the recent changes have brought an explosion in arbitration *provisions*, not arbitration, because the provisions effectively diffuse the disputes altogether. *See generally* Judith Resnik, *Diffusing Disputes: The Public in the Private of Arbitration, the Private in Courts, and the Erasure of Rights*, 124 YALE L.J. 2804 (2015).

82 *See* Webber, *supra* note 6, at 220.

83 *Id.* at 210 ("The primary purpose of arbitration provisions in this context is not to shift shareholder claims from judges to arbitrators, but to eliminate the claims entirely by undermining their economic viability").

big enough on paper, it is not clear that institutional investors would actually pursue a remedy. Evidence from Europe, where only big institutional investors can bring derivative actions, suggest that in reality most valuable claims are not pursued, partly because it is easier for managers to collude and convince the few players who can bring a claim to not bring it.[84] Similarly, in the United States, Professors Bebchuk and Hirst showed that none of the large index funds had been the lead plaintiff in *any* securities class action over the past ten years.[85] They interpret this evidence as suggesting that institutional investors with high-enough stakes prefer, for various reasons, not to vigorously pursue their claims.

Even if one assumes that institutional investors would regularly pursue claims in arbitration, one has to acknowledge that the procedure in arbitration starkly differs from court procedures in ways that limit information production.[86] Discovery tends to be *much* more limited. Depositions are taken only rarely. Plaintiffs' investigations normally do not extract internal company documents. And so on. In theory, arbitration provisions can be amended to demand a more information-extracting, akin-to-litigation procedure. But that would defeat the purpose behind the wave of arbitration provisions.[87] A key purpose in shifting to arbitration, besides eliminating disputes, is limiting the negative publicity from disputes. Confidentiality and privacy are hallmark features in the arbitration procedure. It is therefore hard to imagine companies agreeing to an expansive discovery regime in arbitration.

8.4.3 *Section 220 Requests and Whistleblowing*

As noted above, filing section 220 requests and finding inside informants are two important investigatory tools in shareholder litigation. One could claim that we do not need litigation to employ these channels of extracting information. These are *pre*filing investigatory tools, after all, which would supposedly remain available even if we switch to mandatory arbitration.

[84] *See* Martin Gelter, *Mapping Types of Shareholder Lawsuits across Jurisdictions, in* RESEARCH HANDBOOK ON REPRESENTATIVE SHAREHOLDER LITIGATION 459, 471 (Griffith, et al. eds., 2018).

[85] Lucian A. Bebchuk & Scott Hirst, *Index Funds and the Future of Corporate Governance: Theory, Evidence, and Policy*, 199 COLUM. L. REV. 2029, 2112 (2019).

[86] *See* Jean R. Sternlight, *Creeping Mandatory Arbitration: Is It Just?*, 57 STAN. L. REV. 1631, 1641 n.51 (2005).

[87] *Cf.* Lipton, *supra* note 9, at 639.

The argument that standalone section 220 requests (not in conjunction with litigation) can substitute the informational benefits of litigation is easily refutable. It is inconsistent with the logic of incentives and inconsistent with the law. There is a good reason that section 220 requests are usually filed in conjunction with litigation. A shareholder would be willing to go through the costs and trouble of fighting companies for information only when said shareholder (or, more realistically, a plaintiff's law firm) anticipates a potential financial bonanza down the road. Shareholder litigation provides the supercharged economic incentives needed to make the fight worth it.

Even if we assume proper incentives for filing standalone section 220 requests, the law makes such requests irrelevant from an information-production standpoint. The courts have conditioned granting section 220 requests on confidentiality.[88] If a shareholder wants to enjoy her rights to inspect the books, she must first agree to not diffuse the information she receives. As a result, the only time when section 220 information escapes confidentiality and becomes available is when the requesting shareholder uses the information in conjunction with court filings, such as the initial complaint or as attachments to a motion. In other words, information gleaned from section 220 requests can only affect reputations when it is filed with the court.

The argument that standalone whistleblowing would replace litigation's informational benefits is harder to refute. There is no law prohibiting the release of information coming from whistleblowers outside litigation, and the incentives problem has supposedly been addressed in the Dodd–Frank Act.[89] Still, there exist ample indications that without litigation, the whistleblowing would not make an impact. Litigation adds value to the information revealed by amplifying, certifying, and diffusing whistleblowers' claims. To illustrate, consider *Freund v. Lucent Technologies, Inc.*,[90] where plaintiffs submitted a section 220 request for all the materials that were filed in a whistleblowing action (brought by a former senior official who had been fired in retaliation). While the initial whistleblowing did not reverberate publicly, the *Lucent* litigation made the whistleblower's information more salient and coverable by the media.[91]

88 *See* Radin, *supra* note 58, at 1388.

89 Dodd–Frank Wall Street Reform and Consumer Protection Act § 922, 15 U.S.C. § 78u-6 (2012) (amending § 21F of the Securities Exchange Act of 1934).

90 No. 18893, 2003 WL 139766 (Del. Ch. Jan. 9, 2003).

91 *See, e.g.*, Carol J. Loomis, *The Whistleblower and the CEO*, FORTUNE (July 7, 2003), http://archive.fortune.com/magazines/fortune/fortune_archive/2003/07/07/345538/index.htm.

As the *Lucent* example illustrates, without litigation, such whistleblowing would be akin to a tree falling in the forest where no one is around – did it really make a sound? With litigation, the whistle gets widely echoed by the press.

8.5 IMPLICATIONS

The policy implication of this chapter's analysis is straightforward: recognizing the informational role of litigation puts a thumb on the scales against enforcing mandatory arbitration for shareholder claims. If policymakers and courts nevertheless decide to enforce arbitration provisions, we need to design arbitration procedures that allow more information to come out from arbitration.

At the same time, I want to be careful not to overstate my claim. There are two important qualifications. First, any evidence for the informational benefits of litigation is more qualitative in nature. We know that reputation matters, we know that media scrutiny matters, and we know that litigation matters to media scrutiny and reputation. But we have not yet quantified how much exactly it matters: What is the size of these informational benefits of litigation? Second, and relatedly, even if one is convinced that the size of the informational benefits is significant, one still needs to weigh them against the significant costs of litigation.[92] After all, our aim is not to maximize production of information, but rather to optimize it. Perhaps the tradeoff that mandatory arbitration offers – less informational benefits with less administrative costs – is worth it from a societal perspective. Against this background, let us go back to what we started this short section with: the two immediate policy implications.

First and most basically, the information-production argument puts a thumb on the scales against mandatory arbitration. A thumb on the scales and not a decisive vote, because we only have suggestive evidence. But what we have is enough to caution against replacing litigation with arbitration without first gaining better evidence and a better understanding of the positive externalities of litigation. Securities markets are fraught with asymmetric information and supercharged incentives to cheat. Reputational deterrence is important to their proper functioning. And litigation seems to be important to the proper functioning of reputational deterrence. The direct costs of litigation are well researched and salient to us, while the costs of reputational

92 *See* Amanda M. Rose, *The Shifting* Raison D'Etre *of the Rule 10b-5 Private Right of Action, in* Research Handbook on Representative Shareholder Litigation 39, 52 (Griffith, et al. eds., 2018).

under-deterrence are not. If one has to conjecture, I would surmise that the latter far outweigh the former.[93]

If courts and regulators nevertheless allow companies to adopt arbitration provisions, the second set of policy implications comes in: providing insight into how we would want such arbitration to look. Ideally, in the area of corporate and securities laws we would want arbitration that injects some valuable information into the market. Is there a way to get the cost-saving aspects of arbitration without losing the information-extracting benefits of litigation?

At a minimum, we would want an accessible database of disputes with "explained awards" – arbitrators should include a short summary of who did what to whom, when, and why that is a bad thing. The requirement of explained awards should come from, and be monitored by, the SEC or another regulator. Leaving things to the market will simply not work, as the experience with the Financial Industry Regulatory Authority (FINRA) arbitration forum shows. For over a decade now, FINRA has used a rule that requires explained awards only upon joint requests from both parties.[94] This opt-in mechanism produced "very, very few" actual explained awards.[95] A better design would be to mandate explained awards, or at least set the default differently, so that the parties can opt out of explained awards only upon joint request.

To emphasize: even if arbitration proceeds with a searchable database of disputes and explained awards, it would probably produce much less law-as-source benefits compared to litigation. Most of the impact that law enforcement has on media coverage comes not so much from the outcomes of disputes, but rather from documents that were produced in earlier stages of the process (discovery, depositions, and so on). Arbitration entails much less information-extracting and would surely be less useful to third parties trying to figure out what and how things happened.

8.6 EXTENSIONS: ARBITRATION AND REPUTATION IN OTHER CONTEXTS

We started this chapter by noting that the reputational effects of shifting to mandatory arbitration vary greatly across different contexts. This short section goes beyond the context of shareholder litigation, to demonstrate the various

93 *See* Lynn A. Stout, *Type I Error, Type II Error, and the Private Securities Litigation Reform Act*, 38 Ariz. L. Rev. 711, 713 (1996) (asserting costs of fraud outweigh costs of litigation).

94 Barbara Black & Jill Gross, *The Explained Award of Damocles: Protection or Peril in Securities Arbitration*, 34 Sec. Reg. L.J. 17, 18 (2006).

95 Jill Gross, *FINRA Arbitrator Writes Explained Award to Create Precedent*, Indisputably (June 30, 2017), www.indisputably.org/?p=11070.

factors in play. We specifically focus on the distant context of employment litigation. Mandatory arbitration of workers' claims has gone through two major changes in recent years: one legal (the Supreme Court's *Epic* decision), and one social/cultural (the #MeToo movement). Section 8.6.1 explains how the *Epic* decision affects the market for reputation. Section 8.6.2 looks at the other side, namely, how the market for reputation affects firm's propensity to adopt mandatory arbitration provisions, following the #MeToo movement.

8.6.1 *Arbitration of Workplace Claims*: Epic *Ramifications*

In May 2018, the US Supreme Court's *Epic* decision enforced arbitration clauses with class waivers in employment contracts.[96] Large employers were already funneling workplace disputes to arbitration before *Epic*, and now, when they can effectively eliminate class action, are figured to force such provisions even more aggressively.[97] Can we apply the argument presented throughout this chapter, in the context of shareholder claims, and similarly make a case against mandatory arbitration in the context of employment claims? Is *Epic* bad policy?

The answer is yes, but. Yes, I think that *Epic* would affect reputational deterrence negatively. But I think its effects would be much different than the ones we analyzed in the context of shareholder litigation.

The first difference lies in the "reputation for what" question. While shareholder litigation mostly affects a company's reputation for quality of governance, employment litigation can also affect a company's reputation for quality of workplace relations.

Another, much more relevant distinction lies in the "reputation to whom" question. The likelihood that information from litigation would translate into reputational sanctions vary across different stakeholder groups. When shareholder litigation reveals information on the checks and balances inside companies, investors are likely to do something with the information. They have too much skin in the game not to. In employment litigation, by contrast, it is much less clear that information from litigation will actually change how stakeholders treat the company. The relevant stakeholder group here is usually employees. And with employees, it is less likely that litigation will tell them something they did not already know about how the company treats its workers. Unlike investors, who suffer as outsiders from asymmetric information and

96 Epic Systems Corp. v. Lewis, 138 S. Ct. 1612 (2018).

97 *See, e.g.*, Jean R. Sternlight, *Mandatory Arbitration Stymies Progress towards Justice in Employment Law: Where To, #MeToo?*, 54 Harv. CR-CL L. Rev. 156, 177–78 (2019).

rational apathy, workers are insiders who are directly affected, and have all the incentives and ability to keep informed about the company's action. These workers rarely rely on litigation for new information. And they often do not need litigation for mobilization either. In unionized areas, the union can engage management either directly or through media pressure. After all, the *Epic* decision did not affect workers' ability to mobilize collectively outside the specific context of class litigation.[98] Even in nonunionized areas, workers can arguably mobilize for their causes and enlist the media via non-litigation channels such as social media, as the Market Basket case study illustrates.[99]

What about a different stakeholder group, namely, consumers? On paper, information from litigation on how firm X mistreats its employees can lead consumers to buy less from firm X going forward. Indeed, many survey-based studies document consumers' professed willingness to pay more (less) for the products of companies with good (bad) workplace conditions.[100] Yet I am skeptical that *Epic* would actually change consumers' willingness to pay. For one, as Chapter 5 indicated, evidence shows a gap between consumers' professions in surveys and their actual buying decisions: in reality, consumers purchase based on product quality and price, and little more. And in many of the cases we can summon from memory where consumers were willing to go the distance and boycott a firm for workplace conditions, it was for violations that are not affected by the *Epic* decision at all. The classic example here is issues of child labor in third-world countries, which are not the type of wage-and-hour disputes that would have been litigated in US courtrooms regardless of *Epic*.

Still, I conjecture that *Epic* would have serious reputational ramifications, if only through a different channel: not necessarily through the reputation-for-workplace dimension, but rather through the reputation-for-governance dimension. In other words, ending public dispute resolution of workplace

98 Benjamin Sachs & Sharon Block, *Epic Fall Out: The Supreme Court and Concerted Activity*, ON LABOR, May 23, 2018, https://onlabor.org/epic-fall-out-scotus-and-concerted-activity.

99 *See, e.g.*, WBUR News, *Market Basket Shows Power of Organized Labor without Unions, Sep. 3, 2014*, www.wbur.org/news/2014/09/03/market-basket-labor. Still, one cannot completely ignore the distinction between labor and employment law (unionized and nonunionized, respectively). In the USA, where most workers are nonunionized, losing the channel of litigation as a potential mobilization mechanism cannot be downplayed. *Compare* Jean R. Sternlight, *Disarming Employees: How American Employers Are Using Mandatory Arbitration to Deprive Workers of Legal Protection*, 80BROOK. L. REV.1309, 1313 (2015) *with* Benjamin I. Sachs, *Employment Law as Labor Law*, 29 CARDOZO L. REV. 2685, 2702 (2008).

100 *See, e.g.*, Dara O'Rourke, *Outsourcing Regulation: Analyzing Nongovernmental Systems of Labor Standards and Monitoring*, 31 POLICY STUDIES JOURNAL 1, 4 (2003) ("One bad supplier can significantly damage a firm's reputation and, in turn, its sales and stock value").

claims can have a detrimental effect on accountability in other areas beside workplace conditions. This is because information from workplace litigation may help expose shenanigans in other aspects.

A timely illustration comes from the Wells Fargo phony-accounts scandal. An investigative report by the *L.A. Times* broke the story, showing how pressures from the top of the organization led to shady practices of sucker-punching customers and abusing employees.[101] But how was the *L.A. Times* able to come out with such a story? It turns out that the reporter relied on court documents from wage-and-hours lawsuits filed by disgruntled Wells Fargo employees. A similar, earlier example appears in the Dean Starkman's book on watchdog business journalism we mentioned earlier: in the 1990s investigative reporters were able to link low-rent operators to Wall Street by trolling employment litigation against financial companies.[102] The court documents provided readymade, libel-proof testimonies by former employees, which detailed the lawless culture in the financial companies in question.

Following *Epic*, such workplace disputes are no longer aired in court. The next time a journalist attempts to expose shenanigans by financial companies, such inside information is more likely to remain out of her reach.

8.6.2 *How Reputation Affects Arbitration: the #MeToo Example*

After focusing throughout this chapter on how shifting to arbitration can affect the market for reputation, let us switch to the other side: how the market for reputation can affect the shift to arbitration. When a firm adopts a mandatory arbitration provision, it sends a certain signal to the market. Under certain conditions, stakeholders will view the mere adoption of such provision negatively enough to merit boycotting the firm, and the prospect of a reputational sanction will push firms to drop such provisions or not adopt them to begin with.

A classic illustration came throughout 2018–19, in the context of law firms' employment contracts. Initially, law firms followed the mandatory arbitration trend, forcing their summer interns, associates, and administrative staff to sign contracts with such provisions. And they have gotten away with it, until a social–cultural shift made these provisions more salient and objectionable to their employees. In short, the #MeToo movement happened.

101 E. Scott Reckard, *Wells Fargo's Pressure-Cooker Sales Culture Comes at a Cost*, LA TIMES, Dec. 21, 2013.

102 Starkman, *supra* note 50, at 186–87.

The #MeToo movement increased the saliency of sexual harassment issues. Activist organizations and the media – information intermediaries – started targeting firms who do not do enough to root out sexual harassment. For law firms, specifically, not doing enough about sexual harassment (in our context: trying to force complaints into behind-closed-doors arbitration) started coming with a meaningful reputational risk. The tides turned when a Harvard Law School student group, called the Pipeline Parity Project, started advocating boycotting interviews in firms that force their employees to adhere to such provisions. Fearing reputational damage, one big law firm after another started dropping their mandatory arbitration provisions.[103]

Can the same dynamics – fear of reputational sanctions pushing firms to avoid forcing arbitration – apply elsewhere? I conjecture that it is less realistic outside this specific law-firm-employment context. For one, the issue here is different: sexual harassment is a much more salient issue (at least at the height of the #MeToo movement) than most other contexts in which consumers are forced to sign arbitration provisions without even caring/knowing about them. Further, the target audience is very different: here the target audience – potential employees – are the relatively sophisticated and aware-to-the-dangers-of-arbitration law students.

It all comes down to solving a collective action problem. For investors in company X, it may be better if company X adopts mandatory arbitration; but for investors as a group, it is better that no company adopts such provision. The increased saliency, low complexity, and levels of engagement by student bodies that we witnessed in the law-firm-employment context usually do not apply in other contexts.

[103] *See, e.g.*, Stephanie Francis Ward, *Orrick Follows Munger Tolles in Dropping Mandatory Arbitration Agreements: Will More Firms Follow?*, ABA Journal, Mar. 28, 2018, www.abajournal.com/news/article/orrick_follows_munger_tolles_in_dropping_mandatory_arbitration; Aidan F. Ryan, *Harvard Law School Pipeline Parity Project Celebrates Another Change to Controversial Law Firm Policies*, The Harvard Crimson, Dec. 10, 2018, www.thecrimson.com/article/2018/12/10/pipeline-parity/; Karen Sloan, *#DumpVenable Campaign Launched by Harvard Law Student Group*, The National Law Journal, Feb. 4, 2019, www.law.com/nationallawjournal/2019/02/04/harvard-law-students-target-venable-over-mandatory-arbitration.

Conclusion

Five years after the Polinsky and Shavell article that we opened the book with, the movie *Spotlight* came out. *Spotlight* won the 2015 Oscar for best film by telling a compelling story about investigative reporters holding the Catholic Church to account over child sex abuse.[1] Yet as I was watching the movie, I could not help but see law-and-reputation themes in almost every scene. The *Boston Globe*'s Spotlight reporters could not have done it alone. The legal system helped them.[2] The *Globe* reporters spotted the pattern of abuse by looking at numbers of lawsuits filed against individual priests. They revealed the cover-up by getting internal church documents from motions attached to court files. *Spotlight* is therefore not really a story about investigative journalism holding the powerful to account. It is rather a story about interactions between the media and the courts. Between law and reputation.

The interactions are what produced accountability. Without the legal system generating information in the process of examining individual lawsuits against priests, the reporters would not have had such a powerful story to tell. And without the reporters putting the pieces of the puzzle together, identifying the pattern, packaging it compellingly, and diffusing it widely, the church would not have admitted its mistakes and changed its behavior. The legal system would probably have continued settling and sealing one individual case after another. It took media scrutiny to move the needle.

This book develops a theory of these interactions between law and reputation. It fleshes out how and why such interactions occur, and what outcomes

[1] Spotlight (Participant Media 2015).

[2] Timothy D. Lytton, Holding Bishops Accountable (2008) (a book-length account of how litigation against individual priests and the church played a key role in holding these players accountable).

they achieve. Once we are aware of the interactions, we can design legal institutions with an eye to their reputation-affecting role.

It is intuitive to think that decisions and events in the court of law trickle out and affect the court of public opinion, and vice versa. Yet up to this point legal scholars have tended to assume away complementarities between law and reputation, by treating the two systems as independent of each other.[3] *Law and Reputation* challenges the conventional assumption by mapping the various channels through which the law can influence reputational evaluations, and presenting on-the-ground evidence of such influence. Consider the following data point: communication scientists estimate that between a quarter and a third of the content of business media is dedicated to reporting about companies' interactions with the legal system (regulation, litigation, and corporate governance battles). This data point alone is enough to rid us of the prevalent assumption that law and reputation are independent of each other, and challenge us to start examining how they interact.

The rest of this conclusion offers a brief synthesis of the book's contributions as they relate to existing literature, before outlining potential future extensions of the reputational framework.

RELATION TO THE EXTANT LITERATURE

To clarify some of this book's original contributions, we can juxtapose them with the relevant literature. The Introduction clarified our scope by showing how the questions we are asking differ from the ones that are usually asked in the related literature. This section focuses on how the answers we are providing differ from the ones that others do. The book's original contributions do *not* consist in telling us that reputation matters or that the law matters for reputation. We already know that. The contributions consist rather in exploring *how* the law matters for reputation. Consider the following four examples of gaps in the conventional approach to law and reputation we have sought to narrow.

First, other legal scholars have written about problems with reputational sanctions (usually in the context of making the case for legal intervention).[4]

3 *See, e.g.*, Peter-Jan Engelen, *Legal versus Reputational Penalties in Deterring Corporate Misconduct*, *in* DOES ECONOMIC GOVERNANCE MATTER? GOVERNANCE INSTITUTIONS AND OUTCOMES 71–95 (Mehmet Ugur & David Sunderland, eds., 2011); David Charny, *Nonlegal Sanctions in Commercial Relationships*, 104 HARV. L. REV. 373, 390 n.57 (1990); Yoshinobu Zasu, *Sanctions by Social Norms and the Law: Substitutes or Complements?*, 36 J. LEGAL STUD. 379, 381–82 (2007).

4 *See, e.g.*, Robert Prentice, *Whither Securities Regulation? Some Behavioral Observations Regarding Proposals for Its Future*, 51 DUKE L.J. 1397, 1429–34 (2002).

But the existing analyses focus almost solely on detection costs, suggesting that market players rarely learn about corporate failures in real time. *Law and Reputation* shows that another set of costs – enforcement costs – also looms large. Even when market players become aware of a certain failure, they may under or overreact.

Second, *Law and Reputation* challenges the conventional economic analyses of law and social norms, which treat behavior as either law-complying or norm-following.[5] By spotlighting the existing interdependencies, this book illustrates the need to rethink the conventional approach and its policy implications. We cannot use reputation as a justification for deregulation, at least not automatically. If we scale back the background threat of litigation or regulatory investigations, we risk increasing the costs of reputational sanctions. The issue of complementarities between legal and nonlegal systems should therefore move from the periphery to the center of the law and social norms literature.

Relatedly, even when legal scholars recognize the costs of legal and nonlegal systems, they usually do so by taking a horse race approach: identifying areas where informal, nonlegal systems are supposedly better (less costly) than formal, legal systems. I refocus the debate by looking at different systems as providing multiple-layers control or, as it were, a diversified portfolio. Each system of control has its own unique set of costs. And because the systems' flaws are imperfectly correlated, a combination of several systems cancels out extreme cases of over- or under-sanctioning. The multiple-layers approach is especially suited to the context of complex, atomized markets, where asymmetric information issues abound and any single system alone cannot govern behavior. In other words, one system of control is usually not enough to hold powerful players to account. It takes a village. Recall the Catholic Church's cover-up of sexual abuse, or DuPont's toxic emissions. Only a combination of litigation and media scrutiny was able to stop the continuous harmful behavior.

Finally, *Law and Reputation* highlights the importance of the legal *process*, and in particular the earlier stages of litigation. The rare extant accounts of the reputational role of the law tend to focus on legal outcomes,[6] whereas I focus

5 Eric Talley, *Disclosure Norms*, 149 U. PA. L. REV. 1955, 1960 (2001).

6 *See, e.g.*, Edward M. Iacobucci, *On the Interaction between Legal and Reputational Sanctions*, 43 J. LEGAL STUD. 189 (2014) (the size of legal sanctions affects the reputational-signaling equilibrium by affecting firms' initial decisions whether to commit wrongs or not); Scott Baker & Albert H. Choo, *Reputation and Litigation: Why Costly Legal Sanctions Can Work Better than Reputational Sanctions*, 47 J. LEGAL STUD. 45 (2018) (firms can opt to submit themselves to formal sanctions and thus facilitate better informal control).

on information disseminated in the process of determining legal outcomes. As Chapters 3 and 4 show, for example, two SEC enforcement actions or Delaware trials with identical legal outcomes may generate completely different reputational outcomes.[7] To be sure, I do not claim that my account precludes others. The law produces information in various ways and to various effects. The key is to identify the subsets of cases that are relevant for each type of effect. In corporate law litigation, for example, the filing of a lawsuit or the rendering of a judicial opinion probably generates less reputational impact than the information coming out during the process (such as in the discovery stage or in prediscovery requests to inspect the books). Shifting our attention from the outcomes of legal disputes to the process comes with important implications. If we want to improve information production, we need to rethink seemingly nonsubstantive doctrines such as pleading standards, plaintiffs' rights to demand inside information in discovery, openness of court proceedings, and the desirability of arbitration clauses.

POTENTIAL EXTENSIONS

The interactions between two complex systems such as law and reputation are a vast topic. Accordingly, considerations of brevity and scope have compelled me to leave important angles out of this book, in the hope that future work can address them. Consider the following four specific avenues: engaging in quantitative empirical work to test some of the hypotheses developed here in qualitative methods, elaborating on the hypotheses' normative implications, and broadening the scope of analysis to incorporate other legal fields and other legal systems.

Empirical Extensions

The insights developed here rely on mixed methods, mostly qualitative in nature, such as interviews, case studies, and content analysis. As the Introduction clarified, such methodology makes sense when the aim is to generate hypotheses and indicate the plausibility of the hypotheses – a required step when approaching an undeveloped field. Now that we have chartered the territory of law and reputation, we need to take the next step of

7 In other words, I use the notion of "shadow of the law" differently: instead of having the notion denote how market players consider the backstop of expected legal outcomes they can obtain in the courtroom, I use it to denote the backstop of what information will be revealed should the parties' behavior be evaluated in the courtroom.

building on some of the exploratory work done here and designing more quantitative tests of the hypotheses.[8] As a caveat, I do not claim that my qualitative empirical work here has produced conclusive proofs of my theory or generated external validity in the sense in which the term is used in quantitative studies. What my work has produced, I hope, is a rich theory, one that is valid in the modest sense of prima facie credibility, and that can pave the way for subsequent quantitative probes.

Normative Extensions

Reputational forces do not always promote overall welfare. At first glance, this book can be read as too much of a paean to how reputation incentivizes companies to engage in nice behaviors or avoid bad behaviors. A more accurate statement of my claim is that reputational forces incentivize companies to *appear* moral and competent. In the real world, given asymmetric information, corporate insiders sometimes take actions that appear good but are actually detrimental to their agents. The book alludes to such "bad reputation effects,"[9] for example, in the context of how regulators can co-opt court-induced reputational pressures by responding too aggressively or symbolically. But there is room for more detailed analysis.

Another avenue for future research on the normative aspects of law and reputation is the phenomenon of *reputational spillovers*. We have discussed how legal enforcement actions affect the reputation of defendant companies and businesspeople. But in reality enforcement actions against one company may affect the defendant's peers as well. Outside stakeholders often do not completely differentiate between peer companies' reputations. The revelation of bad news about one company may cause stakeholders to lose trust in the whole industry or market.[10] Such dynamics of spillovers and cascades open the door to interesting normative implications. Consider for example an extension of the "make it look like a struggle" idea from Chapter 3. Counterintuitively, when Delaware courts and the SEC manage to appear tougher than they truly

[8] In methodology jargon, this is called "exploratory sequential mixed methods design": the researcher approaches a new terrain with more qualitative methods, and then once he identifies initial patterns, he looks to corroborate them with a later quantitative stage. The Sage Encyclopedia of Qualitative Research 527 (Given, ed., 2008).

[9] *See generally* Jeffrey C. Ely & Juuso Valimaki, *Bad Reputation*, 118 Q. J. Econ. 785 (2003).

[10] *See, e.g.*, Amar Gande & Craig M. Lewis, *Shareholder-Initiated Class Action Lawsuits: Shareholder Wealth Effects and Industry Spillovers*, 44 J. Fin. & Quant. Anal. 823 (2009). To be sure, reputational spillovers can work both ways: other companies may actually benefit from revelation of bad news about their competitors. David Prince & Paul H. Rubin, *The Effects of Product Liability Litigation on the Value of Firms*, 4 Am. L. & Econ. Rev. 44 (2002).

are on corporate America, they may actually promote overall welfare under certain conditions, by containing reputational spillovers. If the public and politicians overreact to isolated corporate failures, then courts that follow a make-it-look-like-a-struggle strategy may help to restore trust in markets without unnecessarily punishing good companies or committing to overregulation.

Other Legal Fields

We can also broaden the scope of the law-and-reputation argument by applying it to legal fields we did not cover here. The law generates reputation-shaping effects to various degrees even in seemingly remote areas. The book focused on corporate and securities laws, while also discussing product liability, administrative law, and even labor law applications. Elsewhere I touched on applications to public international law.[11] Future research can further extend the applications to classic private law. Consider two examples that I am currently working on.

In tort law, the reputational perspective can shed light on the long-standing debate of negligence versus strict liability.[12] Conventional economic analysis treats the prevalence of negligence regimes as a puzzle: on paper, a strict-liability rule would be preferable as it leads to optimal activity levels. Such an analysis assumes that liability rules affect behavior only directly, through imposing legal sanctions. Yet, as this book showed, liability rules can also affect behavior through producing information. Take medical malpractice, for example. Litigation under a negligence regime produces reputation-relevant information, such as whether the facility was properly maintained, or whether the doctor used the most up-to-date methods. It gives outside observers information that they can use to evaluate whether the problem is indicative of future behavior or not. Do I want to be hospitalized in this facility or operated on by this doctor or not? Litigation under strict liability, by contrast, does not focus on how things happened but only on what happened. It produces much less reputation-relevant information. In that way, negligence regimes affect the activity levels too, albeit indirectly: by producing information, they dictate how many future patients will go to the doctor in question.

[11] Roy Shapira, *Reputation through Litigation: How the Legal System Shapes Behavior by Producing Information*, 91 WASH. L. REV. 1193, 1243–45 (2016).

[12] Roy Shapira & Assaf Jacob, A Reputational Perspective on Liability Rules (2020) (unpublished manuscript) (on file with author).

In contract law, the reputational perspective spotlights a counterintuitive problem in the shift to personalized contracts.[13] Sellers increasingly rely on big data and predictive analytics to identify potential "nudnik" consumers: those consumers who are more likely to voice concerns publicly, such as posting detailed negative reviews online, enlisting the help of the media, or complaining to the regulator. This small group of consumers is an engine of market discipline. They are the ones generating most of the reputation-relevant information on sellers. While most of us do not even notice when we are overcharged by $4 on a takeout order, these nudniks do, and their activism holds sellers accountable. Yet if sellers can now identify who is a nudnik before that consumer even steps into their store, they can effectively silence the nudnik or avoid selling to her altogether. In other words, an unexplored dark side of big data is that it can be used to reduce the expected reputational sanction for overcharging, mistreating a customer, or selling a defective product. This technology is good for companies. It may actually be good for the targeted consumer herself, because sellers often offer her preferential treatment. Yet it is bad for the market overall. Legal intervention may be needed to protect the market for seller reputation.

Other Legal Systems

Another fertile ground for future research is the *comparative* aspects of law and reputation. The examples used throughout the book come mainly from US law. Some of the reason for this is practical: the United States is where I studied, taught, and consulted on law and reputation when I was formulating my ideas. But there is also substantive reason to focus on the United States: the American legal system is more geared toward information production than any other legal system in the world. For one, discovery is the most far-reaching.[14] And plaintiffs and their lawyers enjoy high-powered economic incentives to extract information: the bounty is higher.

Yet, while the reputational effects of the law may be strongest in the United States, logic and anecdotal examples suggest that they apply to some extent in other systems as well. When Oxford's John Armour was assigned to comment on my law-as-source project, he did his own digging, and found that legal sources were indeed behind over half of the top investigative projects in the United

[13] Yonathan Arbel & Roy Shapira, *Theory of the Nudnik: the Future of Consumer Activism and What Can We Do to Stop It*, 73 VAND. L. REV. (forthcoming, 2020).

[14] Érica Gorga & Michael Halberstam, *Litigation Discovery and Corporate Governance: The Missing Story about the "Genius of American Corporate Law,"* 63 EMORY L.J. 1383, 1389 & n.23; 1406 & n.104 (2014).

Kingdom as well. And in a current project where I examine Israel's move to a Delaware-style business court, the early findings are in line with what we saw in Chapter 3: the biggest change from moving to Delaware-style adjudication is not in substantive law but rather in the more intensive media coverage and the reputational effects of the legal disputes. The new business court shapes behavior mainly indirectly. In other, non-common-law systems, the reputational effects seem to be more limited. In Germany, for example, the names of the disputants are confidential. This takes away the ability of investigative reporters to cull court documents to find patterns of misbehavior, as elaborated in Chapter 7.

Along these lines, a promising venue for comparative inquiry is to apply the reputational framework to the "what matters" debate that has been dominating the law and finance literature since the 1990s. The extant literature has been trying to locate the determinants of strong corporate governance and capital markets, searching for systematic differences in either legal, market, or social controls across countries. Yet one important difference has been left relatively understudied: the differences in interactions between systems of control. The reputational perspective suggests the possibility that the variation in outcomes across countries is driven not just by how each system functions in isolation, but also by how the systems affect each other. Systems of control can facilitate each other in one country while crowding each other out in another country. Specifically, when measuring the effectiveness of legal enforcement, we should try to capture the indirect effects too, by asking whether the legal system facilitates better nonlegal controls.[15]

My initial conjecture is that countries with adjudication systems that provide quality information to the market can afford to rely more heavily on market solutions. This is because litigation (or regulatory investigations) that provide information in a timely, accessible, and accurate manner facilitates better reputational control. Such a perspective suggests a new explanation for the relative strength of US corporate governance. Perhaps the genius of American corporate law comes not from well-designed and strictly enforced substantive rules, but rather from civil procedure rules that are geared toward information production.[16]

***

[15] *See, e.g.*, Howell Jackson & Mark Roe, *Public and Private Enforcement of Securities Law: Resource-Based Evidence*, 93 J. Fin. Econ. 207, 210 (2009) (alluding to the potential benefit of public enforcement in facilitating better reputational control).

[16] Gorga & Halberstam, *supra* note 14; John Armour et al., *Regulatory Sanctions and Reputational Damage in Financial Markets*, 52 J. Fin. & Quantitative Analysis 1429 (2017) (on differences in enforcement styles between the SEC and its UK equivalent, including how they affect information production).

This book centers around one overarching point: the law shapes behavior not just through imposing sanctions, but also through producing information. In the course of fleshing out this point and examining the interactions between law and reputation, the book contributes to various debates that have been at the center of academics' and practitioners' attention, such as the desirability of heightened pleading standards or mandatory arbitration clauses.

Delving into the interconnections between law and reputation also sheds new light on age-old policy debates. Two binary camps have been dominating the debate over legal intervention: one camp advocates "leaving things to the market" while the other calls for "ramping up legal sanctioning." Yet those who oppose legal intervention fail to recognize the importance of the legal system for the functioning of market discipline. And those who advocate for more legal sanctions fail to recognize the ability of the legal system to shape behavior *indirectly*, without interfering with business decisions. Sometimes the most effective and realistic way to promote deterrence is not to increase legal sanctions, but to increase the quantity and quality of information production.

APPENDIX A

Interviews

To capture the fuzzy dynamics of how law affects reputation, I conducted in-depth open conversational interviews with veteran journalists, reputation consultants, and litigators. In this type of interview, the researcher introduces a topic in broad strokes, the interviewee talks freely about the interviewee's experience and insights into the topic, and the researcher further probes specific experiences with follow-up questions.

The interviews played an especially important part in Chapter 2's insights on how the law affects investigative reporting. As a way to introduce the topic, I started all interviews with the same research question, namely, "What role do you think that legal sources play in investigative reporting?" I also included in almost every interview some questions about variation across issues and over time, such as "Is it harder as a reporter to hold big government to account than it is to hold big business to account, or vice versa?," and "How have the legal sourcing dynamics you just described changed over time?" When interviewing Pulitzer winners, I asked them specifically, "What role did legal sources play in your [winning project]?" and we went into detail and clarifications.

The interviewing is of course subject to biases. Your interviewees may tell you what they think you want to hear or distort their responses to boost their image. Two factors alleviate such concerns here. First, as Chapter 2 noted, the insights presented here are based on triangulation: not just what journalists say about legal sources when they talk with me, but also what they say when they talk with themselves (tip sheets/syllabi), and what they actually do (content analysis). Second, overstating the role of legal sources is actually the opposite of what a journalist who wishes to boost her image would do. If a journalist tilts her answers in a self-serving way, why would she suggest that she merely piggybacked existing public documents? She is better off claiming more credit to her hard-working, developing-ears-on-the-streets efforts.

In compiling the sample of interviewees, I focused on two groups. For the first batch of interviews I approached journalists who served or are currently serving in big-picture-type positions: directors and founders of investigative reporting centers, heads of academic units of investigative reporting, veteran editors, and so on. I made a concerted effort to approach reporters with varied experiences – as reporters and editors, in broadcast and print media, covering the financial market beat and covering criminal cases, and so forth. The second batch of interviewees were winners of the Pulitzer Prize for Investigative Reporting in 1995–2015. In both groups, roughly two-thirds of the journalists I approached agreed to interview for this project.

Table A1 details the interviews of the law-as-source study. Unless noted otherwise, I conducted the interviews by phone. I then list some of the most helpful and influential interviews I have had in the earlier stages of formulating this book's thesis.

TABLE A1 *List of interviews*

No.	Name	Date	Position
1	Berens, Michael	8/18/17	2012 Pulitzer winner
2	Bergo, Sandy	8/14/17	Director of the Fund for Investigative Journalism
3	Blackledge, Brett	9/25/17	2007 Pulitzer winner
4	Boardman, David	8/16/17	Dean, Klein College of Media and Communication; Pulitzer-winning editor
5	Bogdanich, Walt	9/6/17	2008 Pulitzer winner
6	Carter, T. Barton[1]	8/15/17	Media law professor at Boston University
7	Christensen, Kim	11/20/17	1996 Pulitzer winner
8	Cohen, Sarah	11/29/17	2002 Pulitzer winner
9	Coll, Steve	8/31/17	Dean of Columbia Journalism School; two-time Pulitzer winner
10	Daillak, Jonathan	5/5/17	Executive director of the Loeb Awards
11	Daly, Chris	9/25/17	Journalism professor at Boston University
12	Eisinger, Jesse	6/6/16	2011 Pulitzer winner, 2015 Loeb Award winner
13	Englund, Will	8/17/17	1998 Pulitzer winner
14	Grandestaff, Lauren	8/16/17	Research director at the IRE
15	Graves, Florence	11/6/17	Founding director, the Schuster Institute for Investigative Journalism
16	Green-Barber, Lindsay	8/15/17	Former Media Impact Analyst at the Center for Investigative Reporting

TABLE A1 (*continued*)

No.	Name	Date	Position
17	Horvit, Mark	8/14/17	Director of the IRE; journalism professor at the University of Missouri
18	Ilgenfritz, Stefanie	12/14/17	2015 Pulitzer winner
19	Jaquiss, Nigel	11/1/17	2005 Pulitzer winner
20	Lehr, Richard (Dick)	8/16/17	Communications professor at Boston University
21	Levy, Clifford[2]	11/19/17	2003 Pulitzer winner
22	Lewis, Charles	8/25/17	Head of the Investigative Reporting Workshop
23	Lipinski, Ann Marie	8/24/17	Curator of the Nieman Foundation for Journalism at Harvard; former co-chair of the Pulitzer Prize board
24	Locy, Toni	8/15/17	Professor and Head of the Department of Journalism and Mass Communications at Washington & Lee university
25	MacLaren, Selina	8/31/17	Legal Fellow at the Reporters Committee
26	Mahr, Joe[3]	10/3/17	2004 Pulitzer winner
27	McKim, Jenifer	8/24/17	Senior investigator at the New England Center for Investigative Reporting
28	Mehren, Elizabeth	8/9/17	Journalism professor at Boston University
29	Mendoza, Martha	9/6/17	2000 Pulitzer winner
30	Nelson, Deborah	9/6/17	1997 Pulitzer winner
31	Possley, Maurice	10/6/17	2008 Pulitzer winner
32	Saul, Stephanie[4]	10/18/17	1995 Pulitzer winner
33	Siconolfi, Michael	12/14/17	2015 Pulitzer winner
34	Smith, Jeffrey	9/8/17	2006 Pulitzer winner
35	St. John, Paige	10/3/17	2011 Pulitzer winner
36	Starkman, Dean	2/9/16	1994 Pulitzer winner
37	Tulsky, Rick	8/24/17	1987 Pulitzer winner; former president of the IRE
38	Ureneck, Lou	8/8/17	Journalism professor at Boston University
39	Weinberg, Steve	8/24/17	Professor of journalism at the Missouri School of Journalism; former director of the IRE

[1] In person.
[2] Email correspondence.
[3] Email correspondence.
[4] Email correspondence.

NOTABLE EARLIER INTERVIEWS

Interviews with Communication/Reputation Experts

Email interview with Eric Dezenhall, President, Dezenhall Res. (July 2012);
Telephone interview with Charles Bakaly, Head of the Litig. Commc'n Dep't, Edelman (Aug. 21, 2012);
Telephone interview with Jeff Segal, Founder, MedicalJustice (Nov. 27, 2012);
Interview with Michael Fertik, Founder, Reputation.com (Feb. 11, 2013);
Telephone interview with Rupert Younger, Founder, Oxford Univ. Ctr. for Corp. Reputation (May 7, 2014).

Interviews with Legal Experts

Interview with Richard Clary, Former Head of Litig., Cravath, Swaine & Moore, in Cambridge, MA (Nov. 16, 2012);
Telephone interview with Peter Grossi, Drug-Liability Litigator (Dec. 12, 2012);
Telephone interview with Bruce Carton, Former Senior Counsel, SEC Enforcement Dep't (May 21, 2013);
Telephone interview with a Representative of Courtroom Connect (June 13, 2013);
Telephone interview with Bill Ide, Partner, McKenna Long & Aldridge (Apr. 2, 2014);
Telephone interview with Harvey Pitt, Former Chairman, SEC (May 28, 2014).

Interviews with Media Experts

Interview with Guy Rolnik, Founding Editor, TheMarker, in Cambridge, MA (Nov. 15, 2013);
Telephone interview with Kim Masters, ENTM'T JOURNALIST (June 14, 2013);
Telephone interview with Kim Christensen, Journalist, L.A. TIMES (Jan. 17, 2014);
Telephone interview with Corie Brown, Journalist, NEWSWEEK (Jan. 20, 2014);
Telephone interview with Richard Verrier, Journalist, L.A. TIMES (Jan. 23, 2014).

APPENDIX B

Content Analysis

Aside from interviews, the book rests heavily also on content analysis of media coverage. In particular, Chapter 2 presents content analysis of prizewinning investigative reports. This Appendix describes the process.

Sample: The reason for focusing on Pulitzers and IRE medals is twofold: relevance and convenience. Pulitzers and IRE medals are considered extremely prestigious by the general public and investigative reporters themselves. Sampling such awards gives us a window into standard-setting and impactful investigative reporting. Further, both awards make all relevant parts of a winning project publicly available online, and in many cases contain the entry letter submitted by the newspaper, thereby making it more convenient to figure out how the story came about.

Identifying Sources: To identify the sources of Pulitzer-winning stories we read every entry for each project. A few entries made our task straightforward, explicitly mentioning from the outset how they came up with the story. Most entries, however, drop occasional, sometimes implicit references to sources throughout the project. After all, when journalists write a story, they normally do not start with deep confessions of where they found the information, but rather focus on the story itself. Therefore, locating the sources necessitated careful reading of all the entries. In most cases, we found indications of sourcing incidentally: there would be a lengthy paragraph detailing who did what to whom, which ended in a "the depositions show" phrase. Identifying the sources of IRE-winning stories, by contrast, was straightforward: the IRE database contains not just the finished products (the investigative reports), but also the prize applications forms, where the applicants explicitly detail how their story came about.

We then had to pinpoint the sources that would be considered "legal documents," as opposed to any other public record. To be sure, the distinction is murky. It is best illustrated by the famous Watergate story. In popular culture,

Watergate is associated with human sources – tips from "deep throat." Yet the investigative project actually started when a journalist that covered the police beat went over logs of overnight arrests, and stumbled upon a suspicion that started the digging. For our purposes, going over police logs to find leads does *not* count as relying on a legal source. What happened later in the story (i.e. when Woodward and Bernstein used documents subpoenaed by law enforcement officers to show how the break-in was connected to higher-ups) does.

Weighting Sources: Assigning weights to legal sources' contributions to a project is complicated by the fact that most winning projects have multiple parts, covering different angles of the topic. Each part can rely on varying mixes of sources. Part 1 of a project may rest on information attained by FOIA requests, while parts 2–4 may be based on interviews, and part 5 may draw from depositions. We judged the relative weight of legal sources based on each part's contribution to the overall story and its impact. In most cases, the judgment was made easier by the fact that the Pulitzer committee already narrowed down the articles that are considered a part of the winning projects, listing only the most impactful ones. If the Pulitzer committee identified these parts as essential to the project, we could usually infer that indications of strong reliance on legal sources there meant that legal sources played a strong role in the project as a whole.

Reliability: My analysis of prizewinning investigative projects rested on human-based content analysis. Human analysis is generally considered to increase the validity of analysis but decrease the reliability (relative to computer-based content analysis). In our case of having to code legal sources' roles, three factors mitigate potential problems with reliability. First, unlike in projects with larger samples where coding is assigned to research assistants, in our smaller, exploratory-style sample, I personally coded all entries. Second, I was not the only coder – at least one research assistant separately examined each prizewinning project, and the agreement among us (the intercoder reliability) was relatively high: 0.81. Third, with respect to Pulitzers, I managed to talk with the prizewinning journalist in seventeen out of the twenty-five sampled projects, and directly asked them about the role legal sources played in their reports. Asking the journalists increased the reliability of the specific seventeen projects and, more generally, put our coding to the test. We coded all stories before talking to the prizewinning reporters, and so when their answers confirmed that our coding was accurate in thirteen of the seventeen stories, and actually slightly understated the role of legal sources in three more of the stories, it provided another reason to believe that we did not overstate the role of law as source.

Table B1 details the Pulitzer-winning projects, and our coding of them. Table B2 follows, with details on the coding of the IRE medals.

TABLE B1 1995–2015 *Pulitzer winners for investigative reporting*

No.	Year	Title	Topic	Reporter/outlet	Legal sources' role	Legal sources' type
1	2015A	*Courting Favor*	How lobbyists influence congressmen and state attorneys general	Eric Lipton/ *New York Times*	Medium	FOIA strong; litigation weak
2	2015B	*Medicare Unmasked*	How healthcare providers are milking Medicare money	*Wall Street Journal* staff	Strong–medium	FOIA strong; reg. investigations strong (parts)
3	2014	Series on black lung benefit cases of coal miners	How professionals (lawyers, doctors) help the industry deny benefits from coal miners stricken with black lung disease	Chris Hamby/ Center for Public Integrity	Strong	Litigation
4	2013	Wal-Mart Bribery Abroad Series	Wal-Mart's widespread bribery efforts in Mexico	David Barstow & Alejandra Xanic von Bertrab/ *New York Times*	Nonexistent	—
5	2012A	NYPD Intelligence Operations on Muslim communities series	NYPD's questionable domestic intelligence-gathering practices (clandestine spying program)	Matt Apuzzo et al./ Associated Press (AP)	Medium	Litigation; reg. investigations
6	2012B	*Methadone and the Politics of Pain*	How vulnerable patients were moved from safer pain-control medication to a cheaper, more dangerous alternative	Michael J. Berens & Ken Armstrong/ *Seattle Times*	Medium–weak	Litigation; reg. investigations

(*continued*)

TABLE B1 *(continued)*

No.	Year	Title	Topic	Reporter/outlet	Legal sources' role	Legal sources' type
7	2011	Florida Insurance Market Investigation series	Fleshing out weaknesses (unreliable insurers) in the property-insurance system in Florida	Paige St. John/ *Sarasota Herald-Tribune*	Strong	Reg. investigations strong; litigation (parts)
8	2010A	*Tainted Justice*	Exposing a rogue police narcotics squad	Barbara Laker & Wendy Ruderman/ *Philadelphia Daily News*	Medium	Litigation
9	2010B	*The Deadly Choices at Memorial*	The urgent life-and-death decisions made by one hospital's exhausted doctors when they were cut off by the floodwaters of Hurricane Katrina	Sheri Fink/ *ProPublica*	Strong	Reg. investigations; litigation
10	2009	Message Machine series	How the Pentagon uses retired generals to influence public opinion (and how many of these generals have undisclosed ties to companies that benefited from policies they defended)	David Barstow/ *New York Times*	Strong	FOIA
11	2008A	*Faulty Governmental Regulation of Toys, Car Seats and Cribs*	Lax regulation of baby products	Staff of *Chicago Tribune*	Strong	Litigation; reg. investigations; FOIA

12	2008B	Toxic Pipeline series	Toxic ingredients in products imported from China	Walt Bogdanich & Jake Hooker/ *New York Times*	Strong	Reg. investigations strong; litigation (parts)
13	2007	Two-Year College Corruption series	Cronyism and corruption in the state's college system	Brett Blackledge/ *Birmingham* (AL) *News*	Medium–weak	Investigations, litigation (in later parts)
14	2006	*Investigating Abramoff: Special Report*	The story of lobbyist Jack Abramoff, which exposed widespread congressional corruption	Susan Schmidt et al./*Washington Post*	Strong	FOIA strong; reg. investigations medium
15	2005	*The 30-Year Secret*	Exposing a former governor's long-concealed sexual misconduct with a 14-year-old girl	Nigel Jaquiss/ *Willamette Week*, Portland, Oregon	Strong	Litigation
16	2004	Special: Tiger Force series	Atrocities by an elite U.S. Army platoon during the Vietnam War	Michael D. Sallah et al./*The Blade*, Toledo, OH	Medium–weak	FOIA medium/weak; litigation weak
17	2003	*Broken Homes*	Abuse of mentally ill adults in state-regulated caring homes	Clifford J. Levy/ *New York Times*	Medium	Litigation; reg. investigations
18	2002	*The District's Lost Children*	The neglect and death of children placed in protective care (and the District's role in it)	Sari Horwitz et al./ *Washington Post*	Strong	FOIA; litigation
19	2001	*Seven Deadly Drugs*	How regulatory reforms have reduced FDA's effectiveness and led to approval of unsafe prescription drugs	David Willman/*Los Angeles Times*	Medium	FOIA strong; litigation weak

(*continued*)

TABLE B1 *(continued)*

No.	Year	Title	Topic	Reporter/outlet	Legal sources' role	Legal sources' type
20	2000	The Bridge at No Gun Ri	Killing of civilians during the Korean War	Sang-Hun Choe et al./AP	Nonexistent	—
21	1999	Pervasive Voter Fraud in a City Mayoral Election	Voter fraud in a Miami election	Staff of *Miami Herald*	Medium–weak	Reg. Investigations
22	1998	Series on The International Ship-breaking Industry	How the ship-breaking industry cuts corners in ways that endanger workers' safety and the environment	Gary Cohn & Will Englund of *Baltimore Sun*	Strong–medium	Litigation strong; reg. investigations (parts)
23	1997	*Tribal Housing: From Deregulation to Disgrace*	Cronyism in the federally sponsored housing program for Native Americans	Eric Nalder et al./ *Seattle Times*	Strong	FOIA strong; reg. investigations medium
24	1996	Baby Born after Doctor Took Eggs without Consent	Fraudulent and unethical fertility practices at a leading research university hospital	Staff of Orange County Register, Santa Ana, CA	Medium–weak	Litigation; reg. investigations; FOIA
25	1995	*For Some LI Cops . . . Lucrative Disability*	Abuse of disability pension funds by cops	Brian Donovan & Stephanie Saul/ *Newsday*	Strong	Litigation strong; FOIA weak

TABLE B2 *IRE Medal winners for 1995–2015*

No.	Year	Title	Topic	Reporter/outlet	Legal sources' role	Legal sources' type
1	2015	*Insult to Injury: America's Vanishing Worker Protections*	How states dismantled their workers' compensation programs, ultimately sticking taxpayers with the growing bill for injured workers	Michael Grabell & Howard Berkes/ *ProPublica*	Strong	Litigation; FOIA
2	2013	*The NSA Files*	How communications between US citizens are collected by surveillance programs	Glenn Greenwald & Ewen MacAskill/ *Guardian US*	Medium	Litigation
3	2011	*Assault on Learning*	How school violence goes under-reported, and how government intervention programs amount to little more than paper-shuffling	Susan Snyder & Kristen A. Graham/ *Philadelphia Inquirer*	Weak–medium	Litigation (human sources); FOIA (weak)
4	2010	*Breach of Faith*	Local government corruption in Bell, CA	Jeff Gottlieb & Ruben Vives/*Los Angeles Times*	Strong	FOIA
5	2009	*Toxic Waters*	The flaws in Clean Water Act regulation	Charles Duhigg & Matthew Bloch/ *New York Times*	Strong	FOIA
6	2008A	*Kwame Kilpatrick: A Mayor in Crisis*	Corruption at the municipal level	Jim Schaefer & M. L. Elrick/ *Detroit Free Press*	Strong	Litigation; FOIA

(*continued*)

TABLE B2 (*continued*)

No.	Year	Title	Topic	Reporter/outlet	Legal sources' role	Legal sources' type
7	2008B	*Guantanamo: Beyond the Law*	Abuse and faulty imprisonment of Guantanamo Bay detainees	Tom Lasseter & Matthew Schofield/ McClatchy Washington Bureau	Strong	Litigation; reg. Investigations; FOIA
8	2007A	*The Other Walter Reed*	Mistreatment and neglect of America's war-wounded at Walter Reed Army Medical Center	Dana Priest & Anne Hull/ *Washington Post*	Nonexistent	–
9	2006A	*Beyond Sago: Coal Mine Safety in America*	How coal companies' misconduct and lax regulation contributed to avoidable coal miners' deaths	Ken Ward, Jr./ *Charleston Gazette*	Strong	FOIA
10	2006B	A *Tank of Gas, A World of Trouble*	Tracking the supply chain of gasoline	Paul Salopek/ *Chicago Tribune*	Nonexistent	–
11	2005A	*The High Price of Homeland Security*	How security systems contracts have run amok in the wake of a scare to prevent terrorist attacks	Scott Higham & Robert O'Harrow, Jr./ *Washington Post*	Medium	FOIA (weak); reg. Investigations; court records
12	2005B	*Toxic Legacy*	Pollution by Ford Motors	Jan Barry & Mary Jo Layton/*The Record N.J.*	Strong	Litigation; reg. Investigations; FOIA

13	2004A	*Death on the Track: How Railroads Sidestep Blame*	The railroad industry's shirking of responsibility for fatal accidents through destroying evidence and neglecting to report accidents	Walt Bogdanich/ *New York Times*	Strong–medium	Reg. Investigations; FOIA
14	2004B	*Web of Deceit: The Fall of West Virginia House Education Committee Chairman Jerry Mezzatesta*	Corruption, misconduct, and cover-up by a long-time powerful state legislator	Eric Eyre/ *Charleston Gazette*	Strong–medium	Reg. Investigations; FOIA
15	2003A	*Big Green*	Unethical and illegal practices at the world's largest environmental group	Joe Stephens & David B. Ottaway/ *Washington Post*	Strong–medium	Litigation
16	2002	*Crisis in the Catholic Church*	Widespread abuse of minors by Catholic priests and the church's cover-up efforts	Walter V. Robinson & Matt Carroll/ *Boston Globe*	Strong	Litigation
17	2000	*The Body Brokers*	How private entities illegally profit from organ donations	Mark Katches & William Heisel/ Orange County Register	Medium–weak	Litigation; FOIA
18	1999A	*Invisible Lives: D. C.'s Troubled System for the Retarded*	Cruelty, sexual assaults, and deaths in a multi-billion-dollar state program for the retarded	Katherine Boo/ *Washington Post*	Strong–medium	Litigation; reg. Investigations; FOIA

(*continued*)

TABLE B2 *(continued)*

No.	Year	Title	Topic	Reporter/outlet	Legal sources' role	Legal sources' type
19	1999B	*Deadly Alliance*	Workers' safety issues in beryllium manufacturing, fueled by the US military's demand for the metal	Sam Roe/*Toledo Blade*	Strong	Litigation; FOIA
20	1998	*Rezulin: A Billion-Dollar Killer*	Regulatory failures in ignoring warnings and approving a dangerous diabetes pill	David Willman/ *Los Angeles Times*	Medium	Reg. Investigations; FOIA
21	1996A	*And Justice for Some*	Mishandling of homicide investigations by LA police	Fredric N. Tulsky & Ted Rohrlich/ *Los Angeles Times*	Strong	Litigation; reg. Investigations; FOIA
22	1996B	*Money from Asia: The Democrats' Controversial Campaign Contributions*	How the Democratic National Committee solicited improper donations from foreign-linked corporations and individuals	Alan C. Miller & Glenn F. Bunting/*Los Angeles Times*	Strong–medium	Litigation
23	1995B	*Military Secrets*	How the US armed forces allowed accused sex offenders to escape prosecution or escape imprisonment after being convicted	Russell Carollo & Jeff Nesmith/ *Dayton Daily News*	Strong	Litigation; reg. Investigations

Note: Excludes redundancies with Pulitzers: projects that won both prizes. In years where the IRE Medal was not given to print investigative work, we sampled the award given in the "newspapers: large circulation" category.

Index

Lightning Source UK Ltd.
Milton Keynes UK
UKHW022237101020
371381UK00013B/205

9 781107 186507